The Emotional Self

The Emotional Self

A Sociocultural Exploration

Deborah Lupton

SAGE Publications

London • Thousand Oaks • New Delhi

SAGE Publications Ltd
6 Bonhill Street
London EC2A 4PU

SAGE Publications Inc
2455 Teller Road
Thousand Oaks, California 91320

SAGE Publications India Pvt Ltd
32, M-Block Market
Greater Kailash – I
New Delhi 110 048

British Library Cataloguing in Publication data

A catalogue record for this book is available from the
British Library.

ISBN 0 7619 5601 8
ISBN 0 7619 5602 6 (pbk)

Library of Congress catalog card number 97–062538

Typeset by Photoprint, Torquay
Printed in Great Britain by Biddles Ltd, Guildford, Surrey

Contents

Acknowledgements

An earlier version of some of the arguments presented in this book has been published in a chapter entitled ' "Going with the flow": some central discourses in conceptualizing and articulating the embodiment of emotional states' in *The Body in Everyday Life*, edited by S. Nettleton and J. Watson, published by Routledge, London, 1998. I am grateful to the people who agreed to be interviewed about their emotional experiences and beliefs about emotions for the book, and to Else Lackey for her very competent research assistance as an interviewer. As always, I thank Gamini Colless for his personal support.

Introduction

It is a rainy Sunday afternoon, and for want of anything better to do, you have decided to clear out your desk drawers, which are bulging with papers, some many years old. You pull out the old school reports, letters from friends and lovers, photographs, postcards and birthday cards that you have saved over the decades of your life. You come across a programme from a school musical in which you played a role, your first and only stage part, at the age of 16. You open it up, and peruse the contents, remembering the other students and the teachers who were involved in the production. You smile to yourself as a warm wave of nostalgia for those days overcomes you. You recall the light-hearted fun and camaraderie of the rehearsals, the dedication of the amiable teacher who was directing the musical, the rather creaky but earnest accompaniment provided by the school band, the excited hubbub in the dressing rooms behind the stage when you were preparing for the performance. You recall the nervousness you felt, the butterflies in your stomach, waiting in the wings to go on stage to perform your role in front of an audience including numerous family members and friends.

Then you suddenly remember what happened on the last night of performances. The details of the scene in which you forgot your lines come back to you vividly. You feel your face growing red and hot, just as it did that night several decades ago, as the embarrassment of those moments is relived. You remember how you froze in the middle of the scene, unable to remember what you should say next, and how the other actors stared at you, and how the audience seemed to grow quiet and expectant, waiting for your words. Finally, after what seemed like hours, the words came back to you, and you said them, and the scene went on. Your friends and family assured you after the show that they had not noticed anything amiss, that your performance was terrific. But you secretly knew that they were only trying to make you feel better, and you felt as if you had shown yourself up, been made to look a fool.

This vignette serves to demonstrate several important features of human emotional experience. One aspect is the ways in which emotions are the products of cultural definitions and social relations. There is reference in the vignette to a number of emotions: nostalgia, camaraderie, enjoyment, excitement, nervousness, embarrassment, chagrin. All of these emotions are produced in a social context, through interactions with others. Most of them are accompanied by physical sensations, which are interpreted as specific emotions via knowledge of the social situation as specific emotions. What is also of interest is the ways that embodied sensations and feelings are put into words. In the vignette, there is reference to a 'warm wave' of nostalgia, the 'light-heartedness' of fun and camaraderie, the 'butterflies in the stomach' associated with the feelings of excitement and nervousness, the 'freezing' of thought and physical movement that was part of not being able to recall the lines, the 'redness' and 'heat' associated with the bodily sensations that are identified as embarrassment. Another important feature is the role played by material artefacts as repositories of and cues to emotions: in this case, a school musical programme, which is capable of arousing echoes of the same emotional responses as were experienced at a particular time years ago.

As all this suggests, emotions are phenomena that are shaped, experienced and interpreted through social and cultural processes. Surprisingly enough, however, for some time this concept of emotion was not particularly accepted among sociocultural theorists and researchers, who tended to accept an essentialist notion of the emotions as biological phenomena 'that respond to cross-cultural environmental differences but retain a robust essence untouched by the social or cultural' (Abu-Lughod and Lutz, 1990: 2). Emotions were predominantly seen as originating within the individual, confined to such solitary interior aspects as brain functioning and personality. As Abu-Lughod and Lutz note, 'emotions stubbornly retain their place . . . as the aspect of human experience least subject to control, least constructed or learned (hence most universal), least public, and therefore least amenable to sociocultural analysis' (1990: 1). As a result, many sociologists, anthropologists and other cultural analysts viewed the study of the emotions as the province of the 'psy' disciplines, particularly social and cognitive psychology, rather than as relevant to their own concerns.

Related to this neglect of the emotions was the tendency for social and cultural theorists and researchers to neglect analysis of the body. While sociocultural analyses of the body have burgeoned in the past 15 years or so, for quite some time it was an area of research that few pursued. According to Bryan Turner, one of the major exponents of the new sociology of embodiment, this initial neglect was because 'Any reference to the corporeal nature of human existence raises in the mind of the sociologist the spectre of social Darwinism, biological reductionism or sociobiology' (1996: 37). Social theorists' concern about reducing human behaviour and social relations to biological explanations meant that they tended to go too far the other way, in representing the 'social actor' as virtually disembodied.

A further explanation given for the paucity of research on the emotions in such fields as sociology and anthropology is their supposed contravening of the 'scientific' or 'objective' approach (James, 1989: 17). The emotions have been viewed as irrelevant or disruptive to the project of post-Enlightenment (modernist) academic scholarship, which has tended to privilege rational thought over 'irrational' emotionality. The inextricable relationship between the emotions and embodiment is part of the meanings of irrationality that have tended to accompany the emotions. In western cultures, the embodied nature of humanity has historically been a source of consternation. The body has constantly been presented as threatening to overcome the pureness of thought. In contrast with the clarity and will of the mind, the body is portrayed as primitive, dumbly responding to the passions (Bordo, 1993: 11). In the writings of the ancient philosophers, the body was considered unruly, requiring the continual monitoring of 'reason'. In Christian writings, particularly since the Protestant Reformation, it has traditionally been portrayed as a source of corruption via the temptations of the flesh, drawing people's attention away from their spiritual devotions.

Because the emotions are viewed as embodied sensations, they are considered to be the antithesis of reason and rationality. From this perspective, the emotions are impediments to proper considered judgement and intellectual activity. Emotional expression has also traditionally been associated with 'uncivilized' behaviour, with vulgarity and the lower orders. As Boscagli has observed, for much of the twentieth century, emotions have been considered to be 'the sphere of mass culture and kitsch. He or she who is moved is considered unsophisticated, uncultivated, and part of a mass incapable of keeping the necessary distance from a certain event' (1992/1993: 65). This is far from the ideal of the scholar who seeks the purity of reason, uncontaminated by the subjectiveness of physical sensations, desires and urges.

The dominant 'dispassionate' approach to the emotions in the academy has itself been subject to challenge in recent years, particularly by those taking up postmodern and feminist theoretical critiques of modernist perspectives. Within these strands of thought, emotional experience is considered to be an essential and insightful conduit to knowledge. Emotional responses are viewed as important sources of human values and ethics and as a proper basis for political action. Much feminist writing, for example, as part of the 'personal is political' approach, has used detailed discussion of the author's personal emotional experiences to position more general or theoretical arguments about the cultural and political meanings and implications of femininity and the role of women in contemporary societies. Such works challenge notions of personal experience, the subjective and emotion as irrelevant or disruptive to epistemology and academic theorizing (see, for example, Jaggar, 1989; Gilligan and Rogers, 1993; Jordan, 1993; Ruddick, 1994; Griffiths, 1995).

It is similarly argued by some postmodernist theorists that truth and knowledge themselves can never be free of emotional underpinnings, even though it may be pretended by those who espouse modernist approaches that their route to truth and knowledge is dispassionate,

scientific and objective. For instance, Game and Metcalfe (1996) have
commented on the passionless nature of social scientific inquiry. They
have called instead for a 'passionate sociology' which both acknowledges the emotional underpinnings of academic research, scholarship
and teaching and directs more of its attention to such fundamental
aspects of human existence and social relations as emotional experience.

In the spirit of 'passionate sociology', I acknowledge that as the author
of this book, I have my own emotional investments in it. Writing is
always inevitably a product of subjectivity, whether it is produced under
the titles of fiction or non-fiction. The writer's style and her or his
preoccupations and interests are all inflected through her or his personal
experiences, whether this is brought to the fore or remains as sub-textual.
Particularly for writers in the humanities and social sciences, who
address topics about human experience and selfhood, culture and society, a recognition of the ways in which one's topic has resonances for
one's lived biography is generally part of the process by which insight is
gained. Throughout this book, whenever I seek to make reflections on
emotion, I inevitably use my own experiences and understandings to
provide insight as well as those that I have accessed through others'
writings, or, in the case of the interview material I gathered for this book,
their spoken words.

As noted above, despite the traditional disdain in social and cultural
theory for devoting attention to the details of human embodiment and its
relevance for social action, social relations and selfhood, in recent times
there has been a growth of interest in the ways that sociology may
explore aspects of humanity that were previously taken for granted as
'fixed' or 'biological'. This interest in the sociology of the body potentially includes a greater attention to the sociology of the emotions,
including exploring the relationship between sociocultural meaning and
representation, social interaction and bodily experience. Like the body
itself, emotional states serve to bring together nature and culture in a
seamless intermingling in which it is difficult to argue where one ends
and the other begins. As Lyon and Barbalet contend, 'it is through
emotion (feeling/sentiment/affect) that the links between the body and
the social world can be clearly drawn'. They go on to describe emotion as
'embodied sociality' (1994: 48).

Other writers have also seen the emotions as integral to the main-
tenance of human societies and social relationships. For Finkelstein
(1980: 112), emotions are the 'heart of social discourse', 'emblematic of
human consciousness and intrinsic to public decorum' and thus the
sociology of the emotions should be a foundational question for the
discipline. Denzin similarly argues that:

> Emotionality lies at the intersection of the person and society, for all persons
> are joined to their societies through the self-feelings and emotions they feel
> and experience on a daily basis. This is the reason the study of emotionality

must occupy a central place in all the human disciplines, for to be human is to be emotional. (Denzin, 1984: x)

The cultural anthropologists Scheper-Hughes and Lock, for their part, assert that the emotions, in bringing together private feelings and public moralities, 'provide an important "missing link" capable of bridging mind and body, individual, society, and body politic' (1987: 28–9).

It is these features, these ways of understanding the relationships between the emotions, the self, the body and the social world, that are the focus of this book. Any attempt to describe or discuss the emotions, lay or academic, must confront the fact that the concept of emotion is ephemeral, slippery, difficult to 'pin down'. There is evidence of a major confusion in the academic study of the emotions. The term 'emotion' is both commonly used to denote the constellation of phenomena including somatic, feeling and behavioural aspects, but also more narrowly to refer to the feeling component only (Elias, 1991: 119). Jaggar (1989) has observed that the question 'What are emotions?' is deceptively simple, because there is a complexity and inconsistency in the ways in which the emotions are viewed. Part of the complexity, she argues, is that the emotions cover a wide range of phenomena: 'these extend from apparently instantaneous "knee-jerk" responses of fright to lifelong dedication to an individual or a cause; from highly civilized aesthetic responses to undifferentiated feelings of hunger and thirst, from background moods such as contentment or depression to intense and focused involvement in an immediate situation' (Jaggar, 1989: 147). As such, she contends, 'It may well be impossible to construct a manageable account of emotion to cover such apparently diverse phenomena' (1989: 147).

While the academic literature often attempts to distinguish between 'emotions', 'feelings', 'moods' and 'sensations' in well-defined and precise ways, this often involves a degree of crude reductionism at the expense of acknowledging the grey areas between the categories (Griffiths, 1995: 98–100). These attempts fail to recognize that what we call 'emotions' and how we experience them always gain their meaning as part of a wider sociocultural frame. The very mutability, ephemerality and intangible nature of 'the emotions', as well as their inextricable interlinking with and emergence from constantly changing social, cultural and historical contexts, means that they are not amenable to precise categorization.

The purpose of this book, therefore, is *not* to define, once and for all, what emotions 'are', or to attempt the enormous task of constructing a grand narrative sociological account of how emotions are experienced and understood. There is a vast range of academic literature on the emotions across such diverse fields as physiology, psychology, psychiatry, history, philosophy, sociology and anthropology, to name but some of the major ones. I make no attempt to review this literature comprehensively. My aim is more specific and selective – to engage in an exploration of the ways in which the emotions play a central role in contributing to our sense of self, or our subjectivity. The discussion focuses on the emotional self in the context of western societies – principally Anglophone and western European countries – at the end of the twentieth century. A major theme of this book is that our concepts of our emotions are often integral to our wider conception of our selves, used to give meaning and provide explanation for our lives, for why we respond to life events, other people, material artefacts and places in certain ways, why we might tend to follow patterns of behaviour throughout our lives.

This point in human history is a fascinating time to study notions of the emotional self, for the late twentieth century has witnessed an intensification of discourse and expert knowledges around intimacy and emotional expression. A network of expert knowledges, based particularly on the 'psy' disciplines (psychology, psychiatry, therapeutic psychoanalysis) has developed around the emotions, seeking to measure and survey emotional response and to counsel people on how best to deal with and express their emotions. Self-help books written about how to identify one's feelings and communicate them to others, and how to understand others' emotions, sell in their millions in the western world. In Australia, for example, the second best-selling book in the two-year period spanning 1995 and 1996 was American psychologist John Gray's *Men are from Mars, Women are from Venus*, an explanation of why men and women find it difficult to share their lives. It remained in the list of top-ten best-selling books into 1997.

The mass media devote much of their time to conveying and dissecting the emotions of others, reporting on events that are seen to have emotional significance and evoking emotional responses from their audiences. 'Confessional' televised talk-shows, such as the *Oprah Winfrey* show, require their participants, both the famous and the not-so-famous, to reveal details of their intimate experiences and feelings. Such programmes, indeed, are predicated on their guests revealing the most private and distressing feelings. It is all the better if a famous guest like Madonna can be persuaded to produce a tear in her eye as she recounts the painful feelings evoked by her mother's death, or if the former Duchess of York, Sarah Ferguson, is encouraged to reveal her feelings of shame and guilt concerning her infidelity and the breakdown of her royal marriage to Prince Andrew (both women were guests on the *Oprah Winfrey* show in 1996). In such arenas, the disclosure of emotion becomes commodified in order to attract ratings, the talk-show host acting as confessor figure for the sake of entertainment.

So too, news and documentaries frequently debate issues of contemporary emotional expression. News accounts obsessively portray the emotions provoked by such occasions as public ceremonies or the swearing-in of national leaders and sporting events such as the Olympics and football finals. Images of elite sportsmen and sportswomen leaping for joy after a win, or slumped with despair at losing, are a commonplace device of sports journalism. It has become a standard of news reports to seek out and note the emotional responses of victims of disasters or tragedies, and for journalists to end reports of their responses with a statement noting that psychological counselling was made available to the victims in order to deal with their emotional distress. This last statement has become a marker for the recognition that people are both profoundly emotionally affected by such events and that they require expert attention and help in dealing with and resolving their distress. As Walter, Littlewood and Pickering note of British news reporting of death, there is evidence not of 'emotional avoidance but emotional invigilation, not depersonalisation but an active reporting of the personal' (1995: 585).

The intense interest of the mass media and the public in death and the emotions surrounding it was notably to the fore following the sudden death in August 1997 of Diana, Princess of Wales, from her injuries incurred in a car accident in Paris. Television and radio news stations around the world were quick to broadcast the news of Diana's death and conduct indepth analyses of its causes and aftermath, often disrupting regular programming to do so. The news media continued to devote an extraordinary degree of attention to the emotional aftershocks of the death for several weeks after the event. Diana's funeral, held a week after her death, was a world-wide live media event watched by millions. Media commentary and images returned again and again to the emotional distress – the shock, grief, disbelief and anger – felt by thousands of people, not only in Britain but in other countries, at the death of the Princess. Much attention was paid in the media to the ways in which people expressed their feelings, for example, by leaving 'floral tributes', letters and fluffy toys at Kensington Palace, Diana's former home, and by queuing for hours to sign condolence books.

In the past few years, 'reality' television has become a popular media genre. 'Reality' television documents such real-life experiences of 'ordinary' people as undergoing hospitalization, receiving the assistance of ambulance officers, being arrested by police officers or even getting married. It also includes live television coverage of sensational legal cases such as the murder trial of the famous black American sportsman O.J. Simpson, which attracted fervent interest across the world. In one such Australian television series screened in mid-1997, entitled *Home Truths*, families were given video cameras and asked to film aspects of their everyday lives. The resultant (edited) footage had all the roughness and technical faults of home videos as well as their veracity. Viewers saw women giving birth, parents and children quarrelling, a couple with young children dealing with their financial problems after the husband was unexpectedly retrenched, an adolescent girl coping with adapting to living in Australia after her family had emigrated from eastern Europe, an old woman speaking about her loneliness after having to move to a nursing home. A vital component of the attraction of such programmes

is the ways in which they appear to reveal the emotions of the participants. Despite the banality of their subject matter, they are emotional
spectacles, drawing viewers in because of their apparent authenticity
and truth, allowing us to empathize with others' problems and joys.
There is, therefore, evidence of a current proliferation of discourses
around emotional expression, supported by practices and institutions, an
intense, almost voyeuristic interest in how others experience and display
emotion and an incitement to revealing emotion in both private and
public forums.

The central theoretical perspective used in the book is that of a version
of social constructionism that is informed by a poststructuralist interest
in discourse (patterns of ways of representing phenomena in language),
but is also tempered by a recognition that the sensual, embodied aspects
of the emotion require attention. I explore aspects of the phenomenology
of the 'emotional self ', or how individuals think about, express and give
meaning to their lived emotional experiences, and the sociocultural and
historical underpinnings of this state of 'being-in-the-world'. I am interested not only in how the emotional self is conceptualized and lived in
contemporary western societies, but also in exploring its antecedents, for
our ways of thinking, talking about and experiencing emotion is the
product of layers of meaning built up over time. Such an analysis seeks
to disrupt taken-for-granted assumptions about how we tend to understand subjectivity and embodiment and to identify the conditions in
which these assumptions are developed and reproduced (Rose, 1996:
41).

In Chapter 1, I review two major perspectives on the emotions evident
in the humanities and social scientific literature: the 'emotions as inherent' perspective and the 'emotions as sociocultural products' perspective.
There is an emphasis in the chapter on outlining the social constructionist approach, particularly the attention that is paid in some versions of
social constructionism to the discursive aspects of the emotions, for as I
noted above this is a major concern of the book. Unlike some highly
relativist social constructionists, however, I do not go as far as to claim
that the emotions do not exist outside language, and indeed make a case
in this chapter for 'bringing the body back in' to poststructuralist
theorizing on the emotions.

Chapter 2 identifies some dominant discourses on emotions circulating
in lay accounts. The discussion in this chapter is based on an original
empirical study conducted for the purposes of this book, in which a
group of 41 men and women participated in one-to-one semi-structured
interviews, talking about their own emotional experiences and beliefs
about the emotions. Their accounts were analysed for the recurring
discourses and metaphors that were employed in relation to such issues
as defining the emotions, concepts of 'emotionality' and the 'emotional
person', emotional management, differences in emotional styles between

people, gender and emotional expression, the embodiment of emotion and the relationship between emotion and health states.

The next two chapters build on the discussion in Chapter 2 by exploring in depth the broader sociocultural and historical contexts in which contemporary discourses on the emotions are generated and reproduced. Chapter 3 looks at dominant notions of the body and the self in contemporary western societies, including a review of the antecedents of these notions, and positions concepts of the emotions within these traditions. There is a particular focus in the chapter on identifying and discussing features of the two competing discourses of emotions to which I referred above: that discourse which positions emotion as disruptive, chaotic and evidence of loss of control of the body/self, and that which represents emotion as a source of self-authenticity, humanity and self-expression. This chapter also elaborates upon the current concepts of 'working' upon the emotional self and the role played by the 'psy' disciplines and notions of intimacy and the confession in this project of the self. It ends with further discussion of the beliefs and discourses concerning emotion and health.

Chapter 4 takes up in more detail the issues concerning gender and emotional expression that were introduced in Chapter 2. It looks at features of the archetypes of the 'emotional woman' and the 'unemotional man', including how these have developed in western societies and their implications for contemporary gendered experience. There is a particular focus in this chapter on the symbolic nature of feminine and masculine embodiment and the psychodynamic dimensions of gendered emotion. The chapter also includes a discussion of emotional labour in intimate relationships and the current move towards the 'feminization' of masculine emotionality.

In Chapter 5, I address the topic of the emotional relationships that we have with objects and places. The chapter begins with a general discussion of the role played by emotion in the consumption of commodities and then focuses more specifically on appropriation, or the process by which an object becomes an extension of the self via the strategies of everyday use. I argue that the investment of emotion in objects is often an outcome of appropriation. I then discuss the ways in which objects may serve as the mediators of emotion and the emotions that are associated with particular places, especially in relation to the cultural meanings of 'home'. The chapter ends with a review of the emotional dimensions of leisure activities. In the brief concluding chapter I review the major themes and findings of the book and comment on the complexity of the concept of the emotional self.

1
Thinking Through Emotion:
Theoretical Perspectives

This chapter discusses some of the major ways in which the emotions have been conceptualized and researched in the humanities and social sciences, serving in part to locate the theoretical position from which I have undertaken my own research. Any attempt to review approaches to the emotions is bedevilled by a certain lack of clarity and conceptual confusion in the literature. Similar approaches may be given different names in psychology compared with sociology or anthropology, for example, and even within these disciplines there is a lack of consensus about how to label or categorize the various approaches. Nonetheless, it is possible to identify two broad tendencies in the humanities and social scientific literature. For my purposes here I have termed these the 'emotions as inherent' and the 'emotions as socially constructed' perspectives respectively. I emphasize, however, that the approaches I have grouped under these rubrics represent more of a continuum rather than two discrete categories, and that there is a significant degree of overlap between them.

The chapter begins with a discussion of the theories and research within these two perspectives. More time is spent on describing the social constructionist position and its various versions because it is this approach that underpins the rest of the discussion in this book. As I note, however, it is important not to take too relativistic an approach to the emotions, neglecting their sensual, embodied nature. The chapter ends with an analysis of how the emotional self is always also an embodied self, for it is inevitably through the body that we construct, live and make sense of emotion.

Emotions as Inherent

For exponents of what Bedford (1986: 15) has termed 'the traditional theory of the emotions', an emotion is an internal feeling, or an experience involving such a feeling. While it is generally acknowledged that social and cultural features may shape the expression of emotions in various ways, the belief is maintained that at the centre of the emotional self there is a set of basic emotions with which all humans are born. Even though it may be accepted that the expression of these emotions may differ from society to society, this does not detract from the fact that such emotions are always pre-existing. Emotional states are therefore located within the individual. They are genetically inscribed, and thus are inherited rather than learnt. Research from this perspective, which is sometimes referred to as the 'positivist', the 'essentialist' and the 'organismic' as well as the 'traditional' approach, is generally directed towards such tasks as identifying the anatomical or genetic basis for the emotions, showing how emotions are linked to bodily changes, seeking to explain the function served by inherent emotions in human survival and social interaction or identifying which emotions are common to all human groups.

Some exponents of the 'inherent' perspective view emotional states as physiological responses to a given set of stimuli: for example, the 'flight or fight' response to a fearful situation. An emotion, in this view, is equivalent to the embodied sensation or a collection of sensations, such as flushes, visceral clutches, raising of the hair on the neck, that occur as a response to a stimulus. They argue that one becomes angry, for example, in response to an anger-provoking situation, and this feeling of anger generates physical sensations which enables one to deal with the situation to protect oneself. There is the suggestion in much writing within this perspective that the physical sensations provoked by an emotion, as 'instinctive reflexes', are relatively uncontrollable, although the extent to which they are subsequently acted upon may be mediated by conscious will. As the writer of a medical encyclopaedia put it:

> Civilization demands self-control, and self-control is learning not to act as emotion dictates. Even this is more than anyone can manage at all times, and reflex physical responses to emotion can hardly be controlled at all. A man can more or less learn not to punch someone on the nose whenever he is angry, but he cannot stop his pulse from racing, or a host of internal adjustments of which he is not even aware. (Wingate, 1988: 166)

As this quotation suggests, for many advocates of the 'emotions as inherent' perspective, the emotions are viewed as part of the animalistic legacy in human development, subject less to thought and reason than to impulse. Charles Darwin's theory of emotions, which viewed them as common to both animals and humans and based upon primitive states of physiological arousal involving innate instinctual drives, is highly influential to this conceptualization. Darwin published a book entitled *The Expression of the Emotions in Man and Animals* in 1872, in which he sought to establish a continuity of emotional expressions, as represented physically, from lower animals to humans. He theorized that the emotions were central to survival, by constituting reactions to threats and dangers in the immediate environment, as well as signalling future actions or intentions.

The neurophysiological approach takes up this individualistic and biological perspective by focusing its attention at the micro-level of human anatomy. Neurophysiological models of emotion have been very

dominant in psychological research, underpinning the efforts of psychologists since the foundation of the discipline to achieve recognition as
a science by engaging in research involving observable phenomena
(Gergen, 1995). Research from within this approach focuses on brain
functioning, with emphasis placed on identifying the biological factors
that relate perception to physiological response in humans, often by
using animal models (such as rats or cats). Specific parts of the brain are
identified as the sources of different types of emotion: the limbic system
for 'primitive' or 'instinctive' emotions (such as fear or disgust), the
frontal cortex for 'thinking' emotions (or those that are seen to be
mediated by experience and cultural understandings, such as jealousy or
embarrassment). For example, research has been carried out comparing
male and female brains using imaging techniques in the attempt to
identify differences between men's and women's brain function and the
relationship of such anatomical features to gender differences in emotional expression (Douglas, 1996). Other research has attempted to
discover how brain lesions or other damage of parts of the brain might
affect emotional expression. Attention is also paid in neurological
research to identifying the pathways by which the chemicals involved in
transmitting impulses to various parts of the brain work to incite
emotional response (see several of the chapters in Strongman (1992) for
examples of this type of research).

Recent writings in the field of what has been called 'evolutionary
psychology' have reformulated the Darwinian emphasis on the role
played by emotion in human survival. It is suggested in this literature
that the evolution of humans via natural selection favoured genotypes
that supposedly fostered social co-operation and reciprocal altruistic
tendencies, including the propensity for affection, gratitude and trust. It
is argued that unpleasant emotions, such as anxiety or anger, also serve
to enhance survival. Fear and its associated 'flight' behaviour, for example, are seen to act to separate the individual from the source of danger,
while anger is viewed as destroying a barrier to the satisfaction of a need
(Plutchik, 1982: 546). Emotions are thus portrayed as functional, 'total
body reactions to the various survival-related problems created by the
environment' (1982: 548).

Some theorists adopting this approach have attempted to systematize
the emotions. Plutchik (1982), for instance, attempts what he terms a
'psychoevolutionary structural' theory of emotion. He defines an emotion as 'an inferred complex sequence of reactions to a stimulus',
including 'cognitive evaluations, subjective changes, autonomic and
neural arousal, impulses to action, and behavior designed to have an
effect upon the stimulus that initiated the complex sequence' (1982: 551).
Plutchik suggests that 'there are eight basic adaptive reactions which are
the prototypes, singly or in combination, of all emotions', including
incorporation (of food or new stimuli), rejection (the expelling of something seen to be harmful), protection, destruction, reproduction, reinteg-

ration (response to the loss of something deemed to be important), orientation and exploration. He argues that these are all adaptive behavioural patterns related to survival, and that there is a set of 'primary' emotions which correspond to these patterns: ecstasy, vigilance, adoration, terror, amazement, grief, loathing, rage, anger, annoyance, disgust, boredom, sadness, pensiveness, surprise, distraction, fear and apprehension.

Appraisal and Emotion: Cognitive Theory

Cognitive theories of emotions, found mostly among social and behavioural psychologists and philosophers, are less biologically essentialist than several other 'inherent' approaches. While exponents of this approach maintain the conviction that there are some emotions that are universal to all humans, and that emotions have their basis in physiology, they have sought to identify the extent to which emotional behaviour is mediated through judgement and assessment of the context. From the cognitive approach it is argued that humans make judgements in relation to the physical sensations they feel when deciding what emotional state they are in. This approach builds on the writings of the early psychologist William James in his *The Principles of Psychology*, first published in 1890. James claimed that emotion begins with an initial bodily sensation (or set of sensations) in response to an event which is evaluated cognitively and labelled as a particular emotion: 'we feel sorry because we cry, afraid because we tremble' (James, quoted in Gergen, 1995: 8). From this perspective, therefore, the physical response is seen to *precede* the emotion and is interpreted in certain ways based on judgement of the situation. This is clearly a different approach from those perspectives I described above, which generally begin with the premise that emotion *causes* or is *equivalent* to physical sensation.

Cognitive theorists are thus interested in the interrelationship between bodily response, context and the individual's recognition of an emotion. They focus in particular on the ways in which environmental conditions are appraised, leading to an emotional reaction, but may also be regulated (controlled or voluntarily enhanced) in response to individual experience and the sociocultural system of norms about emotional expression in which an individual is located. This process of appraisal is represented as being related to the individual's understandings of how events might affect her or his well-being. Appraisal, therefore, may be viewed as a product of socialization, for how a situation is appraised by an individual from one culture may differ from the appraisal given by another individual from a different culture. The physiological responses that are produced in response to the appraisal, however, are generally regarded as fixed and universal across cultures and times: it is the interpretations of the context that are variable.

Like the psychoevolutionary perspective, the cognitive approach tends to see emotions as functional, as coping responses. Mesquita and Frijda, for example, describe appraisal processes in functional terms as 'a series of checks with respect to a set of dimensions such as positive or negative valence, causation by someone else or the self, blameworthiness, outcome uncertainty, controllability, and modifiability. A series of such checks describes the emotional significance of an event' (1992: 180). They go on to state how various emotions prepare individuals for 'action', impelling them to respond in certain ways to the situation: for instance, the readiness to protect oneself from danger as part of the experience of fear.

Folkman and Lazarus (1988: 310) give the examples of anger, which they see as usually including an appraisal of a harm or a threat in the immediate environment, and happiness, which they describe as including an appraisal that 'a particular person-environment condition is beneficial'. They define two types of cognitive appraisal, the primary form involving the question 'What do I have at stake in this encounter?', contributing to the quality and intensity of emotional response, and the secondary form of appraisal taking the form of the question 'What can I do?'. According to Folkman and Lazarus, the answer to the second question influences the kinds of coping strategy that will be used to deal with the demands of the situation. Problem-focused forms of coping will be more likely to be used if the situation is appraised as amenable to change, while emotion-focused forms of coping are more likely to be used if the outcome is appraised as unchangeable (Folkman and Lazarus, 1988: 310).

Most models of emotion proposed by cognitive theorists still tend to treat emotion as states of physiological arousal. While the cognitive approach does take into account social norms and contexts around emotional states, it has been criticized for drawing too artificial a distinction between emotion and thought, or between a feeling or bodily sensation and the accompanying interpretation of that feeling or sensation as 'an emotion'. There is therefore a tendency in these accounts for the 'private', individual world of sensation to be contrasted with the 'external' world of observation, intellect and calculation (Jaggar, 1989: 149–50). The cognitive approach may also be criticized for holding too linear and rationalistic a perspective on how emotions are experienced. The ways that the emotions are described in some of this literature represents them as somewhat sterile entities, the outcomes of a logical sequence of information processing such as is performed by computers. There is little sense given of the details of the sociocultural context in which the meanings of emotions are developed, including such aspects as power relations, historical conditions or individuals' membership of social groups. Rather, emotion is treated dominantly as the experience of a self-interested, atomistic individual.

Emotions as Sociocultural Constructions

The other major approach to emotions I have identified in the humanities and social sciences adopts a social constructionist perspective. To describe emotion as socially constructed means that it is always experienced, understood and named via social and cultural processes. Social constructionists, therefore, tend to view the emotions to a greater or lesser degree as learnt rather than inherited behaviours or responses. At a general level, social constructionists tend to be interested in identifying and tracing the ways in which norms and expectations about the emotions are generated, reproduced and operate in specific sociocultural settings, and the implications for selfhood and social relations of emotional experience and expression.

Within the perspective offered by social constructionist approaches to the emotions, however, there are a number of different foci and inflections. The 'weak', or less relativistic thesis of social constructionism concedes that there is a limited range of 'natural emotion responses' that are biologically given and thus exist independently of sociocultural influences and learning (Armon-Jones, 1986: 38). Exponents of the 'weak' thesis, therefore, although taking more of an interest in the social and cultural aspects of experiences and understandings of the emotions than many of the researchers I have grouped under the 'emotions as inherent' perspective, have some things in common with these researchers (and this is where the distinction between the two tends to blur).

One exponent of the 'weak' thesis is the sociologist Theodore Kemper. He contends that the emotions are 'rooted in our evolutionary nature' which is also 'ineluctably social' and goes on to assert that 'there are no emotions that are purely internal or context-free' (1991: 301). In his own research, Kemper (1987) has identified four physiologically grounded 'primary' emotions: fear, anger, depression and satisfaction/happiness. He sees these emotions as universal to all humans, as manifested very early in human development and as having survival value, emerging from evolutionary processes. Kemper (1987) describes such emotions as guilt, shame, pride, gratitude, love and nostalgia as 'secondary' emotions which are acquired through 'socializing agents'. He claims that the 'primary' emotions are altered in some ways through 'socializing agents' to become 'secondary emotions'. Kemper views guilt, therefore, as a form of 'socialized' fear (of punishment for inappropriate behaviour), while shame is anger (with the self) which has been 'socialized' and pride is 'socialized' satisfaction.

The 'strong' thesis of the social constructionist approach is that emotion is an irreducibly sociocultural product, wholly learnt and constructed through acculturation. For exponents of the 'strong' thesis, emotional states are viewed as purely contextual and cannot be reified as separate entities: they are not inherent or pre-existing, waiting to be studied by the researcher. They claim that the words we use to label a set of phenomena such as internal states, thoughts and behaviours as an 'emotion' are generally selected in relation to a particular situation and are often used to rationalize reasons and actions. It is in bringing together these understandings, feelings and behaviours with the logic of situation and rationale that the sense of which emotion is involved begins to emerge (Griffiths, 1995: 100). Emotion is thus viewed as an intersubjective rather than an individual phenomenon, constituted in the relations between people.

Exponents of this perspective see emotions as self-reflexive, involving active perception, identification and management on the part of individuals, and indeed, as created through this reflexiveness. Lutz describes emotions as 'culturally constructed judgments, that is, as aspects of cultural meaning systems people use in attempting to understand the situations in which they find themselves' (1985: 65). As such, emotions are viewed as dynamic, changeable according to the historical, social and political contexts in which they are generated, reproduced and expressed. Attention is paid to the ways in which emotional phenomena are given different meanings which have wider social and political implications.

One of the most prolific exponents of the 'strong' social constructionist approach is the social psychologist Rom Harré, who has asserted that 'there is no such thing as "an emotion". There are only various ways of acting and feeling emotionally, of displaying one's judgements, attitudes and opinions in an appropriate bodily way' (1991: 142; see also Harré, 1986). He suggests, therefore, that an emotion is not an entity unto itself, separate from the bodily experience and expression of the emotion. Harré emphasizes the moral meanings of emotions. In relation to the emotion of 'anger', for example, he contends that:

> By reifying 'anger', we can be tempted into the mistake of thinking that anger is something inside a person exercising its invisible and inaudible influence on what we do. But to be angry is to have taken on the angry role on a particular occasion as the expression of a moral position. This role may involve the feeling of appropriate feelings as well as indulging in suitable public conduct. The bodily feeling is often the somatic expression to oneself of the taking of a moral standpoint. (Harré, 1991: 142–3)

There is also an implication of self-assessment in this description. That is, Harré suggests that individuals do not 'spontaneously' feel and express an emotion. One 'does' an emotion instead of 'having' an emotion.

Cultural anthropologists have played an integral role in the 'strong' social constructionist project by conducting cross-cultural comparisons of emotional expression and understanding, with an emphasis on small-scale, non-western cultures. Such research is directed at demonstrating the lack of universality of emotions across cultures (see Heelas (1986) for a comprehensive review of this literature). It therefore points to the fragile nature of the category of 'emotion' by emphasizing that emotions are understood in various ways in different cultural milieux: 'The prevalent assumption that the emotions are invariant across cultures is replaced here with the question of how one cultural discourse on emotion may be translated into another' (Lutz, 1988: 5). Lutz (1988) notes that for anthropologists studying cultures other than their own, the difficulty of attempting to identify and understand the emotional lives of people in that 'strange' culture is related to the difficulty of understanding their moral system. If it is assumed that the expression of emotion is not simply a matter of drawing from a common pool of emotions shared by all humans, as the 'inherent' approach would have it, then the research question becomes oriented to identifying cultural views and expressions of 'that which is real and good and proper' (Lutz, 1988: 8).

Social historians of emotion have taken a similar approach, but have directed their attention towards the ways in which conventions around emotions have changed over different historical periods within rather than across cultures. For instance, Stearns (1995) has shown how grief has undergone several reformulations in Anglo-American societies in the past two centuries in response to economic demands, religious expectation and demographic changes. He claims that grief tended to be minimized before the nineteenth century but became a dominant emotion in the Victorian era almost to the point of obsession. By the late nineteenth century, mourning rituals were flourishing and grief and sorrow were major topics in popular culture and private letters and diaries. By the early years of the twentieth century, however, there is evidence of a turn against grief rituals as 'vulgar and morbid', and parents were advised to keep signs of grief from their children. Stearns links these changes with a dramatic reduction in mortality rates, particularly for infants, between the late nineteenth century and the early decades of the twentieth century. He contends that by the latter period, extended engagement in grief and mourning rituals had become impractical because of the demands of steadily advancing industrialization. A decline in religious certainty and a move away from the embrace of emotional intensity towards emotional restraint also weakened grief culture.

Such social histories provide valuable insights into the shifts in notions of emotion across time within cultures. They emphasize the contingency of current taken-for-granted assumptions about emotional behaviour and the ontology of emotion and point to the importance of identifying the broader social and economic changes that are associated with changes in concepts of emotion and emotional experience.

Emotion and Power: Structuralism

Structuralism is a dominant perspective in the sociology of the emotions. While it shares similar preoccupations with the cognitive perspective in studying the link between appraisal of the situation and emotional response, structuralism goes even further in focusing attention on the macro-social aspects of the context in which emotions are experienced and understood. Many exponents of this perspective, however, still retain the notion that there is some universal, biological basis to at least some emotions, and could therefore be described as adopting a 'weak' rather than a 'strong' social constructionist position. They often take a functionalist line, viewing emotions as supporting human survival. Hochschild, for example, defines emotion as 'a biologically given sense, and our most important one. Like other senses – hearing, touch and smell – it is a means by which we know about our relation to the world, and it is therefore crucial for the survival of human beings in group life' (1983: 219).

From the structuralist perspective, emotions are viewed as being shaped by social institutions, social systems and power relations. This approach sees individuals' emotional states as directly associated with their position in the social system and their membership of social groups, such as their gender or social class. The more radical of those writers who may be grouped under the rubric of structuralism adopt a Marxist perspective in critiquing the social inequities implicated in emotional experience. Marx himself fulminated against the feelings of boredom, resentment, bitterness and despair that were produced in members of the proletariat as an outcome of their oppressive living and working conditions and their alienation from the expropriated products of their labour as part of the capitalist economic system. As Marx and Engels proclaim in their *Manifesto of the Communist Party*: 'Not only are [the proletarians] slaves of the bourgeois class, and of the bourgeois State; they are daily and hourly enslaved by the machine, by the overlooker, and above all, by the individual bourgeois manufacturer himself. The more openly this despotism proclaims gain to be its end and aim, the more petty, the more hateful and the more embittering it is' (1848/1982: 41–2).

The early sociologist Emile Durkheim was also interested in emotion, but from a functional structuralist rather than a critical or 'conflict' structuralist perspective. He referred to the importance of social norms in rituals in his writings on religion, particularly his *The Elementary Forms of the Religious Life* (1912/1961). Durkheim asserted that through these rituals high emotions are generated, which in turn serve to cement together social bonds and generate collective solidarity. He termed this kind of emotion 'collective effervescence'. His work suggests that social order is not simply maintained via 'rational' thought or reasoned action, but is also fundamentally underpinned by affective ties which are developed at the group level.

One area of interest in structuralist research is the role played by such emotions as shame, guilt and embarrassment in maintaining social order and underpinning social relations. For Scheff (1990), pride and shame are the 'primary social emotions' because they serve as 'intense and automatic bodily signs of the state of a system that would be otherwise

difficult to observe, the state of one's bonds to others'. They are 'instinctive signals' which communicate the state of a social bond: 'Pride is the
sign of an intact bond; shame, a severed or threatened bond' (Scheff,
1990: 15). Shame, he argues, is generated through constant self-
monitoring of one's behaviour. For that reason it is the most important
social emotion in terms of its self-regulating function and its relationship
to gauging what others think of one's behaviour. Scheff argues that
conformity to 'exterior norms' is rewarded by others' deference and a
feeling of pride, while non-conformity is punished by non-deference and
feelings of shame, providing an explanation of why people conform to
norms and how social control operates (1990: 95).

Kemper (1991) is also interested in the ways in which emotion is
generated as part of power relations between individuals. He argues for
an equation whereby social actors have a certain amount of power. In
their interactions with another actor, he suggests, emotions will flow due
to the actors' realization of either loss or gain of power. Thus, for
example, in any one social interaction of two actors, 'if one actor loses
power or the other actor gains it, the emotional outcome is some degree
of fear or anxiety. If one actor gains power and/or the other actor loses it,
the emotional outcome is likely to be a sense of security' (Kemper, 1991:
319).

As well as directing their attention at how emotions serve a function in
the maintenance of social order, many structuralists are interested in the
reverse relationship: the social ordering of emotional expression, and the
rules and norms underpinning emotion 'work' in various social contexts.
The concept of emotion 'work' differs from that of the 'control' or
'suppression' of emotion in that it is not merely about stifling or
suppressing feeling, but also about constituting feeling, bringing it into
being in response to awareness of social norms about what one *should* be
feeling. As Hochschild has put it, 'By "emotion work" I refer to the act of
trying to change in degree or quality an emotion or feeling' (1979: 561).
She goes on to claim that 'Emotion work becomes an object of awareness
most often, perhaps, when the individual's feelings do not fit the
situation' (1979: 563). This definition suggests that at least some emotions
do not 'naturally' occur as instinctive responses, but must be produced
by the individual as a deliberate, reasoned social strategy.

Emotion work operates through 'feeling rules'. For instance, people
are expected to be happy at weddings and birthdays and sad at funerals.
If these rules are flouted, it is argued, the individual is generally
subjected to social censure of varying degrees, ranging from the expression of mild disapproval and admonitions to 'cheer up' to outrage
(Hochschild, 1979, 1983). While accepted as given when 'all goes well', it
is when these rules are broken that the individual stands out as a
'deviant' other, provoking anger or frustration in others. Thus the
person's expression of emotion comes to be socially shaped and subject
to a high degree of management.

As noted above, some writers within structuralism have adopted a critical perspective, influenced by Marxist theory, on the ways in which emotions have come to be regulated in contemporary western societies. One of the most influential is Hochschild (1983), who argues that the management of the emotions has become increasingly commercialized. According to Hochschild, the number of 'emotion workers' has been rising since the early decades of the twentieth century. This term refers to individuals who are paid to adjust their feelings to the needs of the customer and the requirements of the work situation (for example, flight attendants, prostitutes, social workers, debt collectors and sales workers). Emotional management, Hochschild claims, has become progressively less voluntary and amenable to change on the part of the individual over the course of this century: feelings have therefore become harnessed to economic imperatives.

In her empirical research exploring how flight attendants are trained to manage their 'real' feelings to present a pleasant, smiling countenance to their customers, Hochschild (1983) contends that the institutional rules of emotional management and expression that are adopted by the attendants in order to perform their jobs have a personal cost. Flight attendants must repress their 'real' feelings in dealing with passengers. If they are angered or irritated by offensive behaviour, frustrated, afraid or tired, they cannot overtly show this, because of airline policy about how attendants should present themselves. In doing so, in putting on a 'false demeanour', they are progressively alienated from their 'real feelings' and 'real selves'. According to Hochschild:

> There is a cost to emotion work: it affects the degree to which we listen to feeling and sometimes our very capacity to feel . . . when the transmutation of the private use of feeling is successfully accomplished – when we succeed in lending our feelings to the organized engineers of worker-customer relations – we may pay a cost in how we hear our feelings and a cost in what, for better or worse, they tell us about ourselves . . . the worker risks losing the signal function of feeling. (Hochschild, 1983: 21)

Hochschild calls this 'the commercial distortion of the managed heart' (1983: 22). Running throughout Hochschild's critique, therefore, is the notion that there is a more 'real' or 'true' self that needs to be freed from the imperatives of the labour market, so that what she sees to be more 'authentic' emotional responses may be experienced and expressed. Her approach to emotion 'work' suggests that the less emotions are regulated by social norms, the better.

Structuralists have some important insights to offer in terms of noting differences in emotional patterns between social groups and highlighting the role of power and political structures in the management and expression of emotion. Some exponents of this approach, however, appear to be rather formulaic in their understandings of how emotions are produced, seeing a specific structural condition of a social relationship as invariably producing an associated emotion. Some theorists adopting the structuralist approach have even attempted to use mathematical-statistical methods to predict emotions (see research reviewed in Kemper, 1991: 320–2). The social actor in structuralist accounts often tends to be represented as passively shaped (and sometimes as coercively manipulated or controlled) by 'feeling rules'. Particularly in critical approaches, norms of emotional management are portrayed as prescriptive, constraining and restrictive of selfhood, serving to support institutions, the economic system and social inequalities and to regulate and maintain the prevailing social order to the detriment of individuals' emotional welfare. There is little sense of individual agency in these accounts.

Emotion and Selfhood: The Phenomenological Approach

For writers adopting the phenomenological perspective, the experience of emotion is viewed as integral to our selfhood and the ways in which we assess and deal with others, including in moral terms. Emotion, thus, is viewed as a phenomenon worthy of profound philosophical inquiry. This approach can be identified in the writings of Jean-Paul Sartre, for whom emotions were cognitive estimations and moral judgements of the individual's place in the world (Finkelstein, 1980: 112). For phenomenologists, an individual's 'lived experience', or the self-understandings and judgement built up from an individual's membership of and experiences in a particular social milieu, is the key to the emotional experience. As Finkelstein has put it: 'The individual's feelings of distress, anxiety, boredom, alienation, love, sympathy, and so on, are manifestations of the personal and private apprehensions the individual has made of the world. As such, emotions are emblematic of the individual's understanding of self, others and the social milieu' (1980: 119). The phenomenological critique of a simple physiological approach to the emotions is that behaviour or awareness of behaviour are not emotions. Rather, phenomenologists claim, it is the individual's *interpretation* of bodily sensations that is the emotion. Finkelstein defines emotions as 'stances towards the world, emblematic of the individual's apprehension of it and moral position within it: how the individual feels becomes how the individual sees' (1980: 119).

The definition of emotion rests on an individual's judgement of the situation, which itself is a product of acculturation and part of 'being-in-the-world'. The concept of 'being-in-the-world' is an integral part of the philosophy of the phenomenologist Merleau-Ponty, who considered emotion to be inevitably part of individuals' interactions with others. Merleau-Ponty argued that physical sensation can only ever be understood and defined as 'emotion' in the interpersonal context in which it is experienced. Emotion, therefore, is much more than sensation or an inner state: it is a relational, or intersubjective, phenomenon which joins us to others and is produced via our interactions with others (Crossley, 1996: 47–8).

The sociologist Norman Denzin took up and developed this approach to emotion in his book *On Understanding Emotion* (1984). He notes in the early pages of the book that 'The voluminous literature on the emotions does not contain any serious phenomenological account of the essential features of emotionality as a lived experience' (1984: vii). Denzin's work was designed to fill this void by offering a phenomenological account of 'the inner and outer worlds of emotional experience' with the central thesis that 'self-feelings lie at the core of the emotional experience' (1984: vii). For Denzin, emotions are nothing less than central to the ontology of human existence. He argues that 'People are their emotions. To understand who a person is, it is necessary to understand emotion' (1984: 1). He goes on to contend that 'to consider only the biological body . . . independent of the lived body, and the person's consciousness of his or her body as the source of his or her emotion, is to treat the body as a thing and to locate emotion in disorders of the body' (1984: 20).

Denzin's central research question was: 'How is emotion, as a form of consciousness, lived, experienced, articulated, and felt?' (1984: 1). He asserts that emotionality locates the individual in the world of social interactions. While the emotions may be experienced as inner feelings, they are generated through interactions with others: 'A person cannot experience an emotion without the implicit or imagined presence of others' (1984: 3). He points to the subjective nature of the experience of emotions and notes that the labels applied to emotional experiences are subject to change and different interpretations. Denzin argues that what he calls 'self-feelings' are any emotions that a person feels. Emotions include both those feelings that people direct towards the self, and also to others. But emotions are always self-referential: 'An emotional experience that does not in some way have the self, the self-system, or the self or self-system of the other as its referent seems inconceivable' (1984: 50). Emotions, therefore, also provide a means by which a person is able to work towards self-knowledge.

It is this self-referential dimension of emotion that Denzin argues is absent in the physiological, stimulus-response approach to the emotions: 'Emotions are not things; they are processes. What is managed in an emotional experience is not an emotion but the self in the feeling that is being felt' (1984: 50). While emotions such as anger may not have their origin in the self, they are always referred back to the self that feels (1984: 50–1). Emotions, therefore, are not the outcome of a linear sequence of events and responses, but rather emerge in a hermeneutic circle, in which emotional thoughts merge and run together and are responses to previous interpretations, understandings and experiences: 'The temporality of emotional consciousness becomes circular, internally self-reflective, and encased within its own experiential boundaries. The future, the present, and the past all become part of the same emotional experience.

What is felt now is shaped by what will be felt, and what will be felt is shaped by what was felt' (1984: 79).

Another dimension of emotions to which Denzin points is the self-justification involved, or the ways that emotions 'carry or call for justification within the person's present world of involvement' (1984: 53). That is, in western societies at least, one cannot experience an emotion without wanting to come up with some justification or reason for why one is feeling this emotion. Denzin terms these justifications 'emotional accounts' and argues that these accounts are basic to an understanding of self-feeling (1984: 53).

For example, a person undergoing an important job interview may find herself experiencing certain bodily sensations she interprets as 'feeling nervous'. These sensations may include a tightened stomach, rapid breathing, pounding heart, a feeling of hotness, sweaty palms, jerking movements of the foot, a dry throat and mouth, quavering voice and flushed neck and face. Members of the interview panel will not be able to observe some of these bodily signs but may well notice others, and also come to the conclusion that the individual is 'feeling nervous' rather than, for example, demonstrating anger or fear, both of which emotions include similar bodily processes. That the individual is experiencing these bodily sensations in the first place is because of her situated knowledge and interpretation of the context in which she finds herself: the important job interview. She, and those observing her, interpret the sensations she feels and demonstrates as 'nervousness' rather than 'anger' or 'fear' because of their culturally specific understandings that such situations generate this type of emotion rather than other emotions. They decide that this emotion is wholly appropriate and even expected, given their shared understandings of the nature and meanings of the situation. Should the woman be experiencing such sensations having a peaceful meal at the dinner table with friends or family, however, and find herself unable to locate a socially appropriate reason for such sensations, she may define them as 'inappropriate', perhaps causing further emotional states of worry and anxiety.

Emotional feeling and expression is part of what Denzin refers to as the 'interpretive', everyday practices of the person. These practices, he argues, 'involve a constitutive core of recurring activities that must be learned, taught, traced out, coached, felt, internalized, and interiorized, as well as expressed and exteriorized. They must be practiced over and over. They become a part of the taken-for-granted structures of activity that surround and are ingrained in every individual' (1984: 88). For Denzin, the practices of the person reveals the self. Emotionality, he argues, attaches to these interpretive practices, which operate at two levels: the practical level, or the actual doing of the practice, and the interpretive level, the evaluation and judgement of that practice. The practice may be embodied, such as exercising, or disembodied, such as thought:

An 'emotional practice' is an embedded practice that produces for the person an expected or unexpected emotional alteration in the inner and outer streams of experience. Such practices may be recurring – for example, lovemaking, eating, drinking, exercising, working, or playing. Emotional practices place the person in the presence of others and often require others for their accomplishment. Emotional practices are both practical and interpretive. They are personal, embodied, and situated. Unlike purely cognitive practices, which are taken for granted and not emotionally disruptive of the flow of experience, emotional practices make people problematic objects to themselves. The emotional practice radiates through the person's body and streams of experience, giving emotional coloration to thoughts, feelings, and actions. (Denzin, 1984: 89)

Denzin identifies 'pretended emotion' as occurring in situations where people know that they should feel and express an emotion but do not 'really' feel the emotion. In this situation, Denzin argues, emotions are 'distorted' or are 'spurious'; 'deep' emotions are contradicted by 'surface' emotions (1984: 75–6). As this would suggest, Denzin's approach to the emotional self is similar to that of writers like Hochschild, in that he sees some forms of emotion 'work' as distorting the 'true' self. However, phenomenologists are less likely than structuralists to consider some emotions as inherent. They would rather see them as 'manufactured aspects of social reality' (Finkelstein, 1980: 119). As such, their perspective on emotion approaches the 'stronger' rather than the 'weaker' end of the social constructionist continuum.

The phenomenological account of emotions is important to an understanding of the ontology of the emotional self because of the insights it offers on the relationship of emotion to selfhood. It moves well away from the overly rationalized and prescriptive view that is often presented in structuralist accounts by focusing more attention at the meaningful, dynamic and moral nature of emotion. There is also a far greater sense of individual agency in relation to people's emotional experience provided by phenomenological accounts. Phenomenologists tend to be less interested in the role played by more macro factors such as social structures, institutions and power relations in individuals' emotional experience.

Emotion as Discursive Practice: Poststructuralist Perspectives

Another dimension of emotional experience is the rendering of bodily sensations into language. An emphasis on discourse (or patterns of words used to describe and explain phenomena) emerges from recent developments in poststructuralist theory, particularly as it has been influenced by the writings of Foucault and Derrida. The central argument of this perspective is the constitutive role played by language. For poststructuralists, discourses do not simply reflect or describe reality, knowledge, experience, identity, social relationships, social institutions and practices. Rather, they play an integral part in constructing them: 'Discourse is a practice not just of representing the world, but of signifying the world, constituting and constructing the world in meaning' (Fairclough, 1992: 64). The words used in relation to emotions, therefore, are not assumed to be simply labels for 'emotion things', describing pre-existing entities or natural events. Rather, they are seen as 'coalescences of complex ethnotheoretical ideas about the nature of self and social interaction' and as 'actions or ideological practices' serving specific ends as part of the creation and negotiation of reality (Lutz, 1988: 10). It is clear from these statements that poststructuralist perspectives fall towards the 'strong' thesis end of the social constructionist continuum.

An example of the poststructuralist perspective is a discussion by Fischer (1993) on the concept of 'emotionality', particularly as it is used in describing women. Fischer argues that because the term 'emotional' has so many meanings, it is impossible to claim that members of one gender group (or that matter, one ethnic/racial or age group) are inherently more 'emotional' than those of another group. Emotionality should not be viewed as an individual personality trait or property of a particular social group, but as a culturally constructed and responsive category. Fischer contends that the social science instruments which attempt to measure differences in emotional experience and expression themselves act to constitute what they are searching for rather than identifying 'inherent' or 'natural' differences between men and women.

Poststructuralist approaches to the emotions, therefore, privilege the role played by language and other cultural artefacts in the construction and experience of the emotions. Indeed, Abu-Lughod and Lutz (1990: 10) argue for a perspective that views emotion as 'discursive practice'. As they point out, such a focus on discourse 'leads us to a more complex view of the multiple, shifting, and contested meanings possible in emotional utterances and interchanges, and from there to a less monolithic concept of emotion' (1990: 11). They contend that this 'new' approach recognizes the constituted nature of emotion via language, sees emotions not as internal states, but as about social life, and acknowledges the power relations inherent in 'emotion talk' (1990: 2). Harré and Gillett (1994) have also discussed in detail the 'discursive approach', which they argue has transformed the psychology of the emotions. For advocates of discursive psychology, the emotions are thought of as 'actual moments of emotional feelings and displays, moments in which we are "feeling annoyed" or in which we are "displaying our joy" in particular circumstances in a definite cultural setting' (Harré and Gillett, 1994: 146). The physical adjuncts of emotions are viewed as incidental to the emotional state, while the social world is regarded as primary, particularly the linguistic practices used to define emotions.

To focus attention on the patterns of language used to describe emotions moves towards an understanding of how we interpret bodily sensations and represent them to ourselves and others as 'emotions'. According to Lutz, deconstructing the discursive and cultural aspects of emotion does not preclude the use of the term:

> After deconstruction, emotion retains value as a way of talking about the intensely meaningful as that is culturally defined, socially enacted, and personally articulated. It retains value also as a category more open than others to use as a link between the mental and the physical . . . and between the ideal or desired world and the actual world. (Lutz, 1988: 5)

In poststructuralist writings, the notion of the fragmented rather than the unified self is privileged. The term 'subjectivity' has been adopted in the place of 'selfhood' or 'self-identity' to describe the manifold ways in which individuals understand themselves and experience their lives. The concept of subjectivity incorporates the understanding that self-identity is highly changeable and contextual, albeit within certain limits imposed by the culture in which an individual lives. Subjectivity is produced, negotiated and reshaped via discourse and practice.

A poststructuralist perspective would therefore tend to reject the notion that there is such a thing as a 'true' or 'false' self that exists separately from social and cultural processes, as writers like Hochschild and Denzin have contended (see discussion above). Rather, it is understood that notions of the self are constituted through these processes and thus are inseparable. From the poststructuralist perspective, therefore, the existence of 'feeling rules' and the emphasis placed on emotional management in all contexts of life is part of the way in which the body and the self are governed and constituted. Discourses on emotional management and conduct are inevitably part of human subjectivity. They cannot be stripped from the self, leaving the 'true' self behind, for different discourses construct the self in different ways. It is through discourses on emotions, therefore, including 'feeling rules', that the emotional self is shaped and reshaped as a continuous project of subjectivity.

In an analysis of the discourses of love and romance, for example, Wetherell argues that even in the case of what is seen to be the 'overwhelming' emotions of passion and romantic love, the experience and feeling is always inevitably identified, labelled and constructed through narrative and language. Thus, when people 'in love' describe their feelings to themselves and each other:

> the discourse analyst says that it is not the case that every woman and man in love magically find themselves uttering, creating and discovering afresh, for the first time, these words as the mirror or reflection of their experience, although they may well feel they are doing just that. The words instead are second-hand, already in circulation, already familiar, already there, waiting for the moment of appropriation. (Wetherell, 1996: 134)

The notion that emotions are constructed via discourse does not necessarily imply that people are passive actors in this process. The relationship between subjects, discourses and practices and emotions is not a simple, predictable one. Jackson argues, for example, that the process of 'being in love' is active rather than passive, an action of locating oneself within 'scripts' or discourses of love: 'Those who feel themselves to be "in love" have a wealth of novels, plays, movies and songs on which to draw to make sense of and describe their passion' (1993: 212). She points out that women tend to be socialized into a form of 'emotional literacy' in relation to love and romance – for example learning a romance narrative by reading romance novels or magazines and watching soap operas on television – in ways that men are not. As a result, 'Women often find men emotionally illiterate precisely because men have not learnt to construct and manipulate romance narratives or wider discourses of emotion' (Jackson, 1993: 216). As this would suggest, there is no inherent reason why women might be 'better' at 'reading' emotions than men. Rather, it is the gendered acculturation, including the discourses to which they have access and which seem to 'make sense' for them, in which individuals engage throughout their lives that shapes their capacity to identify and experience emotions.

Another integral tenet of the poststructuralist approach is the dynamic nature of discourse, and the subsequent dynamic nature of subjectivity. Discourses on emotions, as themselves social products, are constantly shifting and changing, competing with each other for prominence, with some coming to the fore at some historical moments, and others receding into the background. It may be argued, therefore, that there are alternative positions and locations from which emotions can be taken up, interpreted and understood. As Hearn has contended, 'it is more helpful to see discourses as both *producing* people assumed to be "subjects" that are or are not emotional, and *produced* by people assumed to be subjects. In both senses subjects do emotions, they do not just happen "automatically"; they have to be *done*' (1993: 148, original emphases). People may choose from those discourses that are available to them or seek to resist dominant discourses, albeit within certain constraints. Their resistance or opposition to dominant discourses, as well as their desire to take them up, may spring from a conscious decision, but may also take place at the unconscious level. It is for this reason that an understanding of the psychodynamics of emotional experience is important to include in a sociocultural exploration of the emotional self.

Emotion and the Unconscious: The Psychodynamic Perspective

Both structuralist and poststructuralist analyses may be criticized for representing the human subject as a largely rational, autonomous individual whose motivation and behaviour emerge from and are manipulated by conscious thought processes. Emotionality, however, would seem to be a phenomenon that also incorporates meanings derived from the 'extra-rational', or that which precedes or is beyond rationality. Psychoanalysis, both as a therapeutic practice and a body of theory, is interested in delving beneath the conscious level of meaning. As such, the psychodynamic perspective offers some valuable insights for understanding the unconscious dimensions of the emotional self.

While psychoanalytic theory played an important role in the development of sociological theory earlier this century (for example, in the work of Talcott Parsons on human motivation and action), it has since lost favour among sociologists, beginning from the 1970s and the influence of social structuralism. Contemporary sociologists interested in emotion have thus tended to neglect the contributions of psychoanalytic perspectives. One major exception is Denzin, who has argued the following:

> My body and my stream of consciousness are moving emotional sites. They are filled with emotional memories, childhood experiences, semirecognizable images of my parents (missing and absent fathers and mothers), and interiorized images (imago) of myself as a distinct object and subject. My dreams, fantasies, and conversations are played out in the dramas of my primordial family situation. I relive my past, emotionally, in the present. I do so in terms of the repertoires of feeling, expression, repression, distortion, and signification that were acquired in my original family situation. These repertoires of feeling and thinking are today reworked through my present situation as it comes toward me from the past. (Denzin, 1984: 43)

As this excerpt suggests, emotions are often felt or experienced at the unconscious rather than the conscious level of experience. Emotions may be expressed in dreams or fantasies rather than put into discourse, and thus may at times be 'extra-discursive' as well as 'extra-rational'.

The concept of the unconscious, or the place in the human psyche where repressed thoughts, fantasies, drives, desires and motivations reside, constantly threatening to re-emerge into consciousness, is integral to psychoanalytic writings. The unconscious is formed through social experience and in turn shapes human action. It was Freud, of course, who first began the project of psychoanalysis and developed the notion of the unconscious, originating in his clinical work as a neurologist with 'hysterical' women in the late nineteenth century. More recent psychoanalytic theory, especially in its formulations revising Freudian theory and incorporating Lacanian and Foucauldian theory (see, for example, Henriques et al., 1984), recognizes the interrelationship between emotion, sociocultural processes, discourse, individual experience and the unconscious. As such, it may be considered as a social constructionist approach, although some of those who take up psychodynamic perspectives are closer to the 'weak' end of the social constructionist spectrum in arguing that some emotions are universal to all humans (see, for example, Craib, 1995).

For psychoanalytic theorists, emotional investments are central to understanding subjectivity, motivation and action. It is argued that the unconscious is a potent source of emotional response, particularly for those emotions that we may find unpredictable or for which it is difficult to construct a 'rational' explanation when we experience them. Psychodynamic perspectives focus attention on individuals' biographies of their early relations with caregivers and other family members, with a particular interest in the ambivalences inherent in people's intimate relationships with òthers. A major tenet of psychoanalytic theory is the inevitability of the repetition of features of early relationships – particularly those individuals may have had as an infant or young child with their primary caregivers – throughout adult life and in other important relationships. Most unconscious feelings, fantasies and neuroses, according to Freud, originate in the pivotal psychic process occurring in early life, the Oedipal crisis, when the young child goes through individuation from the mother. This is achieved by the child turning away from the mother towards the father, who symbolically stands for the external world, the world beyond the mother's body. For Freud, this point of development was crucial to the state of people's future emotional well-being and their adult relationships with others.

Central to understandings of human behaviour as they are articulated in psychoanalytic theory are the concepts of the unconscious defence mechanisms by which people deal with feelings that are potentially destructive to the self, such as anxiety, fear, envy, hate and emptiness. These mechanisms include splitting, introjection, projection and projective identification. By these unconscious defence mechanisms, unacceptable or painful inner aspects of the self or emotions are removed from the self and transferred to other people or things. Splitting involves the unconscious separation of 'good' and 'bad' fantasy objects in the individual's inner world. Projection involves the pushing out of the 'good', and more often the 'bad', feelings from the inner world to something or someone in the external world. Introjection is the reverse: both 'good' and 'bad' things from the external world are taken into the self, or internalized (Minsky, 1996: 85–6). In projective identification, the parts of the self that are externalized and located in another are then recognized in the other, although not as originating within the self. This may at best lead to empathy, at worst with identifying and attacking negative aspects of the other or losing a sense of self (Stein, 1985: 10).

Psychodynamic approaches need not be limited to an individualized perspective on the emotions. Rutherford notes that emotions, moods and fantasies are central to the construction and maintenance of 'individual political and cultural identifications with specific social relations, institutions and values' (1992: 79). Understanding the psychodynamics of such identifications can explain why individuals make a deep emotional investment in conforming or supporting these social relations, institutions and values. Freud himself was interested in the role played by unconsciously felt emotions in the formation of social groups. He saw the emotional ties keeping groups together as involving idealized fraternal love but also paranoid hostility and aggression in response to other groups. Individuals within groups may project destructive feelings such as anxiety and fear into the group, so that the group takes on these emotional characteristics (Segal, 1995: 192–5). Segal (1995: 196–7)

observes, for example, that political groups often seem to be the reposit-
ory of the collective feelings of superiority, messianic missions, convic-
tions of rightness and paranoia about others felt by their members. She
argues that the most clear projection of negative feelings at the collective
level occurs in the context of war, where the group of which one is a
member is positioned as perfect and blameless and the enemy as an evil
inhuman or subhuman monster upon which are projected feelings of
badness, fear and guilt.

Many of these ideas originated with Freud but have been elaborated
by other influential psychoanalysts, including Melanie Klein (see Klein
(1979) for a collection of some of her major writings). Klein's object
relations theory focuses on the unconscious aspects of the relationship
between infant and mother in the pre-Oedipal stage (that stage before the
child begins to individuate itself from the mother and turn towards
the father). Klein was particularly interested in the anxieties, fears and
emotional ambivalence experienced by the dependent, helpless infant in
its earliest relationship with its mother, who is viewed by the child as
'the whole world', as omnipotent. As part of normal development, she
argued, the infant moves between viewing the mother's breast with love
(when it provides satisfaction and comfort) and with frustration, envy
and hate (when it denies satisfaction). In preserving the mother/breast as
'good' for the infant, a splitting between the good and bad breast occurs
that results in the severance of love and hate. Following this pattern,
throughout adulthood parts of the self (including those considered by
the individual to be both 'good' and 'bad') continue to be split off and
projected on to other people and things.

Other feminist writers have taken up a Kleinian psychoanalytic
approach to argue that intimate relationships in adulthood (for both men
and women) will inevitably involve a continual tension between the
desire for autonomy and the desire for closeness with another. Hollway's
writings (see, for example, Hollway, 1984, 1989, 1995, 1996) are particularly valuable in bringing together object relations theory and contemporary poststructuralist theory in the context of feminist critique. She
argues that because people experience the world at least partly through
their interactions with others, intersubjective relations are important to
an individual's negotiation of meaning, discourse and power. Hollway
uses psychodynamic explanation to theorize why individuals make
emotional investments in particular discourses, why they choose to take
up some rather than others. She contends that people's tendency to
project their feelings upon others means that to a greater or lesser degree,
feelings of anxiety and vulnerability are always part of intimate relationships. Hollway has found in her research looking at men's and women's
experiences of intimate relationships that people often sought to protect
themselves against vulnerability and used particular discourses in the
attempt to achieve some power. For both men and women, Hollway

found, desire and need for the other was experienced as a loss of power, even as 'humiliating', as one woman put it (1984: 247).

Hollway argues that men, in particular, tend to construct women as the inferiorized Other as part of their defence against anxiety and vulnerability and their attempts to live up to the masculine ideal of self-mastery. While men need closeness and desire with the Other (the woman), they tend to seek it through sexual activity, where their need can be translated into the less threatening 'male sex drive' discourse: ' "Sex" as male drive therefore covers for the suppressed signification of "sex" as intimacy and closeness' (Hollway, 1984: 246). Women, by contrast, are expected to conform to the 'have/hold' discourse that privileges love, security and romance in heterosexual sexual relations, and portrays their sexuality as a lack. Men construct themselves as the object of this discourse, foisted upon them by women. (See Chapter 4 for further discussion of Hollway's work on gender, intimacy and emotion.)

The psychodynamic perspective on emotional experience and subjectivity goes beyond what has been seen as a tendency towards 'discourse determinism' and a representation of the social actor as overly rational in some poststructuralist writings. It recognizes that the provenance of emotions cannot always be consciously identified, even while they motivate human action, and that emotional states may never be adequately expressed through discourse. Psychoanalytic theory provides a view on the individual that sees subjectivity as multiple and contradictory and incorporates the notion of inner conflict springing from the repression of desires and emotions that constantly threaten to return. In recognizing this contradiction and ambivalence at the heart of subjectivity, the potentially disruptive nature of the unconscious, the psychodynamic perspective goes some way to providing a theoretical basis for the emergence of resistance to social norms and expectations. Individuals are viewed as actively participating in their own domination as well as resisting it, disrupting as well as conforming to convention because of emotional investments, desires and fantasies that they themselves may be unable fully to articulate. As Henriques et al. have asserted, 'psychoanalysis gives space to our fundamental irrationality: the extent to which will or agency is constantly subverted to desire, and the extent to which we behave and experience ourselves in ways which are often contradictory' (1984: 205).

Embodiment and Emotion: Bringing the Body Back in

Critics of the social constructionist perspective, particularly that offered by the 'strong' thesis, have argued that there is a general reluctance on the part of constructionists to acknowledge the bodily effects of emotions: 'The bodily component remains "hedged", harnessed closely to culturally mediated thought' (Lyon, 1995: 253; see also critiques by

Freund, 1990; Craib, 1995). As I explained at the beginning of this
chapter, while I have argued for acknowledging the integral role played
by discourse in constructing emotional experience, I do not wish to go to
the extreme relativist position by neglecting the role played by our flesh
and blood – our bodies – in emotion. The importance of the body for the
emotional self is not simply that emotional experience is related to bodily
sensation, but also that notions of the self are inevitably intertwined with
embodiment (that is, the ontological state of being and having a body).
Embodiment is integral to, and inextricable from, subjectivity.

An emotion is produced in discourse to the extent that it is named and
described using language. This process of naming and describing serves
to interpret a constellation of bodily feelings as a particular 'emotion'.
But language is not the only means of constructing and expressing
emotion. While it is important to recognize the discursive nature of the
emotions, their bodily 'presence' or manifestation is also integral. As de
Swaan has vividly put it in relation to jealousy and envy, they are 'gut
feelings, often acute and painful physical sensations, "stings and pangs"
with which the body reacts to others, and sometimes with such imme-
diacy that it may appear as if it did so without the intervention of
language, consciousness, or the self, working entirely on its own' (1990:
168). Indeed, language can frequently sadly fail our needs when we try
to articulate our feelings to another person. Facial expressions or bodily
movements and other physical signs can often be far better indicators of
a person's emotional state than words. Such fleshly manifestations,
indeed, frequently 'betray' emotional states even as an individual may
seek to cover them over or deny them using language. People who
protest that they are not embarrassed, for example, yet display a bright
red flush on their face, can do little to prevent others interpreting their
state as embarrassment.

To argue for the importance of recognizing the role of the body in
emotional experience is not to veer back towards a view that sees the
emotions as 'inherent' instinctive and pan-cultural bodily responses to
stimuli. My perspective on embodiment assumes that human bodies
themselves are not simply 'natural' products. Rather, adopting the social
constructionist approach, I see our experiences of embodiment as always
being constructed through and mediated by sociocultural processes.
Bodies, within certain limits, are highly malleable. The ways in which we
perceive our bodies, regulate them, decorate them, move them, evaluate
them morally, and the ways in which we deal with matters such as birth,
sexuality and death, are all shaped via the sociocultural and historical
context in which we live. Freund (1990) argues that it is vital to avoid the
split between viewing emotion as the product of biophysical processes or
else as a purely socially constructed phenomenon. He prefers to see
emotion as a 'mode of being', or a relationship between embodied
selfhood, thought and existence (1990: 458).

The ways in which individuals understand, experience and talk about emotions is highly related to their sense of body image. As Grosz explains it, the body image

> is a map or representation of the degree of narcissistic investment of the subject in its own body and body parts. It is a differentiated, gridded, and ever-changing registration of the degrees of intensity the subject experiences, measuring not only the psychical but also the physiological changes the body undergoes in its day-to-day actions and performances. (Grosz, 1994: 83)

The body image shapes individuals' understanding and experiences of physical sensations. It influences how they locate themselves in social space, how they conceptualize themselves as separated from other physical phenomena, how they carry themselves, how they distinguish outside from inside and invest themselves as subject or object (Merleau-Ponty, 1962: Chapter 3). One's body image is first developed in the earliest stages of infancy, but is subject to continual changes as the individual moves through life (Grosz, 1994: 83–5). Body image is also highly culturally specific: for example, studies have revealed that people from western cultures tend to describe emotions as having far more physiological effects than do those from some other non-western cultures, such as Japanese and Samoan (Mesquita and Frijda, 1992: 189–90).

Elias (1991) points to the importance of learning for humans and their potential for communication in connecting biological predispositions with sociocultural processes. He contends that there is no emotion in adult humans that is not in some way influenced via learning, referring to 'learning' in the sense not simply of formal education, but in the broader sense of acculturation into a social context via interactions with others and the physical world. The learning process inheres in learning how to distinguish certain bodily sensations and feelings or states of mind, as they are evoked in particular social and cultural contexts, as emotions. From this perspective, the physicality of the emotions are interbound inextricably with sociocultural meanings and social relationships.

It may be argued, therefore, that the socioculturally constructed nature of emotion is in both the engendering of bodily states and in their interpretation and naming as emotions. This is not to deny that these bodily states are not 'real', with obvious physiological components. It is to contend that if they are not interpreted and named as emotions, then they are simply not emotions, they are merely a collection of bodily states or sensations. There is a world of difference between a physical feeling and an emotion, even where the embodied sensation may be the same. Miller makes this point in relation to the emotion of disgust: 'Disgust is a feeling *about* something and in response to something, not just raw unattached feeling. That's what the stomach flu is. Part of disgust is the very awareness of being disgusted, the consciousness of itself' (1997: 8; original emphasis).

There is, therefore, a reciprocal relationship between embodiment and sociocultural processes in emotional experience. There is a range of embodied sensations, sounds and movements – tears, increased heart rate, clenched stomach, sweating, dry palms, elation, smiling, laughing, frowning, starting, shouting and so on – that all humans have the capacity to experience and express as emotional states. It will depend on the acculturation and personal life experiences of individuals in what ways these sensations, sounds and movements are understood and experienced as emotions, or as other phenomena. While virtually all humans are born with the anatomical equipment to smile and laugh (a mouth, vocal chords, appropriate facial muscles), the contexts in which people smile and laugh and the interpretations that a smile and a laugh are given by the actor and others who may be present are clearly shaped by sociocultural dimensions. Weeping is also predicated upon the physical ability of the body to produce tears, but tears are produced (or stifled) in response to sociocultural conditions.

The bodily senses are vital to producing emotional states. As Rodaway says of smell: 'Olfaction gives us not just a sensuous geography of places and spatial relationships, but also an emotional one of love and hate, pain and joy, attachment and alienation' (1994: 73). Smells and tastes prepare or construct emotional states: the smell and taste of coffee invigorates and prepares one for the day ahead, the smell of dinner cooking as one walks in the door prepares one for the end of the working day, the time in which to relax and enjoy a cosy evening at home, the faintest whiff of a fragrance worn by a past lover may evoke vivid memories of that person and the emotional dimensions of the shared relationship, the rich, sweet taste of chocolate evokes the meanings of comfort and luxury and the associated emotion of pleasure. Bad odours or tastes, conversely, create emotional distress or disturbance, or at the least, a sense of unease or discomfort (Corbin, 1994; Rodaway, 1994). So too, sound is implicated in emotional states. Sounds can be profoundly terrifying, provoking fear, or grating, causing irritation, annoyance, frustration and even fury (for example, the ear-splitting party next door that prevents sleep). They may also be soothing, exciting or provoke ecstatic feelings, and may also be the source of extreme embarrassment, should one emit sounds considered to be socially inappropriate (see Bailey (1996) for an interesting account of the sociocultural and historical dimensions of noise).

In terms of the sense of touch, the sensation of silky, smooth or dry textures tends to create pleasure, while mushy, sticky or slimy textured substances frequently provoke repulsion and disgust (see Lupton, 1996a: 114–17; Miller, 1997: 60–4). Touch, particularly the touch of another person, is highly emotionally laden, linked as it is to our earliest, diffuse, pre-discursive knowledge of the world as tiny infants as well as to our most significant relationships in adulthood. The touch of a loved one is pleasurable, while that of a stranger or someone we distrust is intensely discomforting. As Synnott has put it, 'Hugging and snuggling, pinching and punching, shaking hands or holding hands, linking arms, patting heads, slapping faces, tickling tummies, taking pulses, stroking and striking, kissing foreheads, or cheeks, or lips, or anywhere. . . . They all involve touching and skin contacts, and convey without words a wide variety of emotions, meanings and relationships' (1993: 156).

Sight, perhaps, as the sense considered the 'noblest' and most reliable in western societies (Synnott, 1993: 207), is the sense for which we are most consciously aware of the link between emotion and sensation. Ugly or discordant sights may provoke in us a sense of unease, irritation, disgust or fear, while those that we consider to be beauteous tend to evoke feelings of harmony, joy, pleasure or delight. Christian writings, for example, have constantly evoked the divine beauty and light of God as evidence of His majesty and omnipotence, presenting the emotions evoked by these visual attributes as joy and ecstasy compared with the despair and grief of darkness (Synnott, 1993: 209).

The emotions aroused by the senses are associated with another important aspect of the emotions – their evocation in response to the violation of accepted codes of behaviour. As Synnott (1993: 191–2) points out, Shakespeare's writings were particularly redolent in linking the senses with moral meanings. In *Hamlet* he refers to 'foul deeds rising', of a murderous act smelling 'rank' and 'to high heaven', and of the state of Denmark being 'rotten' with ill deeds and corruption, while in *Macbeth* there is reference to the smell and appearance of blood on a murderer's hand failing to diminish even after repeated washing. Emotion acts as a means of distinguishing oneself from others, of reinforcing norms and moral meanings that serve to set oneself and one's group apart from others at the same time as they reinforce social bonds. As Miller notes of the emotion of disgust, 'Disgust helps define boundaries between us and them and me and you. It helps prevent *our* way from being subsumed into *their* way. Disgust, along with desire, locates the bounds of the other, either as something to be avoided, repelled, or attacked, or, in other settings, as something to be emulated, imitated, or married' (1997: 50, original emphases). A person who stands too close to oneself, who one considers smells strange or bad, who is too noisy or has an inappropriate accent according to one's cultural assumptions, may provoke a range of emotions, including disgust, revulsion, anger, fear and anxiety. These emotional responses are interbound with cultural assumptions about what is considered 'ugly' or 'beautiful', 'foul' or 'fragrant', 'clean' or 'dirty', 'pure' or 'contaminated'.

Not all emotional states may necessarily be understood as having observable or perceptible bodily sensations. Love, for example, may be described as involving a racing pulse or heightened physical sensations (particularly if it is understood to be 'romantic' love) but it may also be a far more diffuse ontological experience that is less overtly experienced bodily. Pride is an emotion with which few distinct bodily sensations may be associated. Pride may be recognized, or 'felt in the head', but not 'in the body' (although sometimes it can be experienced bodily, particularly if it involves pride in relation to another, as in a 'swelling heart', a 'lump in the throat' or 'tears of pride'). While anger is commonly understood to be experienced bodily (through tenseness of the muscles, increased pulse rate, shouting and so on), it is also possible to feel angry about something without experiencing these sensations. Emotion thus at times may fall between the cognitive and embodied dimensions of experience, in a sort of 'space' for which there is no appropriate word (here again, language proves inadequate to the task of representing emotional experience).

Nonetheless, taken at its most general level, all emotions, as well as all thought and action, can be described as 'embodied' simply because they are experienced by humans who are inevitably embodied, and who perceive and understand the social and material worlds necessarily through the body's senses. This notion is found in Merleau-Ponty's writings on the phenomenology of human existence, where he emphasizes that one's 'being-in-the world' and one's knowledge of the world are through one's body (see, for example, Merleau-Ponty, 1962). There is therefore no 'inner' or transcendental realm of intelligence, thought or perception which can be separated from embodiment. As Merleau-Ponty argues, the body itself is a sentient being, mediated through physical presence and perceptual meaning. All knowledge is developed through the body. One perceives the world and constructs notions of reality through the body and its senses: 'The body is our general medium for having a world' (Merleau-Ponty, 1962). Being-in-the-world involves not only thought and bodily action but also emotionality. All of these are interrelated in ways that cannot easily be separated from each other because they are part of the same phenomenon of lived experience.

Lakoff (1987, 1995) similarly contends that structures of conceptual thought are based in bodily experience because humans are embodied. Perception, body movement and physical and social experience all contribute to thought. Thus, those concepts that are themselves not grounded in experience, that are abstract, inevitably employ metaphor, metonymy and imagery derived from embodied experience. He argues that emotional concepts are clear examples of abstract concepts that have a grounding in bodily experience (1987: 377). These insights raise the question of why certain linguistic choices are made in the first place in relation to feelings, embodied or otherwise. Why, for example, is anger, passion or embarrassment described as 'hot'? Can it not be the case that the embodied sensations that are identified as emotion may have led to this discourse, rather than the other way around (the discourse creating the embodied sensation)? In other words, do embodied sensations contribute to the production of discourse rather than being the outcome of discourse?

Lakoff's (1987) analysis of the metaphors used in describing anger acknowledges that physical sensation may be the basis of the discursive network that has arisen around this particular emotion. His analysis first identifies the physiological correlates of anger according to 'folk' understandings: increased body heat, increased internal pressure (the circulatory system and muscular tension), agitation and interference with accurate perception. He then looks at the metaphors associated with these physical correlates. Body heat, he argues, is discursively rendered through such expressions as 'getting hot under the collar', 'a hot-head', 'a heated argument' and 'all hot and bothered'. Internal pressure is expressed through such expressions as 'I almost burst a blood vessel'. Both physiological sensations may lead to a reddened face and neck, expressed as 'scarlet with rage', 'red with anger' and 'flushed with anger'. Agitation is discursively denoted with the terms 'shaking with anger', 'hopping mad', 'quivering with rage', 'all worked up', 'excited', 'all wrought up' and 'upset'. Terms relating to the physical experience of interference with accurate perception include 'blind with rage', 'seeing red' and 'so mad I couldn't see straight' (1987: 382–3).

Lyon and Barbalet (1994) argue further that emotional embodied expression is a means by which the body is not simply passively inscribed or moulded through discourse and practice, but is active and agential: 'Emotion activates distinct dispositions, postures and movements which are not only attitudinal but also physical, involving the way in which individual bodies together with others articulate a common purpose, design, or order' (1994: 48). Emotional states, thus, are forces through which human agency may be stimulated and expressed bodily. The basis of their argument is the work of Durkheim on the role played by emotion in ritual and human ties (referred to above). Drawing on his writings, Lyon and Barbalet contend that the lived experience of embodied emotion often precedes and activates social action. Thus, for example, collective political action is often stimulated by emotional response. Mellor and Shilling (1997) also emphasize the sociological significance of Durkheim's notion of 'collective effervescence'. Such a perspective, they assert, goes beyond the 'rational' approach to human sociality and social relations by emphasizing the extra-rational, sensual, passionate nature of collectivity. It also emphasizes that the production of emotion may occur not only at the level of the actions of the individual body, but from the experiences of bodies grouped together, such as in the rituals of prayer and song in religious activities or marches and drills in the army, which create certain emotions as part of embodied action (Lyon and Barbalet, 1994: 55).

Concluding Comments

This chapter has reviewed several major perspectives in the humanities and social sciences used to address the topic of the emotions. To summarize, physiological, psychobiological and psychoevolutionary approaches tend to take an essentialist view, seeing emotion predominantly as universal and inherent in all humans and as equivalent to physical responses. Exponents of the cognitive approach, although still regarding emotions as inherent phenomena, go some way towards incorporating a focus on social processes, interested as they are in the relationship between conscious evaluation and physical sensation in the identification and labelling of emotional states. Within the social constructionist perspective, there are a number of approaches with differing foci. Structuralist approaches explore the ways in which social structures, power dynamics and membership of social groups shape the expression and experience of emotional states and how 'feeling rules' in turn operate to shape emotional expression. Phenomenologists direct their attention primarily at the sociocultural meanings of emotions at the micro-level, including their importance for the ontology of selfhood and personal biography and in the construction of moral judgements. Poststructuralist approaches are interested in the discursive construction of emotional experience and how individuals participate in this process by adopting or resisting dominant discourses. Psychodynamic perspectives explore the extra-discursive and extra-rational dimensions of emotional experience by addressing how the emotions underpin human motivation and action in ways of which we are often not consciously aware.

My own theoretical approach, as developed in the remaining chapters of this book, attempts to bring together many of the foci developed under the rubric of 'emotions as social constructions'. I am interested in the lived experience and social relational dimension of emotion, including the role played by such factors as gender and power relations in emotional experience. However, I avoid the notion of the 'true' emotional self that tends to be articulated in structuralist and phenomenological accounts for a poststructuralist perspective on subjectivity that sees it as dynamic and shifting, and as constituted, rather than distorted or manipulated by, sociocultural processes. I acknowledge that discourse plays a vital role in constructing and shaping emotional experience, but assert that it is important not to slip into 'discourse determinism'. The extra-discursive, or the interaction of sensual embodiment with sociocultural processes and the influence of the unconscious in emotional experience, also require incorporation into an understanding of the ontology of the emotional self.

2

Recounting Emotion: Everyday Discourses

As I argued in Chapter 1, one way to understand the sociocultural nature of emotions is to examine the discourses surrounding them, or the patterned ways of rendering embodied sensations or internal states of feeling into words so as to convey their properties to others. Surprisingly enough, given the strong interest in the interaction between discourse, subjectivity and social relations that has emerged in the humanities and social sciences in recent years, very few studies have been published thus far that have attempted to look at the discourses people in western societies draw upon when talking about the emotions (for notable exceptions see Lakoff, 1987; Lutz, 1990).

To address this issue, I conducted an interview study, held in Sydney in 1995. Forty-one people were recruited into the study using personal networks and snowball sampling (that is, using initial contacts to make more contacts). The group could therefore not be described as a 'random sample', although a concerted attempt was made to recruit people from a variety of sociodemographic backgrounds. (See the Appendix for a full list of the participants and their sociodemographic details.) Twenty-three women and 18 men participated, ranging in age from 19 to 72 years. Seventeen of the interviewees were aged 40 or less and 24 were aged 41 or older. People from a range of occupations participated, including tradespeople, clerical workers, sales staff, community workers, teachers, university students, managers, lawyers and academics. One participant was unemployed and six were retired. All but four of the interviewees were Anglo-Celtic or northern European in ethnicity (the exceptions were born in Australia of Anglo-Italian, Maltese, Anglo-Indian and Indonesian-Dutch parentage) and all but three were of Australian birth (the exceptions were born in Britain, emigrating to Australia as children or adults).

The aim of the study was to focus in detail on people's personal biographies of emotional experience, their understandings of emotion and emotional management and the ways that they related emotion to their concept of selfhood. In the interviews the interviewees were asked what they thought an emotion was, to name some emotions, to describe how these emotions 'felt' when they were experiencing them and to discuss where they thought emotions came from, whether they thought it was important to control one's emotions, which emotions they

thought were most difficult to control and which easiest, whether
they thought that different types of people were different in the ways
they felt and expressed emotions, what they thought happened if people
do not express their emotions and the purposes that emotions served.
The interviewees were also asked questions relating to the experience of
emotion in their own lives, including whether they saw themselves as an
emotional person, whether there had ever been times when they had lost
control of their emotions and whether there were any conventions about
emotional expression in their family of origin. As well, they were asked
to describe the earliest and a more recent memory of a strong emotion
they had felt.

All the interviews were audiotaped and transcribed. I analysed the
interview data both using these transcripts and listening to each tape.
This was so as to be able to hear the tone of people's words as well as
reading them – particularly important, I thought, given the subject
matter. Because my primary interest was in the discursive aspects of
emotions as they were articulated in these interviews, a discourse
analysis approach influenced by poststructuralist theoretical perspectives
was employed. The idea was to combine the focus on exploring individuals' lived experiences of everyday life that has been a central
emphasis in traditional phenomenological research, with the interest in
the constitutive role played by discourse that has emerged from poststructuralist perspectives.

As argued in Chapter 1, from the poststructuralist perspective subjectivity is fragmented, dynamic, continually produced, reproduced,
constituted and reconstituted, and highly contextual. Discourse mediates
people's views and experiences of reality and their embodied sensations,
both when making sense of these themselves, and when explaining them
to others (including interviewers). The focus of an analysis such as this is
therefore not so much on to what extent the participants are conveying
an 'objective' reality, but how they express their understandings and
experiences of reality incorporating both contradictory and overlapping
discourses. It is assumed that there is a commonly shared pool of
discourses to which people have access and upon which they draw when
describing their experiences. This pool of discourses is not static, but is
subject to constant flux in response to broader sociocultural events and
trends. The focus of the discourse analysis is in identifying which
particular discourses tend to be used by people when 'making sense' of
phenomena and conveying narratives of their experiences to others. This
chapter discusses the discourses used by the study participants when
recounting issues in relation to how they define the emotions, how
'emotionality' and the 'emotional person' are described and evaluated,
their experiences and thoughts about the management of the emotions,
the differences that may be observed among individuals or members of
social groups in terms of styles of emotional expression, issues of gender

and emotional expression, the embodied sensations associated with emotion and the relationship between emotion and health states.

Defining the Emotions

In the interview study, when the interviewees were asked to respond to the question 'What is emotion?', quite a diversity of response was given. Some people found it very difficult to articulate what they thought an emotion to be, finding it easier simply to name some emotions. For those who could give an explanation, emotion was most commonly described as a 'feeling': 'I think an emotion really is the way you feel about something, whether it be sad, happy, cross' (47-year-old woman). This feeling was often described as being evoked in reaction or relation to something else: 'Emotion is a feeling. You know, if you get angry, that's an emotion, if your heart fills up with love for your children, all that's emotion' (62-year-old woman). As Lutz (1985: 78) has argued, emotions are commonly viewed as a subset of feelings, the visible, expressive aspect of feelings. Feelings are understood as sensations within the body/self that require interpretation to be rendered into emotions. Most people, she contends, stress that feelings are physical but may also be opinions. There is, therefore, a rather contradictory approach to feelings in the tension between the concept of feeling as an opinion (as in the statement 'This is how I feel about this issue') and as a physical sensation ('I feel pain').

Emotions were also dominantly described as a means of self-expression: 'An emotion would be a way that a person expresses their feelings towards a particular scenario, scene or happening' (34-year-old man). More specifically, some people saw emotions as messages or signals of one's feelings and thoughts, both to oneself and to others: 'Emotions are for communicating, for telling people how you feel. You know, emotions create the real smiles, the real looks of love in your eye or the creases of frowns on your face' (45-year-old man); 'Emotions work to convey to oneself how one is responding to a situation' (31-year-old woman). There is the suggestion in these words that emotion is a means of self-authenticity, a route to truth, and some people made this explicit in their explanations: 'in a sense [emotions] allow us to stay true to ourselves' (44-year-old man); 'Emotions create your being, they are really what your heart says' (45-year-old man).

For several people, emotion was thought of as a personal resource, even as a source of pleasure: 'They are for enjoyment and the full enrichment of life, I think' (55-year-old man); 'They're there to allow us to live our lives out to the full' (44-year-old man). Related to this discourse is another that represents emotion as an essential part of life: 'I think emotions are firstly for the self. You've got to have emotions, otherwise you wouldn't be able to live, because you can't live without love, and I guess you can't live without expressing some form of anger

sometime, and all the other emotions' (36-year-old woman). Most interviewees contended that the emotions are the seat of humanity, distinguishing us from other animals or from inanimate objects like machines:
'It would be pretty boring if you didn't have emotions wouldn't it? We'd
just sort of be like robots' (47-year-old woman); 'If you didn't show
emotion, you'd be like an animal or something – it's being human'
(54-year-old man). As a 21-year-old man commented, it is difficult to
imagine what life would be like without emotions: 'It's like trying to
imagine what death is like – you can't really imagine it.'

The interviewees had particular difficulties explaining clearly how it is
that emotions are generated. As one woman noted, 'it's something I've
never thought about, it's just there, it's part of you. Like you've got
hands and you've got feet, you've got emotions!' (66-year-old woman). It
was generally agreed, however, that emotions came from 'within' the
self: 'They come from within, obviously, they're part of who we are,
they're part of our nature, so they're there all the time' (44-year-old man).
For some, emotion was described as a state of mind, influencing more
generally one's stance towards oneself and the world: 'I think an emotion
is a state of mind that affects your outlook, that affects the way you think
and feel about things at that particular time' (30-year-old woman). In a
related discourse, emotion was seen as a product of thought: 'Emotion is
an inner welling up of thoughts that could be expressed, I guess, at two
extremities, one being extreme happiness or extreme despair or anguish'
(44-year-old man).

There was a suggestion in most people's accounts that the mind and
the body interact in producing emotion:

> Emotions have to come from the mind, because there's so much of emotion
> that you can't really touch. . . . I don't mean that your mind rules your
> emotions, because if your mind ruled your emotions then you probably
> wouldn't have them. But it's probably between how you feel in your heart and
> how your mind processes that feeling. (49-year-old woman)

> An emotion for me is a feeling. It's a sort of physical experience that has
> physical sort of effects that you feel. It's also a state of mind and there's an
> interrelationship between the two, so that usually it's the state of mind that
> leads to physical effects, although sometimes physical effects can affect your
> state of mind. So if you're feeling tired or run down or jet-lagged or
> something, then that can have a real effect on your state of mind and make
> you feel perhaps a bit depressed, or down, so it sort of goes the other way as
> well. (31-year-old woman)

Several people used the concept of the soul, or the spirit, to describe the
ontology of emotions and how they are generated:

> I think they're generated, like through your soul. 'Cause I think everybody has
> a soul, and emotion comes from somewhere deep within you and I don't
> necessarily think it comes from the mind so much. I mean the mind is
> thinking, but I think it is the soul for me that generates those feelings. (36-year-
> old woman)

> I honestly feel there's more to me than my brain and my body. And I think that my emotions can come from a mixture of everything. So emotions come from within, it's more than inside, it's just part of everything. It doesn't come just from the heart, it's part of my soul, my spirit. (25-year-old woman)

This notion of the emotions, interestingly enough, tended to be articulated by female rather than male interviewees. Conversely, the idea that emotions have a physiological component, are 'hard-wired' into the body or brain, was more often expressed by male interviewees. A 55-year-old man commented, for example, that 'Emotions come from basically our physiology. We're set up to display emotions.' He asserted his belief that it is important to 'train' children 'as early as possible that they must be masters of themselves. The mind is the control, if you don't use your mind to control your life, then you are subverting its natural function.' As this suggests, there was the implication in some of the men's descriptions of the emotions that they were part of a 'less civilized' heredity. For instance, a 49-year-old man said: 'I think the emotions might have been a sort of, prehistoric thing, that we could have before we could speak.' This opinion was echoed in the words of a 30-year-old man: 'I suppose they're simply all part of that reactive-nervous-system part of us that as more primitive beings tended to dictate what we did before our sort of more cognitive sides took over.' Emotion was commonly juxtaposed and contrasted with rationality: 'Emotion is that response of our personality that perhaps is distinct from reason to some extent' (50-year-old man).

Emotion was also described by most people as an inherent force that emerges in response to a stimulus: 'I guess they're triggered by us, in a sense finding ourselves in a context or a relationship with people where there are triggers that generate one or the other' (44-year-old man). However, emotion was also described as learnt, or as the product of experience over the course of one's lifetime:

> Emotions come through experience, accumulated experience, probably on a number of levels: personal, family, ethnicity, and the surrounding culture. (45-year-old man)

> I think they're something that we have learned, something that has happened as we grow, and we've felt this feeling and we've put a label on it, you know, as an emotion, we are taught to label it as well. (41-year-old woman)

Some interviewees sought to differentiate between individual emotions and how or where they were generated: 'Love, they say, it comes from the heart, but it feels as if it's in your chest, it overflows, sort of thing. Anger, I think that's more the brain. Sadness, I think that comes from the heart too' (62-year-old woman). Some emotions were seen to be more 'at the surface' and thus more readily expressed while others were 'built up' over time: 'There has to be a buildup over a bit of time, especially for sadness. I mean, happy's kind of more instant . . . hurt's got to be built up too, so I think it's over a process of time really, that they build up' (30-year-old woman).

'Emotionality' and the 'Emotional Person'

The interviewees were asked if they would describe themselves as 'an emotional person'. The majority, regardless of gender, agreed that they did see themselves as such: only seven of the 41 interviewees denied that they were an emotional person. Being an emotional person, however, was represented in different ways. For some, it meant responding emotionally in a volatile manner. For example, a 30-year-old woman, who was pregnant at the time of the interview, said that she thought she had become more emotional during her pregnancy, meaning that her feelings were both intensified and less controlled: 'I think that I was always like that, but I think pregnancy emphasizes it even more. So if you were a little angry with somebody before, you're a lot angrier with them now. The joy inside even seems to be enhanced, which is nice, but the anger is still, you know, just as strong as that too.' This woman said that she has noticed that people caution others to be careful around pregnant women, 'because she'll snap your head off'. She didn't understand this before, but does now that she herself is pregnant: 'You just seem to get like this feeling, instantly, and you just go for it . . . you really feel that you want to say what you think.'

Being an emotional person, therefore, may mean demonstrating one's emotions openly as well as feeling them intensely. Others agreed with this definition when describing themselves as 'emotional': 'I tend to be fairly bubbly and effervescent so if I'm sad, each part of me shows greatly, if I'm sad, it's overwhelming sadness, if I'm angry, it's overwhelming anger, if I'm happy, it's overwhelming happiness' (46-year-old woman). A 66-year-old woman saw herself as 'very emotional', adding that 'I'll cry at the movies, I'll cry at some story on TV, I'm very affectionate in as much as I'm demonstrative, I'll give anybody a kiss and a cuddle'. This description of emotionality suggests that it means one's emotions are readily evoked by appropriate stimuli (for example, sad stories in the media) and that one finds it easy to demonstrate loving emotions to others. For other interviewees, being an emotional person meant that other people were aware of oneself as responsive and empathetic. For example, a 47-year-old woman said that she saw herself as an emotional person because: 'I'm a person that usually other people will come to talk about things, and sometimes I find it's really hard to – if I'm comforting somebody, I'm probably going to be crying as well as they are.'

Some people's descriptions of emotionality, however, did not include the notion that being emotional necessarily involved openly displaying one's emotions. Rather, being emotional was glossed as having sensitivity to the plight of others, being able to feel for others, even if one does not demonstrate these feelings. Thus, for example, a 43-year-old man saw himself as emotional because: 'I have a lot of compassion for a lot of different things and people. I don't express it that openly, but sometimes

I think, "Well, how can people just shrug those things off and not sort of have those feelings?"' Similarly, a 36-year-old woman said that she would very much see herself as an emotional person because: 'I feel a lot about things, and about people. . . . I do get very emotional about things, particularly people I care about and love. And if they're hurt, or whatever, then I feel very strongly about that.' Emotionality was also represented as being highly conscious of one's feelings. A young man, aged 20, described himself as emotional because 'I'm very aware of how I feel'.

Some people presented themselves as being essentially an emotional person 'inside' but thought that others might not be aware of this because of their skills in emotional management, their ability to hide their feelings. For example, a 31-year-old woman said that she sees herself as 'a highly emotional person. I do get very agitated about things, I get very anxious about things, I can get very excited about things.' Nonetheless, she thinks others see her differently:

> I don't think that – apart from my husband who has seen me completely lose control, I think he would probably see me as an emotional person because he sees me at my most stressed, my most angry, my most excited – but I think virtually everyone else, including my family, would probably not describe me as an emotional person. Particularly people who know me at work, I think they would see me as a very calm, collected, highly controlled person because I do take steps to – I actually do consciously present myself in such a way. Because I think that that's important and that's the sort of persona I want to present.

Many of the above interpretations of emotionality tend to represent it as positive, as demonstrative of finer qualities such as sensitivity, humaneness and the capacity for empathy, a certain refinement of feeling that sets one apart from others who may have more blunt or subdued emotional responses. A smaller number of interviewees represented emotionality as having less positive qualities or implications. Some people described their experience of being an emotional person as being unable to avoid their feelings, to make them go away, meaning that they found themselves somewhat at the mercy of their emotions. These people were also more likely to describe being very emotional as having negative aspects, and to represent themselves as 'too emotional':

> I let myself feel too much. A lot of people get through life and if they feel something coming along that they don't want to deal with, they can bury it. I can't. I don't really think it's a bad thing in the long run, but it can be pretty difficult. I'm a very moody person and it can be very difficult sometimes, you know, swinging from a high mood to a low mood. (25-year-old man)

Most people's descriptions of themselves as 'emotional' or 'not emotional' tended to suggest that they had maintained this personality feature over the course of their lives. Some of the older interviewees, however, argued that people may change as the years go by, often becoming more emotional than they were in their younger days, and related this to their own experience. For example, a 50-year-old woman said that she used not to be an emotional person, but had changed: 'A few years back I was very much in control of my emotions, as far as outward emotions go. But now I find myself much more softer. If I feel like letting the tears drop, then I do.' A 45-year-old man said that as he gets older he finds that he is less tolerant of people who annoy him and is more likely to demonstrate this: 'When I was young I would hide emotion. Now I'm more prone to show it.' Related to this view was the notion that as people change, the way they feel changes as well: 'Emotions don't change, the person changes, I think, and then the emotion changes, because the person changes. Because an emotion is not a thing, it's a person, it's what's coming from a person, their personality or their soul or whatever. So I think that if people change, then their emotions change with that' (36-year-old woman).

The small number of interviewees (seven) who said that they would not describe themselves as an emotional person included both men and women. Here again, there was evidence of somewhat different inter-pretations of what emotionality (or lack thereof) means. One interpre-tation of unemotionality represented it as lacking the capacity to express emotion openly to others. For example, a 54-year-old man said: 'No, I don't think I am an emotional person. .... I feel a lot of emotion but I find it difficult to show it. . . . I don't like to show my emotions, to cry, for instance, I would never do that.' There is the implication in his words that being 'emotional' is more than having the capacity to feel emotions acutely – it also involves being able to show these feelings to others. Similarly, a woman, aged 44, said that she could control her emotions, and therefore did not consider herself to be an emotional person: 'I tend to bottle up things inside rather than upset people.' Another woman, aged 58, said that she did not think she was an emotional person because by comparison with others she does not respond emotionally: 'I can get het up about things, but not like I see some people do.'

Other self-described 'unemotional' people demonstrated some chagrin at what they saw to be their incapacity to express emotions easily. One 34-year-old man, for example, said that he was concerned that he was not as emotional as he should be: 'I'd like to be, not because I'm hard, but things that people would normally cry about, I find hard to cry.' He went on to say that sometimes he will feel sentimental, and to him that was a good sign that he had softer feelings: 'Seeing starving kids on TV, sometimes that will bring a tear or two to my eye and to me that's good to do it.' Men in general tended to be more concerned than women about what they saw to be their inability to express emotion 'properly' (see discussion below on gender issues). For some of these 'unemotional' people, however, emotionality was represented negatively. For instance, a 30-year-old woman who did not see herself as an emotional person said that: 'I think I'm quite a level-headed person, so I think I think about things before I say things. So emotions like anger, which are easily expressed by other people openly, I don't. I sort of think about things before I say them I think.' Emotionality in this interpretation involves irrationality and loss of control over one's emotions, a tendency not to think before expressing one's feelings.

Emotional Management

When asked if they thought it was important to control one's emotions, many of the interviewees strongly supported the notion that ideally one should feel able to express them. As a 47-year-old man commented: 'I think that we'd be a hell of a lot better if we let our emotions take over a lot of the time. No, I don't think it is a good thing to control your emotions, you should let them go.' It was argued that emotions should be expressed for several reasons. These included allowing others to know how you feel so as to facilitate relations with them: 'You should express your emotions because then people know where you're really coming from. They know how you *really* feel, and it may hurt people, but I do believe it's better for them to know how you really feel about things' (45-year-old man). Emotional expression was seen as a human need, with control represented as constraining and repressive: 'If you control your emotions too much, you're just wringing your own life out of yourself ' (49-year-old woman); 'If everybody controlled their emotions, we'd all be walking around like zombies!' (66-year-old woman). Such a release of the emotions was also commonly described as a more 'honest' process. Many interviewees made reference to the 'damage' that could be caused to one's mental or physical health by 'bottling up' one's emotions (see further discussion of this below).

While the majority of interviewees supported in general terms the notion that emotions should be expressed when possible, a small number were less certain on this point. They were more adamant about the importance of maintaining control over one's emotions in most situations. These interviewees were generally older men and women (aged over 50), suggesting a generational difference in concepts about emotional management. A 55-year-old man, for example, represented emotions as powerful and potentially dangerous: 'We certainly need to be in control – emotions are dangerous servants, if not fearful masters and we need to set a control.' A 66-year-old man noted that controlling one's emotions facilitated control of the self: 'While you're controlling your emotions you're in control'. He went on to say that: 'Overly emotional people, I think perhaps that should be controlled a little more. I think that I've got control over my emotions and I think other people should do the same.' For a 72-year-old woman, control of one's emotions was described as important to maintain privacy: 'I think that if you're a private person, I don't think it's good for other people to know what your emotions are.'

Despite their general agreement that it is important to express one's feelings to others, the interviewees also frequently noted that this was not always possible or appropriate, and that the context in which the emotions were felt should be borne in mind: 'It is dependent on what you're doing, where you are and who you're with' (34-year-old man). Many people, therefore, sought to stress the importance of a fine degree of emotional management, at which judgement was exercised as to the best way and most appropriate time and place to express one's emotions:

> I think it's important to control them, but if you over-control them you probably would suffer in other ways. Because I think your emotions are there as a safety valve to allow you to be able to get over that thing . . . you can't let your emotions control you, but you've got to let your emotions be expressed. (50-year-old woman)

> I think that if emotional expression is going to do some damage to someone, yeah, I'd control it. I'm sure there'd be a point at which you'd say, 'Now let's be rational about this.' But at other times, I go with the feel, rather than control it, I allow it to sort of flow through me, and that's more healing than bottling it up. But if it's detrimental to someone and you're doing it for the sheer reason of, 'I'm out to let you feel awful and lash out,' then no, I think one should control that. (46-year-old woman)

Emotional expression was commonly represented as 'natural', with 'culture' or 'society' serving to restrain it in certain ways. There were, therefore, two dominant meanings contained within the discourse of emotion as 'natural'. The first, referred to earlier in the chapter, related to emotion springing from a more 'primitive' origin, located in that part of the brain that was largely instinctive rather than controlled by reason. The second meaning is that of 'natural' emotion as being more authentic.

When the emotions appear to 'take over' and the mind seems to have no control over their manifestation, this can be experienced as frightening. One woman, aged 46, described this happening when she had a nervous breakdown:

> It's just when you're completely, your emotions just take over so much, there's no turning back, your body just says, 'I've had it!' And it's just overwhelming . . . it so bowls you over, so that you're frightened and you think, 'Oh there's nothing I can do about it.' And it fills you with overwhelming sadness and overwhelming anger, the whole feeling is just overwhelming.

The interviewees' accounts suggested that in practice, most emotions, even the strongest, could be controlled or managed in some way if enough effort were exerted. For example, most people considered it important not to allow negative emotions such as depression, self-doubt and fear to 'take over' oneself. Some could describe how they had exerted a conscious effort to avoid this:

> I seem to be able to lift myself out of sadness and depression feelings by just rationalizing them and saying to myself, 'Just think about something else. And if that's upsetting you or you're feeling down, then for God's sake pick yourself up and stop being such a loser!' (31-year-old woman)

The interviewees were asked to describe which emotions they personally found most difficult to control. For most people, the emotions they nominated were the most distressing emotions such as grief, feelings of loss, anger and sorrow. This was for several reasons, one of which being that such emotions were generated from a breakdown in, or loss of, a close relationship with others, or a reaction to someone letting one down. Many of these most important, and therefore emotionally charged losses, are of parents, close family members or partners. For example, a 45-year-old man said that the feelings of loss he felt in relation to his brother's death were very difficult to control: 'There is probably not a day that goes by that I don't miss him, and there is definitely a hole in my life. And I think that's why I become very emotional when I think of him.'

It was argued that because these close relationships are seen as so important, and have lasting ramifications, it is difficult to control the intensity of feeling:

> There's things like you've broken off with someone and you're feeling sorry for yourself or something like that. Things like that are often hard to control because you can't just switch them on and off. Like if you're angry, maybe you can go and see a film or do something nice, but I think that very strong emotional feelings about people, you can't just forget them very easily. (43-year-old man)

A 50-year-old woman had recently split up with her husband, who she had discovered was having an affair. She spoke about the pain her husband's betrayal of her had caused, and how this had badly affected her self-esteem. She said that she tries not to dwell on her sadness, seeking to control it: 'Within reasonable bounds I try to say to myself, "Well, it's no good thinking about bad things that might happen, think about the good side of things." ' Nonetheless, feelings of sadness and rejection in relation to her marital breakdown have often swept over her, and she has found this difficult to control:

> I mean your relationship with another person, if you can't get that right – well, you've allowed a person to get closer to you than anyone else except maybe your parents or a very good friend. And when it doesn't work out, it's like something's been ripped out of yourself, it's part of yourself in a sense that has gone as well. So I feel sad about that, but all in all I just try not to dwell on it.

These negative emotions were also described as difficult to control because there is an imperative to do so, to reduce suffering and bad feelings. Feelings that are seen as positive, such as joy and happiness, were viewed as requiring little control because there is no need to exercise such control: 'If you love someone, then you should allow that love to be seen, I don't think you should restrain it too much. It's important to let that person know how you feel and it's good to have that outlet' (44-year-old man). Similarly, a 20-year-old woman noted: 'When it's a bad emotion, like when you're angry, then you should learn to control it. But if you're really happy, then I don't see any point in stopping being happy, I think you should let people know and maybe it would rub off on other people.'

Emotions viewed as difficult to control were also described as more intense or volatile compared to other emotions. Anger, in particular, was described as a more 'surface' emotion that was therefore difficult to control compared to some other emotions: 'Anger is kind of like an instant thing that just goes aaaah, and comes straight out' (30-year-old woman); 'Sometimes it's necessary to control anger, but what you'd really like to do is punch somebody on the nose. But you can't just do what you'd like to do, you do like to keep it under control' (47-year-old woman). Some people, however, said that they found anger the easiest emotion to control, because they had done so throughout their life-time and had become habituated to it or 'practised' at it. As one 49-year-old man put it: 'Anger, for me, is the easiest emotion to control, because I've had that much practice at it. I never *really* get angry now.'

Many people referred to the undesirable effect losing one's emotional control can have on other people. This was particularly the case when they were talking about anger, which of all the emotions was seen as negative in terms of the effects it could have on one's relationships with others:

> You have to control your anger, because you can hurt other people. I mean you *have* to control your anger, I really believe that. You should let other people know that you're angry but you do have to learn how to control it. There has to be a limit to what you would do when you're angry and you have to set those limits for yourself. You could do dastardly things if you allowed yourself the emotion of anger, or hate even, jealousy, things like that. (49-year-old woman)

> I have felt emotions in my life that if I'd followed through with them, I would have committed holy murder! I feel those emotions have to be controlled. (41-year-old woman)

It was evident from the interviewees' accounts, therefore, that the reactions and feelings of others were a vital dimension in regulating the ways in which one expressed or suppressed one's emotions. One woman gave the example of how emotions such as grief and sorrow must sometimes be controlled for the sake of others: 'If you need to be strong for someone else you need to have a certain control over your emotions' (47-year-old woman). There was also the suggestion by some interviewees that losing emotional control may be the effect of presenting oneself in an undesirable way, and therefore should be avoided in some situations. As a 44-year-old man argued, he was concerned about what other people would think of him if he lost control of his emotions, worrying that they would see him as 'a person that's not in control, a person who is erratic, a person who is unhinged'. A 25-year-old man similarly commented that: 'It doesn't always pay to show your emotions in public because they can leave you pretty defenceless with other people.'

Formal situations, such as in the workplace, where one is expected to present a 'professional' or 'rational' self, were given as examples by several people of the importance of controlling emotion on some occasions. For instance, a solicitor, aged 30, said that he often felt angry with the lawyers from other firms he was working with, but 'there are rarely situations where it would be worth my while to lose my temper'. He said that if he lost his temper in front of clients 'it would seem to be unprofessional, because I'm meant to be detached and not be emotionally involved in situations and not lose my temper. And if I lose my temper then the other person is likely to lose theirs, and it makes coming to a commercial agreement much harder.' For women working in a professional context, emotional control may be considered even more important than for their male colleagues, because of the labels that are so easily given to women as being 'too emotional'. A female academic, aged 31, described her consciousness of the need to maintain emotional control at work, so as to avoid the stereotype of the emotional woman and be accepted as a professional:

> I think that if you take your work very seriously, if you want other people at work to see you as a serious person, as a rational person in control – which are all things that are valued in most workplaces, and particularly in the workplace that I'm in, which is a very professionally oriented, cerebral sort of workplace – then I think it's highly important to control your emotions. So I think, for example, if you're in a meeting with colleagues and you disagree with them, then it's very important to do so in a manner that's not angry. It's important to be assertive, but you shouldn't ever show anger, you shouldn't show distress. You never, ever cry in front of anyone that you work with, particularly people who are superior to you and will make judgements about you in relation to promotion. And I would never ever do that, never ever cry in front of someone. And I would definitely take steps not to show overt anger or distress, or even overt happiness, I suppose, or elation.

The interviewees noted that there is generally less control exerted over emotional states in private, or less formal settings, such as when an individual is alone, or with family or close friends. In this context, they argued, there may be little or no conscious control over the emotions, and emotion may be spontaneously expressed. Yet self-monitoring continues even in 'private', as demonstrated by the narrative provided by a 25-year-old woman, who described how she had lost control of her emotions once when she had an argument with her partner at home. During the argument her partner stopped talking and began to ignore her, which infuriated her, so she looked around for a means of expressing her rage:

> First I went into the bathroom, really wanting to smash something, but kept thinking that there were too many valuable things in the house I'd regret if I smashed, so I kicked a hole in the door. It felt good, but I really needed to lose control completely, like smash lots of plates, so after I kicked the door in, I

didn't know what else to smash. I felt incomplete, because I hadn't fully lost control, I'd only half lost control. If I had like a big bookshelf that I could have toppled over, that would have done it for me. I obviously wouldn't allow myself to completely lose control, because my head kept coming in and saying, 'No, if you smash that, you'll regret it!' because, you know, your mother gave it to you or whatever. So I suppose I wasn't completely angry, completely enraged, because otherwise I would've lost it.

As indicated by this woman's narrative, the absolute loss of control may be rarely experienced. Even in moments of extreme emotionality, internalized policing may take place, regulating behaviour. If the emotion is felt very strongly, even the most determined attempts to control it may ultimately fail but may still have some mediating effect on its expression. In another example, a 31-year-old woman provided an account of how she sought to maintain control as a 16-year-old attending her father's funeral. She said that despite her best efforts, she found it impossible in the end to avoid weeping because of the intensity of her grief:

I remember going to the funeral, and it obviously wasn't the situation that I wanted to be in. I was very upset that my father had died, and I didn't really want to cry in front of people who were there because I didn't feel it was appropriate. I didn't want them to see me break down, I really didn't want to place myself in that vulnerable position. So I just wanted to go along there and be in control and not lose control. And I remember that as the service began, when the person who conducted the funeral started to speak about my father, I remember staring at the carpet and I still remember the pattern on the carpet and the colours because I was staring so hard and trying so hard. I remember feeling that I wasn't going to be able to stop myself from crying. And eventually I did cry, I just could not control it, I was just so overwhelmed with sadness and unhappiness that I did start to cry in a very quiet manner.

While this woman's attempts to control her grief were not successful to the extent she would have liked, her expression of emotion was still moderated. Although, for example, she said she was 'overwhelmed' by sadness and unhappiness, her eventual tears were shed 'in a very quiet manner' rather than in a noisy or more demonstrative manner, and she did not jump up or run from the room or do anything that would be considered inappropriate in the circumstances. Her determination not to lose full control, and her beliefs about what kind of behaviour was appropriate under the circumstances, still shaped the way she expressed her deeply felt emotion.

These accounts suggest that there is therefore a delicate balance that must be maintained, involving monitoring of the situation and context, considering the ramifications for others and for oneself in the expressing of emotion. As a 43-year-old man commented: 'It's difficult, because on the one hand you might control your emotions and bottle them up. On the other hand, you obviously can't express your emotions at all times because it becomes very impractical.'

Emotional Styles: Differences between People

While the interviewees generally agreed that all humans have emotions (for this is an essential and inevitable dimension of the human experience), people were said to be different in the way they felt and experienced emotions: 'I suppose it's what makes people different – some people you think of as being really bubbly and happy and whatever, and some people you think of as being really morose' (47-year-old woman); 'people's responses to things are different, so what might make me angry or frustrated won't make somebody else angry or frustrated, so I think it's a combination of external factors and how you react to those factors or environment' (30-year-old woman). There was a strong suggestion in many people's accounts that 'being different' was part of being 'an individual': 'People are different in expressing their emotion because they are individuals. I mean, they have different personalities, they have different souls, different mind-sets' (36-year-old woman).

Thus, for example, it was thought that the same situation can provoke different emotional reactions from different people. This may be a matter of individual perception or personality type as well as differences in individual's life experiences. As a 43-year-old man put it, some people are very emotional about animals, while others are not: 'So I guess emotions come from what is important, or seems important . . . we all see what is important differently.' Another man, aged 40, noted that in response to the same event: 'Some people get upset, some hold it back, some talk their heads off, some don't talk at all, some drink.' Others argued that people may feel the same kinds of emotion but express them differently: 'We all feel the same but we just have different ways of showing it. Some people don't show it, but they feel it inside, and others, at a drop of a hat, they'd cry and throw tantrums and carry on' (62-year-old woman).

Despite the common view that emotions are inherent, developing 'within' the self (see discussion above), there was also strong agreement among the interviewees that modes of emotional expression are, at least to some extent, learnt. They contended that most important in this learning process was a person's family background, which was seen to influence strongly the way she or he learns to express emotions. A 30-year-old woman observed, for example, that it is difficult for some people to express emotions, 'because I think they've been taught to shut them off for so long, right through their childhood or through, you know, just their upbringing. Like, your parents may say, you know, "Now don't cry now or don't do this now," or "Wait until we get home before you do that." '

Some people said that with their own children they have made a deliberate attempt to avoid repeating the patterns of emotional acculturation they had experienced in their family of origin. For instance, a

46-year-old woman spoke about how her mother had taught her to control her emotions, and that she disagreed with this: 'I can remember saying from day one, when I had my babies, I won't accept how my mother had done it with us. These children will be allowed to express how they feel. I decided that whatever it was, whether happiness or sadness, that we all had a right to show that.' Another woman, aged 62, responded in the opposite way. She felt that her parents made too much fuss 'about every little thing'. Therefore, when she came to have her own children, she decided that she wasn't going to be like that and fuss too much over her children when they were ill. For example, when her children needed stitches for wounds, she remembered she would say to them: 'You just don't scream, it will only take longer and when you go to the doctor, the doctor will sew twice as hard and it will take twice as long to do it. So if you stay quiet it will be all over in a flash and there's no problem.'

The notion that one's emotions are 'natural' was referred to earlier in this chapter. This notion also emerged when people were describing the differences they perceived between children, who were positioned as being more in a state of 'nature', and adults, who had gone through the processes of socialization and therefore were more restrained or 'artificial' in their emotional expression. Children were described as being far more open to their feelings and less self-controlled when it came to emotional expression, and therefore more 'honest' about their emotions, than adults:

> Children seem really open about it, they just blurt it out or they feel it instantly, like they're either laughing at something or they're crying at not getting a chocolate biscuit or things like that. I think they're quite honest, because they don't know the difference. (30-year-old woman)

> Children are much more honest than adults, because adults learn to control their emotions . . . generally, if they're in a happy environment they will just express themselves willy-nilly. It will just come out, be it anger, or love or whatever. That's the way it should be. (36-year-old woman)

I noted above that there was evidence of a generational difference in attitudes about the importance of emotional control among the interviewees, with some older people expressing the belief that such control is important. Those older people who particularly valued tight control over the emotions tended to make disparaging comments about younger generations, and their disapproval of the way that children were now brought up by their parents. They complained that parental control had been relaxed far too much, that children were not properly disciplined, and that this resulted in outbursts of emotion that were inappropriate. As a 66-year-old woman commented:

> I think that the young children are really over the top now with their emotions, I think the young mothers are different too. It makes me very annoyed, because I think they don't have control over them, and I think children need some parental control, otherwise they feel lost. It gets me very upset when

children are allowed to do exactly what they like. That's what's wrong with society, there's just no discipline at home.

When the interviewees were asked if they thought that different groups tended to approach emotional expression in different ways, a distinction was often drawn between, on the one hand, the traditional Anglo or western European approach, and on the other that of Latin, Mediterranean or Middle Eastern cultures. The former group were described as emotionally self-contained and less expressive, while the latter group were positioned as more emotionally labile and openly expressive of their emotions: 'A red-blooded southern Italian person is far more likely to be outward in expressing emotion than a northern European person' (30-year-old man); 'The Middle-Eastern women, like when they grieve and stuff, they wail and hit themselves, scratch themselves and stuff. And then you've got Middle-Eastern men who go into the complete range [of emotion]' (25-year-old woman).

For most of the people who made reference to this difference, the 'open' approach was seen as superior, because it involved greater release of the emotions: 'I do like the Italians' style of things, because they do express themselves and they go over the top and also they've got an appreciation of things' (40-year-old man); 'Southern European races tend to get far more excited about things, which I think's great' (47-year-old woman); 'I think we drew the short straw there, the English and the Anglo-Saxons, they're not good compared to – I always thought the Jews were good at [emotional expression], and the Italians and the French' (49-year-old man). Here again, however, a smaller number of interviewees were less positive about such openness of expression, and this approach tended to be expressed by older people. One example is a 62-year-old woman (herself of Anglo-Celtic ethnicity), who recounted that when she had been giving birth to her children, she noticed differences among the other labouring women in terms of ethnicity. She said that Italian-born women were screaming a lot more: 'They've probably been brought up like that, that if you're hurt, you yell and you scream, if it's hurting you carry on, you don't cover up.' She contrasted this behaviour with her own, noting that she was also going through the process of giving birth, but managed to control herself and keep quiet. Her words indicated her disapproval of what she thought to be 'uncontrolled' behaviour on the part of the Italian women she had observed, with the implication that they had not borne their pain in labour as stoically as she thought was proper.

Gender and Emotional Expression

The interviewees were asked to discuss whether they thought men and women were different in the way they felt and expressed their emotions. Some simply responded that 'people are people', and as such, men felt the same kinds of emotion as women. Few argued that there were inherent gender differences in the expression of emotions. Most people agreed, however, that the social norms and expectations around masculinity and femininity shaped differences in emotional response between men and women. For example, a 25-year-old woman gave examples of the ways that gender influences emotional expression, drawing on her own experience:

> Men don't show their fear, because they're supposed to be warriors and protectors, and they don't show their sadness, so when they feel sad or fearful, they show anger. And women, they are not supposed to show their anger, and I suppose to a certain extent they're not supposed to show their fear either but turn it into sadness. . . . I control my anger because it's not okay for women to get angry. Men get angry and women cry. That's the way I've been brought up – whenever I felt angry, I used to burst into tears and now I don't, but I suppose I find it hard to express anger, so sometimes I just don't do anything.

Several other people commented on the social opprobrium directed at men weeping and women becoming angry, pointing this out as the major difference in hegemonic notions of masculinity and femininity in relation to emotional expression. As a 44-year-old woman opined: 'Men would probably like to cry but I think they hold a lot of it in.' She noted that she had been married to her husband for 25 years and had never seen him cry. As a result of this socialization, she contended, men tended to approach life with a more 'hard-hearted' attitude. Her husband, in particular, she said, demonstrates this approach: 'He can take a lot more knocks and things than what a woman can.' Other interviewees commented on the differences they had perceived between men and women in terms of men's tendency to avoid confrontations, to be silent when they were angry or frustrated with their partner during a domestic argument or to simply 'walk away' during such a confrontation. It was argued that in contrast, most women preferred to 'have it out', to discuss problems and to describe their feelings:

> I've found, particularly with my husband, that it was quite a long time before I understood him and knew what he was thinking or feeling about things, because he was quite controlled and didn't let me know what his emotional situation was for quite a long time after I first met him. And over the years he has begun to open up and now he often talks about how he feels about things, although sometimes he says, 'Well look, no, I don't *want* to talk.' And I say, 'Well fine, OK, I don't need to hear it.' But he *has* changed over that time. And I must say I do prefer – if somebody is reacting to me in a cold manner, or a changed manner, whether it be a past lover or my husband or whatever – I do feel as if I want to know what's going on and I do feel better if I do know, whereas men don't seem to have that need to know what's going on. (31-year-old woman)

It was noted by some that men behaved the same way with other men: 'Men hardly ever express their emotions to each other. I don't think there'd be another man that I'd express my emotions to since at school' (49-year-old man). This did not mean, however, that men did not feel the same kinds of emotion that women did, or to the same degree of intensity, but rather that they 'kept the emotions in' to a greater extent:

> Men seem to hold onto this concept of what they're allowed to express perhaps more than women. Maybe also women feel that they can be more emotional. I'm sure men can be just as emotional . . . men tend to show less feelings like nurturing, but I'm sure that's because they're conditioned that way. (50-year-old woman)

> I think once again it's just a matter of the way people have been brought up. I think that men are, particularly, it's probably stereotyping, but in a lot of cases are brought up to shoulder the burden, not express emotions. I think if men talk about it, it's in a jokey, blokey sort of way. (30-year-old woman)

Only a minority of the interviewees expressed the view that women have a greater inherent capacity for emotional expression compared with men. These people tended to be older men, who made such comments as:

> I think that the woman is able to protect and keep the heart of the man. If the man's got the wisdom to see that and the woman has got the wisdom to show that as well, then I think it can be a powerful thing in the relationship . . . the woman is more emotional, she is the nurturer, she bears the offspring, there's a real difference between a man and a woman and emotion's central to that. (55-year-old man)

> I think women would be more sensitive than men, women have a different type of control over their emotions. I think women are stronger than men emotionally, because of a lot of things they put up with. A woman has an in-built ability to control her emotions. (66-year-old man)

Most people's comments about gender differences suggested that men were in some way deficient because they had not learnt to show their emotions and to dissect emotional states at great length with their partners when there was a problem. Some women said that they found it difficult dealing with what they found to be a discrepancy in emotional styles between their male partner and themselves. For example, a 66-year-old woman who had been married for over 40 years said that her husband very rarely displayed his feelings, even to her in private. Over the years of the marriage, she said, she had found this at times immensely frustrating, because she felt that it was difficult to get close to her husband without knowing how he really felt about things: 'Because I'm emotional, I would love it if my husband could express some of his emotions, because I think it would make us closer. . . . I have seen him, in our married life, angry with me probably about three times. . . . I do think that you have to share things.' She said that she has never really felt emotionally close to her husband but 'we will go on like a pair of old shoes, comfortably together'. This woman thinks, however, that her husband has missed some good things in his life by not being emotionally sensitive or demonstrative: 'I think that if you show or feel greatly either great love or great disappointment, then I think that's a good thing.'

It was not only women who thought that men might be 'missing out' by not engaging well enough with their emotions. Men themselves, especially those who were in the 40s or younger, frequently commented on their own perceived need to be 'more emotional', or to display their emotions more openly to others, particularly to their partners and close family members. The majority of men interviewed in the study commented that they thought men were circumscribed by hegemonic notions of masculinity and emotional expression, and that the 'female approach' was better:

> Women are much better at expressing their emotion, in a general sense, they are more prone to wear their heart on their sleeves. And in their ability to do so they are probably better off, they're mentally healthier, because they are able to express their emotion as it comes, it's much more natural. And that is the problem with our society – it's still got those patriarchal overtones, whereas the male, it's still not cool to wear your heart on your sleeve as a male. There's that patriarchal thing, you must be tough. (45-year-old man)

This man went on to talk about how he had changed himself to conform more to the 'feminine' approach, and how this had had a positive effect on his relationship with his wife:

> I certainly do not bother with the patriarchal profile – I cry, I do what I want. My relationship with my wife just couldn't be better – it's enormously spectacular and beautiful and that's because we communicate, we have such great trust now, that I can tell her if I feel right about something, or I can tell her if I'm just feeling bad or I'm feeling low. . . . I don't have to hide that, I don't have to be tough or whatever.

Some men may prefer to embrace counter-hegemonic forms of masculinity as part of their challenging of dominant assumptions. For example, a young gay man made reference to the assumptions about heterosexuality that he also perceived underlying notions of gender and emotional expression, and how these assumptions did not fit into his concept of himself as a man:

> There's always an assumption at work that boys have to perform a certain behaviour, there's always a presupposition of heterosexuality as well, and girls as well. So the socialization of emotions by gender would exist but I find that hard to talk about because I think there's heterosexual assumptions underlying it. So I've never felt that I've really fitted into that model, that boys should express a certain kind of resistance to dealing with emotions. (20-year-old man)

It was apparent from the interviews, in terms of how much the male interviewees expanded on their answers and went into details about their emotional experiences and feelings, that younger men in general appeared to feel more comfortable about discussing these issues. For instance, one 49-year-old man commented at the end of his interview that: 'I found this very difficult to talk about, because I'm not really in touch with my emotions as much as I'd like to be.' A 54-year-old man poignantly noted how even though he loved his wife very much and wanted to let her know this, he found it difficult to articulate the words or show the emotion: 'I find it hard to show emotion. I want to, and after events happen I say, "Gee, I should have done that." I want to, but I find it difficult.' He added that he found it easier to express loving emotions only 'after a couple of drinks'.

In contrast to these older men, a 21-year-old man was most willing to describe himself as an emotional person, saying that he found it difficult to control his emotions: 'I think that just in certain situations, if I feel something, then no matter how hard I try, it's still going to come out, I can't put up a front.' He went on to speak with apparent lack of embarrassment about the grief he felt at the age of 15 when his grandmother died and how he had wept at that time: 'I think it was good to cry, it wasn't something that made me feel better about the whole situation, but it wasn't as if it was bad.' He also described, in an unselfconscious manner, a more recent occasion involving weeping in public, involving his return from a lengthy overseas holiday when he began to cry tears of joy at meeting his family on arrival at the airport.

Another young man, aged 19, expressed the view that he personally enjoyed wallowing in his emotions and expressing his feelings creatively through art and writing: 'I think it's great to let your emotions control you for a while. I think everything should be let go, to a certain extent. I think it's great to have a cry now and again, I think it's excellent.' He said that he found his relationship with his first serious girlfriend at the age of 17 an opportunity to express his emotions in ways that he had not otherwise experienced in his life thus far. This for him was a revelation, something that opened him up to 'new experiences'. He described how he had gone through a few months of depression after breaking up with his girlfriend, and said that he 'enjoyed' that time, even though he felt down, because he had learnt a lot about himself through introspection: 'It was something I needed to feel at the time.'

Men were just as likely as women to describe themselves as an 'emotional person'. More men than women, however, went on to note that other people may not agree with this self-definition because although they felt emotions keenly, they did not necessarily reveal them to others easily. Here again, a generational difference between men was evident. Older men rather than those in their adolescence or early twenties tended to describe themselves in this way. A 47-year-old man, for example, said that:

Inwardly, yes I'm an emotional person, outwardly to other persons, probably no. I'm a terrible romantic, I'll cry at the movies, but only at home. I think most men do keep the softer emotions to themselves, when they're out with other men, anyway. They have no trouble letting the anger and the macho-type emotions out, obviously, whereas I have a lot of trouble getting the macho emotions out, with other guys. Probably because I'm a softie, I've always enjoyed the company of women, I just feel more at ease with women.

A 66-year-old man described himself in similar terms:

I *am* emotional . . . sometimes I think I'm a little too emotional, but I tend to keep things to myself. I'm not a demonstrative person, everybody will tell you that. They don't really know what's going on in my mind, but I can be quite emotional really. Happiness, the good emotions, I can show outwardly, but the not-so-good ones I tend to bottle up. I really don't know why.

The male interviewees in the study were also more likely than the women to note that they had become 'more emotional' over the course of their lives, learning to identify and express their emotions more easily. This was suggested by a 44-year-old man, who noted that he had become aware of the importance of expressing emotion and had slowly learnt to do this more often. He said that he has recognized more and more emotions as he gets older and he is more aware of his emotional states. This man also noted that he has learnt to vocalize and explore his emotions, whereas when he was in his twenties he would try to deny or ignore them.

It was frequently commented by both men and women that their own parents displayed gendered patterns of emotional expression. The interviewees typically referred to their fathers as emotionally contained or as emotionally absent, particularly in relation to loving emotions. They described their mothers in different terms, as more emotionally volatile or expressive:

My mum lives on emotion, she's an extremely gushy kind of emotional person. . . . My father left when I was six, and I haven't seen him since so I've had a stepfather. But I couldn't tell you what, emotionally, with my stepfather you wouldn't know if he was happy or sad, you just would not know. He's very, very introverted. (25-year-old man)

My dad never showed emotions, so the belief was it took a lot to get my dad riled up. My mother did what most women tend to do, which is turn all of her emotions into tears, so that she could be weak and helpless . . . around my dad I don't suppose anyone really showed much emotion, because he didn't. (25-year-old woman)

Nonetheless, several people also referred to their fathers as 'angry', being able to express at least that one emotion without difficulty, sometimes accompanied by violence. A 36-year-old woman noted, for example, that: 'From a very early age I was always frightened of him coming home. . . . I always wanted my father to love me, and I guess I couldn't understand why he would hit us if he said he loved us, and often-times he used to.' A 49-year-old woman described how her father would not allow open emotional expression in their family when she was a child: 'As far as my Dad's concerned, you're never sick, you never cry, oh, anything like that, there is no up-down, you control yourself and that is it.' Yet her father, she said, was an angry and violent man, and he would regularly fly into a rage and beat her mother. This woman said that she remembered feeling confused as a child, because her father would strike her mother and then start crying, which provoked sympathy: 'You'd want to run up and go, "Oh Dad, don't worry about it!" but you're not really sure whether that's what you're supposed to do.

Like, is this what he wants, or is it not what he wants?' In the face of this uncertainty and violence, her mother, she said, made great efforts to keep things on an emotional keel.

Some interviewees recalled childhood memories of their fathers occasionally showing the emotions of love or grief and said that they found this difficult to deal with because of its incongruity with their fathers' usual behaviour. A 44-year-old man described how his father would never display love for his children openly unless he was drunk, and then he would do so in an overly affectionate and sentimental manner which embarrassed his children. A 34-year-old man recalled seeing, when he was 10 years old, his father in a fit of extreme anger, but also, and perhaps more shocking and distressing and therefore memorable, as weeping.

While most people who discussed their parents referred to their father as either absent or emotionally contained, or otherwise angry and violent, there were some interviewees who noted that it was their father who was the more emotionally expressive parent. A 47-year-old woman, for example, said that her father always showed much more emotion than did her mother, who never really expressed emotion, including love or affection. Her now elderly mother suffers from senile dementia and sometimes suddenly burst into tears. This woman said that she finds it difficult to witness this because she has never seen her mother cry before: 'So to see Mum crying now, I find it really difficult to cope with. Sometimes it makes me feel angry, because I feel like it's emotional blackmail' (47-year-old woman).

When other interviewees described their mothers in negative ways, it was usually in relation to such a narrative: the mother as cold, too emotionally contained, not showing love, rather than being angry or violent, as was the case for most negative representations of fathers. In another example, a 50-year-old woman noted that her now elderly mother is very 'hard' and often says hurtful things: 'I don't think I've ever heard my mother apologize, and I don't think I've ever seen her cry, but she's had me in tears.' She doesn't like visiting her mother very often because of her tendency to be unkind, but then feels guilty for not visiting. This woman noted that she had tried throughout her adult life to approach life differently from the way her mother did: 'I can remember when I first got married, thinking I don't want to be prim and proper like my mother.' She said that despite these efforts, she still has to force herself to show her emotions openly. For example, she would never say 'I love you' to her mother, and her mother had never said that to her.

Embodied Emotion

The interviewees were highly aware of the embodied responses that accompanied emotional states. One man, for example, described the physical sensations accompanying romantic love:

The feelings of love are akin to being high, like drugs will induce, so it's highly, I guess I'd say pleasurable, but there's a lot of similarities to anxiety. You may not eat and you have feelings right through, light-headedness, physical sensations in a whole range of ways. So there's an overwhelming strength of feeling that captivates one, that causes one to feel incredibly high. (44-year-old man)

As this narrative suggests, happiness or the experience of 'being in love' is often embodied as a state of lightness, almost of transcending the weight of the body. This was evident in the words of a 31-year-old woman: 'Extreme happiness feels very, sort of makes me feel very elated, and almost lifted above the ground, above reality, as if you're bouncing along instead of walking under gravity. It's a light sort of feeling, a floating sort of feeling, and just a very uplifting sort of feeling.' These descriptions evoke the 'high' and 'low' opposition, where states of happiness or elation are described as 'high', as in high spirits, or feeling physically high, as if on stimulants. By contrast, the emotions of depression, anxiety or sadness are described as 'feeling low' or 'feeling down' or 'reaching the depths of despair', having the opposite effect physically of dragging the body as well as the spirits down, slowing it, making it feel heavier and more sluggish.

Shweder notes that depression in western societies is articulated as an experience of 'soul loss', a feeling of emptiness, of loss of sense of self or spirit. To be empty is also to be down, low, cut off and hemmed in, as well as in a tactile sense to be dry and cold rather than moist and warm. To 'feel depressed' is 'to feel the blood stagnate in your veins' (Shweder, 1985: 194). Many of these associations are expressed in other cultures, where concepts of emptiness, darkness, dryness and lowness are also used to describe bad or unpleasant feelings. When people are experiencing sadness or depression they are often told to 'pick themselves up'. People are said to 'work themselves up' when emotionally excited, and 'calming down' or 'settling down' when the heightened emotions eventually abate. As a 30-year-old man described it: 'If you've been in a heightened emotional state for some while, I know from my perspective that you tend to come down from that and have a bit of emotional hangover.'

A 21-year-old man described how differently he felt three different emotions – happiness, sadness and anger – according to his bodily reactions and sensations:

If I'm really happy, I'm really jumpy, rushing here, there and everywhere, I just want to show my emotions to everyone else. It's not really in your body, because you're letting it out, so it's not inside. If I'm sad, I'll go into myself, I might listen to a slow song, and just be by myself and not do my normal routine, just want to be by myself and sit and do nothing. I guess you're keeping it inside yourself, sometimes you feel it in your stomach so that you can't eat. Anger is frustration, most times when you feel anger it's when you can't control the situation, so I sort of feel tight. Probably with me it's my shoulders and around my neck, and it's just sort of inside, and there's no real way I can let it out.

In other people's accounts anger also tended to be described in ways that referred to a sense of physical restlessness, tightness or pressure. One 46-year-old woman spoke of the urge to hit or lash out that she experienced when she felt angry, an urge she said she takes care to control because of her concern that she might hurt somebody. This sense of pressure, of needing to express anger physically to relieve a sense of tightness, was also articulated by another woman, aged 31: 'When I'm feeling very angry, there's a sort of tightness of the body. My body feels really tight, I feel muscular tightness almost as if I need to move, or to hit out or hit somebody or throw something. I feel like shouting, I often do when I'm very angry, or slamming doors, or something physical like that.' A third woman described the physical restlessness she experienced when she learnt that her marriage had irretrievably broken down: 'I had to keep walking, my body wouldn't let me stay still, I just walked' (41-year-old woman).

When people describe the bodily experience of emotion, there is often a strong distinction made between 'inside' and 'outside' the body. This is related to how the body/self itself is conceptualized and experienced. In contemporary western societies the 'true self ' is believed to be within the body, locked away in the 'inside', with a sharp dividing line drawn between the 'inside self ' and the 'outside world' (Elias, 1939/1994: 206). As one 50-year-old woman interviewed for the study described it, since she has been in her mid-teens 'I've been aware of an inner self, so there's me in here and there's everything out there'. Emotions are viewed as (partly) constructing the 'true', 'internal' self and are also commonly understood to be internal, generated from within the self in a dark secret place that is somewhat mysterious. It is believed that individuals experience emotions internally first, and then may or may not reveal them to others.

As was evident in some of the interviewees' accounts quoted earlier in this chapter, the ways in which we speak about and experience emotional states draws very strongly on a discourse of 'loss' in relation to the regulation of the body: someone is said to 'lose control' or to 'lose it' if they demonstrate openly their emotions, particularly the more shameful emotions such as anger, hate or jealousy. Tears are one way that emotions escape, but so are other bodily manifestations, such as shouting and laughing where words or incoherent sounds fly out violently from the mouth. To 'lose' one's temper is to relinquish control, to unleash unacceptable feelings. Similarly, maintaining control is understood to involve 'holding on' to an emotion, as in the common phrases 'she held her temper', 'he held in his grief '.

These metaphors signal a concept of subjectivity as a self-contained entity surrounded with borders that one polices, allowing certain phenomena 'in' and others the passage 'out'. As Lutz has argued, 'A discourse that is concerned with the expression, control, or repression of emotions can be seen as a discourse on the crossing back and forth of that boundary between inside and outside' (1990: 73). In some cases, the interviewees contended, it is good to allow the emotions to come 'out' of the self and be revealed for what they are. This is related to the 'open/closed' opposition, which people adopt to discuss the ways in which one's emotions are either revealed, and therefore 'opened' to others, or kept within oneself, and therefore 'closed' to others.

So too, interviewees used the trope of 'covering up' emotions to express the ways in which emotions that are felt are hidden from others. People themselves were described as 'open' in feeling and expressing their emotions or as more 'closed' and 'contained'. The common expression, articulated by several of the interviewees, of people 'wearing their hearts on their sleeve' is a particularly vivid use of this metaphor. To 'wear your heart on your sleeve' is to display your emotions in public, open to the view of everyone, to be particularly transparent and free in expressing one's emotion, to be 'emotional'. As a 49-year-old man remarked of his wife: 'I think she'd wear her emotions on her sleeve most of the time. They're very near the surface and that frightens me sometimes. She explodes, and shouts a lot sometimes.'

A binary opposition between 'hard' and 'soft' types of people was also often made in the interviewees' accounts. 'Hard-hearted' people are understood to be 'cold', not feeling emotions as much as others, or even as more likely to feel such aggressive emotions as anger and hostility, whereas 'soft-hearted' people are easily vulnerable to being overtaken by their emotions, particularly those associated with empathy, sadness and kindness. Men were more frequently described as hard, and women as soft. As one 44-year-old woman said of her husband: 'He's a lot harder, he can take a lot more knocks and things than what a woman can.' The interviewees also very commonly used wet and dry oppositions when describing emotional personalities and the embodied experience of emotion. Being able to let go of one's emotions was described as a 'fluid' or even 'gushy' experience, even if not related to crying. As one 47-year-old woman described emotional expression: 'Normally it's good to go with the flow, to go with the way you feel.' Emotions themselves, then, are conceptualized as fluid entities that may either be tightly held in, if one is a 'dry' person, or allowed to run free from the body, if one is a 'wet' or 'gushy' person. Emotions 'well up' just as tears well up in one's eyes. Emotions are seen to flow in various levels throughout the body and into the outside world. Just as fluids must be 'bottled' to keep them in place and orderly, so too are emotions described as 'bottled up' to keep them under control. Being both too 'wet' or too 'dry' in terms of one's emotions may be seen as negative. For example, a 24-year-old man described his mother as a 'gushy' person, which he viewed as negative: 'My mum lives on emotion, she's an extremely gushy kind of emotional person – I'm an emotional person, but I don't gush.' In contrast, a 49-year-old woman described herself as emotional and perhaps too soft-hearted, but added: 'I wouldn't like to be the sort of person that was cut and dried all the time.'

There is a related temperature metaphor, in which an emotional person, or someone who expresses their emotions freely, is often described as a 'hot' person, or as a 'hot-blooded' or 'hot-tempered' person, while the opposite extreme is described as 'cold', 'cold-blooded' or 'cold-hearted'. To be too 'hot' in one's emotion demeanour is to have lost control over oneself, and is generally thought of negatively, but to be too 'cold' is also seen as a negative attribute: 'some people, I think my mum would be an example of that, find it very difficult to show emotions and appear to be very cold sometimes' (47-year-old woman). In contrast, the person who is described as 'warm' or as 'warm-hearted' is seen unequivocally in positive terms: such a personality avoids both extremes of 'hot' and 'cold'.

Emotions are also described in terms of temperature and how they affect embodiment. Lakoff (1987) has examined these aspects in terms of the semantic system constructed around the emotion of anger in American English. He contends that the general metaphor for anger is 'anger is heat'. This metaphor has two versions, one applied to fluids ('anger is the heat of a fluid in a container') and one to fire ('anger is fire'). Related to these metaphors, particularly that conceptualizing anger as a hot fluid, is the notion that the body is a container for the emotions. Lakoff points out that the metaphor 'seething with rage' is derived from a now discontinued term for boiling fluids. 'Stewing' or 'simmering' of anger indicates anger as a fluid kept hot in a container over a long period of time. As the intensity of anger increases, then the hot fluid is said to 'rise', possibly resulting in a 'towering rage' that becomes less and less easy to control. Intense anger produces 'steam' and 'pressure' on the body/container, so that rage is said to 'barely be contained' or 'bursting out', finally 'exploding' in an 'outburst'. All these terms, Lakoff notes, imply a dangerous loss of control over the contained self, a kind of disintegration or falling apart that is dangerous not only for the angry person but for those around her or him.

I found among the interviewees in my study that anger tended to be described as either cold or hot, depending on the way it is expressed. If kept within and demonstrated through the withholding of emotional expression, anger is described as cold. If released in an outburst of rage, an 'explosion', anger is hot:

> Anger is a very overwhelming feeling, that for me feels just like a rush, a rush of emotions that's very heated. And when I get angry I almost feel like I'm about to explode . . . just sort of a boiling sort of feeling of just feeling overwhelmed by this tension, a lot of feelings that I then need to release. (31-year-old woman)

Among the interviewees, love was also commonly described in terms of temperature, with 'warm' most commonly used as an adjective. For example, a 30-year-old woman described love as 'just a nice warm feeling, nice sort of glow all over, positive thoughts about everything'. A 45-year-old man described how he was recently overwhelmed by his love and pride for his daughter performing in a school concert in a way that combined the liquid and temperature metaphors: 'My eyes bubbled up in tears, and it was beautiful, I was so proud, just so proud, it made me feel great. It's just that nurturing emotion you have when you have your own kids, it was just a wonderful warm feeling, a feeling of pride, a feeling of immense love, it's just very special.' Here again we see 'warmth' as being represented as the desirable middle point between the extremes of 'hot' and 'cold'. A warm feeling is one that is pleasurable and not too disruptive. It is not conceptualized in terms of pressure or tension. If one lets out one's warm feelings, they are released gently and easily, not as an explosion of force.

As noted above, the embodied feelings that people experience in relation to emotions are often articulated in terms of the 'tightness' or 'pressure' that people feel in their bodies. Anger or anxiety in particular are embodied in such a way. Sometimes the 'pressure' of the emotions is described as such that even if the individual tries to hold them in, to 'bottle them up' or 'keep a lid' on them, they escape anyway. This conceptualization uses a dam metaphor, where the body is conceptualized as an inner flood of emotions that are held back by the external skin and the will but may be released in a rush of fluid. A 31-year-old woman used metaphors of fluidity to describe how expressing her anger through shouting and throwing things made her feel better:

> As soon as it happened I'd just feel much better, because I'd just feel like this huge build up of very strong feeling that I just felt as if I couldn't contain. And I would just sort of let the floodgates open, and it would all come flooding out. And I would do all those things, I'd shout and scream and carry on and it would almost feel as if I'd emptied myself of these emotions.

As Lakoff (1987) pointed out, the 'steam' metaphor is also frequently employed to conceptualize emotion. As a 50-year-old woman described her response to tension in terms of pressure caused by steam: 'There's been times when really, as I say to the doctor, I feel as if my head's going to blow off, you know, like a kettle or something.' Steam is both wet and hot, the result of a boiling liquid. When one expresses particularly strong emotions, such as anger, one is said to 'let off steam', as if the body were a kettle or engine. Some individuals are described as 'bubbly', meaning happy and optimistic, which is again a liquid metaphor that recalls movement: boiling water or effervescent drinks. The oft-used phrase, 'stiff upper lip' to describe the supposed Anglo-Saxon approach to controlling emotion is a particularly vivid example of metaphor in portraying an image of a tightly held body part, kept from quivering, kept stiff rather than fluid, in the process of maintaining emotional control.

Emotions and Health States

The interviewees were asked whether they thought there was a link between styles of emotional expression and health states. Most people agreed that there was a strong association between holding in one's emotions, not expressing them openly, and suffering psychological or physical problems or illnesses. Being unable to express one's 'true' feelings, therefore, is seen not only as a source of unauthenticity or dishonesty, but is viewed as potentially harmful to one's physical or psychological health. A common phrase used by the interviewees was that 'it is healthier' to express one's emotions, to 'let them out' rather than control or contain them. A holistic notion of health was generally employed in this discourse, in which mental perceptions and the body were seen to be intimately interrelated: 'Most of our illnesses, in my opinion, are guided by your mind, so if you've got a healthy mind you have a better chance of having a healthy body' (34-year-old man).

The relationship between health and the emotions was also seen to reside in the extent to which people felt able to express their emotions openly. As a 49-year-old man commented, a failure to express one's emotions meant that:

> In this modern society, I believe that's why so many people get ill, or put stress on themselves. I really believe that one of the biggest creators of illness, particularly with emotional or mental illness, is people's inability to express their *true* feelings. And a lot of it stems from what they think the person that they're dealing with thinks, not what they really think, so they're living their lives through another person, not really how they feel.

The dam metaphor was frequently employed to describe the process by which emotions can be physically or mentally destructive, again representing emotions as liquid or steam: 'I think that if you let things bottle up then you're creating negative energies that are I think quite likely to increase exposing yourself to illnesses' (30-year-old woman); 'If you're under pressure and you're not doing anything to relieve that pressure, something's going to go wrong somewhere' (21-year-old man). It was argued, thus, that expressing negative emotion can mean that it is removed from the body. In contrast, keeping emotion 'inside' is harmful:

> If you suppress emotion – it's like holding your breath in, you know, and I don't think that's right, somehow. If you are really angry with someone, depending on the situation, I just think you should let them know, and say, 'Excuse me, but that's not right, and I'm really angry with what you've said.' I think it's a matter of learning to void things properly instead of being really, really angry, you know, that horrible anger. . . . I just think everyone should express emotions a lot more – it's healthier! (30-year-old woman)

Such a pent up of force could result in a metaphorical explosion, involving a sudden rushing out of emotion: 'It builds up inside and then it just goes off like a big bombshell if you leave it too long' (20-year-old woman); 'I think that you need to be able to express your emotions through some sort of medium, otherwise it may all come out in one horrible, violent episode' (30-year-old man). The notion of the body as a machine, propelled by steam or another hydraulic force, is evident in these understandings of the relationship between emotion and health. The mechanical image of the body has been very prevalent in both lay and medical explanations of health and illness since the industrial revolution (Herzlich and Pierret, 1987). It suggests that ill health is caused by some mechanical failure, a breakdown of parts – or in the case of the emotions, as a build-up of pressure (steam or fluid) in the machine that if not released may cause internal damage to the workings.

Although they easily made the link between health and emotions, most of the interviewees were rather vague as to the actual process by which emotion is translated into illness or disease. Some people adopted a discourse using the concept of pent-up emotions as parasitic, turning 'bad' inside the body if not released and 'eating' away at or attacking body tissue: 'Emotions eat you up, I think that if you're continually not expressing them, they will eat you up inside. They could become ulcers, arthritis' (49-year-old man); 'If you don't express emotions, I think it can kill you. It internalizes if it doesn't get released, it turns into something horrid and kills us, so there must be a way to release that' (41-year-old woman). One man, a tree lopper by trade, used the metaphor of 'dry rot' to describe the process by which emotions may turn physically destructive within the body. This notion of repressed emotion as 'eating away' at the body moves away from the mechanical body image to another metaphor that evokes the sense of illness as being the product of a kind of organic process of dissolution of bodily tissue. In this metaphorical model, emotions are understood to 'turn in' upon the body, to invade and destroy tissue because they are not released: 'Passion moves inward, striking and blighting the deepest cellular recesses' (Sontag, 1989: 46). Cancer has often been represented in a similar way: from medieval times to the present it has been conceptualized as like a hungry animal gnawing at internal flesh or as a kind of rotting (Herzlich and Pierret, 1987: 56).

The link between emotional repression and cancer was directly made by some interviewees. A 47-year-old woman, for instance, described a friend of hers who had gone through a painful divorce after she had discovered her husband was having an affair: 'She was really bitter and twisted about it.' The friend had recently died of cancer, which the interviewee traced back to her first troubles in her marriage. She argued that her friend had lost the will to fight the illness because of her despair over her marriage breakdown:

> I think that part of her just didn't want to get better anyway, because she just didn't really care how she felt anymore. She didn't care about her health. She didn't care about what she ate, she didn't care about how she looked after herself, she didn't care about her medical treatment and things, and really, she just let herself die.

A 49-year-old man similarly voiced his opinion that his brother, who died of cancer at the age of 42, was affected by his negative emotions: 'The angst that is created through anxiety can affect you greatly, particularly the stomach, the nerves. That's what happened to my brother – his cancer was basically created through his grief and his anxiety.'

Cancer was not the only specific disease mentioned as being caused by emotional repression, however. Some people linked pent-up emotion with a wide range of illnesses. Conditions such as high blood pressure, heart disease, general fatigue, stomach problems such as ulcers, allergies, over-use of drugs and alcohol, arthritis, depression and suicide were all suggested to be outcomes of emotional repression. In addition to cancer, a 25-year-old woman listed AIDS, anorexia and bulimia, obsessive-compulsive disorders and mental disorders as the outcomes of 'bottling up' emotion. She went on to observe that: 'If you gave me a list of diseases, I'd probably say all of them were caused by not expressing your emotions, like stubbing your toe and getting a cold, they're all messages.' There was a suggestion in some people's accounts of the relationship between emotion and health states of a moralistic discourse, in which people who did not express their emotions and became ill as a result were positioned as failing, or as deficient in some way. This was most obvious in the interview of the 25-year-old woman referred to above, who asserted that: 'I sometimes get annoyed with some people. I mean, I've got friends who seem to be sick all the time, and I think, "Well, you're sick because you want to be." Somewhere deep inside in the emotions, you let yourself be like that.'

Concluding Comments

The interviews with people about their emotions identified a series of recurring discourses and metaphors. Several dominant discourses related to the ontology of emotion and how it is conceptualized in terms of selfhood. These include: emotion as a means of self-expression; emotions as signals or messages of one's thoughts or feelings; emotions as a means of self-authenticity; emotions as a personal resource; emotions as the seat of humanity; emotion as an essential part of life; emotion as primitive; emotion as the opposite to rationality/reason. Other discourses related to how emotion is generated, including the following: emotions as coming from within the self/body; emotion as the product of thought; emotion as instinctive response to a stimulus; emotion as the interrelation of mind and body; emotion as part of the soul; emotion as the product of experience or learning.

In the interviewees' accounts, emotional people were described in generally positive terms as empathetic, compassionate, sensitive, demonstrative, expressive, open and capable of intense feeling, but also as sometimes being at the mercy of their feelings, as irrational and less

controlled. People saw themselves quite emphatically as either 'emotional' or 'unemotional', but it was also acknowledged that people can
change over time, particularly in becoming more emotional as they get
older. The notion that one should attempt to express one's emotions
rather than keep them 'within' the body/self was generally supported,
unless the emotions were negative and destructive, the context was seen
to be inappropriate or such expression might hurt other people. Too
much control over one's emotions was represented as potentially damaging, inauthentic or artificial and less 'honest'. It was generally argued
that men and women were socialized differently in relation to emotional
expression, and that men needed to learn to express their more tender or
vulnerable emotions more openly. A generational difference, however,
emerged at various points, particularly in relation to older people of both
sexes being less likely than younger people to champion the 'open'
expression of emotion.

Emotions themselves were represented metaphorically in a number of
dominant ways: as inside or outside, as high or low, as hot, cold or
warm, as tight or light. People themselves were portrayed as either open
or closed, hard or soft, hot, cold or warm and wet or dry in terms of how
they felt and expressed their emotions. The discourse of emotions as
fluid entities affected by temperature and pressure was very dominant.
The mechanical metaphor of the body was predominant in people's
descriptions of the body and emotional experience, particularly in relation to the possible consequences of emotional repression, as was the
metaphor of internal rotting or gnawing and the dam metaphor, representing the body's boundaries and the will as holding the fluid emotions
within.

Having established that these often contradictory discourses and
metaphors are dominant in people's explanations of the emotions, the
next step is to place these discourses and metaphors in their broader
sociocultural and historical context. The next chapters go on to do this,
focusing first in Chapter 3 on concepts of the body/self as they relate to
notions of the emotions, and then in Chapter 4 on the gendered dimensions of emotion.

3

Emotions, Bodies, Selves

In the previous chapter, a series of recurring discourses and metaphors used by people to conceptualize and describe emotional states and experiences were identified. In this chapter, I seek to contextualize these discourses and metaphors, locating them in their broader sociocultural and historical settings. I begin with a discussion of how the 'open' body/self that was dominant in pre-modern times changed over the centuries into the more 'closed' body/self that has become characteristic of the late-modern era. This overview positions contemporary concepts of the body/self, and by extension, those of the emotions, by identifying their antecedents. Then follows an analysis of the two major notions of emotions circulating today, each of which is in tension with, and takes its meaning from, the other. The first is a product of the negative discourses on emotion that position it as dangerous, disruptive or humiliating, and portray emotionality as evidence of lack of self-control. The second is the contrasting positive discourses on emotion that represent it as authentic evidence of humanity, selfhood and the proper basis of judgement and morality. I go on to look at concepts of contemporary emotional management and the role played by the 'psy' disciplines, followed by a discussion of intimacy and the confession. The chapter ends with an analysis of the associations that are commonly made in contemporary discourses between health states and emotions.

Notions of the Body/Self and Emotion: From Pre-modernity to Modernity

In western societies the self is currently perceived as an autonomous individual, constantly moving between the need to 'connect' with others and the need to maintain a sense of individuality. Contemporary notions of embodiment similarly privilege self-discipline and autonomy, maintaining oneself as distinct from other bodies, keeping one's bodily boundaries tightly regulated, shut off and distinct from others' bodies. This concept of the body/self is itself a historical artefact, the product of a number of major social and cultural changes since the Middle Ages, including the transition from feudalism to capitalism, the Renaissance, the rise of the modern European state, the Enlightenment, the Industrial Revolution and the emergence of capitalism. In what follows, the development from the 'open' to the 'closed' body/self is traced, with the implications for how the emotions are conceptualized highlighted throughout.

The 'Open' Body/Self

The concept of the emotions as fluid entities, which, as noted in Chapter 2, is dominant in contemporary discourses in western societies, has its antecedents in the ways in which bodies/selves were conceptualized and experienced in medieval times. In the Middle Ages in Europe there were many threats and dangers to human health and life for both peasantry and aristocracy alike. The most extreme of these threats and dangers were hunger, cold, epidemic disease and war. The presence of the supernatural was taken for granted, incorporating notions of a vengeful God with that of an evil Satan (Muchembled, 1985).

Historians of the period argue that in those times of great uncertainty and fear, where death seemed ever-present, where the work of the devil was viewed as everywhere, where there was little thought of the future, emotional states were expressed far more freely and openly, with little concern about their consequences. People were inclined to sudden changes of mood, to expressing what appears to modern sensibilities as 'uncontrolled' joy, hatred and anger. Violent acts were common, public executions, with the bodies left to rot as a warning to others, were standard punishments, and the torturing or killing of animals for the pleasure of seeing them suffer was considered a harmless sport. Few regulations existed to encourage people to engage in self-restraint in relation to sensual pleasures and emotional expression, and as a result, impulses tended to be followed without thought for the need to control or moderate them. Those regulations on behaviour that did exist tended to be enforced by external authorities, such as the Church, rather than being reliant on people's capacity for voluntary self-discipline. The body was very much a public body, with little sense of personal privacy. Very few bodily actions, including urinating, defecating and washing, took place in private, and there was little or no modesty, embarrassment or shame associated with these acts. People thought nothing of sharing common pots of food, bathing facilities and beds with strangers at inns and spitting and blowing one's nose with one's fingers were common practices (Elias, 1939/1994; Muchembled, 1985).

As this suggests, the body was far less contained, privatized and controlled in the Middle Ages. It was not yet conceptualized as discrete, isolated from the network of social relations or the physical world surrounding it. Instead, the body was understood as essentially porous, allowing a constant interchange of the elements between inside and outside the body: 'open to the world in all its orifices, unbounded, abusive, devouring, and nurturing' (Greenblatt, 1982: 5). In her analysis of body images in medieval and early modern German culture, Roper notes a 'literature of excess' in which the body was imagined as 'a container for a series of processes: defecation, sexual pollution, vomiting. Fluids course about within the body, erupting out of it, leaving their mark on the world outside. The body is not so much a collection of joints and limbs, or a skeletal structure, as a container of fluids, bursting out in every direction to impact on the environment' (1994: 23). Muchembled similarly argues that for people living in medieval France, one's body was perceived as a microcosm, a world which embraced forces that were pleasurable and that 'gushed forth through the orifices of the lower body' (1985: 78).

The self was also conceptualized as far less contained and autonomous in the medieval period. Men and women were taught from childhood to see themselves as connected and interdependent parts of a larger whole of the family or community (Gillis, 1988). Falk (1994: 20) describes this 'open' body/self as characteristic of societies in which the boundaries between 'inside' and 'outside' are largely defined in collective terms. Rather than the self being considered as individualistic, it is viewed as the 'group-self ', in which there is a continuous merging between individual and group identities.

It has been contended by some historians that this concept of the body as open and permeable was generally the source of corporeal pleasure rather than dismay or anxiety (Roper, 1994). In Bakhtin's (1984) study of descriptions of the carnivalesque in Rabelais's writings, he notes that the carnival and the feast provided an occasion for people to enjoy the unbounded nature of their bodies, the lack of regulation between 'inside' and 'outside', the overtaking of the mind by the body and the passions. Bakhtin describes this notion of embodiment as the 'grotesque' body, subject to few restrictions or regulations: its most distinctive character, he argues, is its 'open unfinished nature, its interaction with the world' (1984: 281). Nonetheless, concepts of health and ill health in the medieval period were strongly related to the notion of the 'open' body as constantly threatened with invasion by sinister forces or spirits. A series of taboos subsequently existed to police the body's openings and its fluids, particularly in such circumstances as illness, death, childbirth, sexuality and excretion, when the body was viewed as being especially open to the outside (Muchembled, 1985: 72–5). Amulets, charms and exorcisms were often used as remedies for mental torment or distress such as anxiety, despair, misery, grief and guilt, seen to protect people against the dark forces of evil that could possess them (MacDonald, 1981: 215–17).

The humoral model also drew on a notion of the body that saw it as comprising fluids. In this model, which was formulated in ancient times but remained dominant in Europe until well into the eighteenth century, the body was believed to contain four fluid 'humours' – black bile, yellow bile, blood and phlegm. It was thought that an excess of one humour over the others resulted in an imbalance that could cause illness, and also in the expression of certain personality traits (Nutton, 1992). The substances of blood and yellow bile were related to the characteristics of a 'warm' tempered person; the sanguine individual who was hearty, cheerful and florid in complexion on the one hand, and the choleric person who was angry and quick-tempered on the other. In contrast, black bile and phlegm were understood to result in a 'cool' tempered individual, either sad or apathetic. While these temperaments were considered to be natural 'outcomes', for even in healthy people the balance of the humours was seldom exact, it was believed that extreme variations could contribute to mental disorders, predisposing individuals to dangerous excesses of the passions characteristic of their particular temperaments (MacDonald, 1981: 186). Popular remedies for humoral imbalances included purgatives with emetics (to cause vomiting) and laxatives and blood-letting with leeches or via surgical incisions, the idea being to restore the bodily balance by expelling excessive humours (1981: 187).

The Emergence of the 'Civilized' Body/Self

Most historians point to the social changes occurring in the early modern European states in the sixteenth and seventeenth centuries as pivotal in the emergence of what came to be the ideal of the disciplined, individual, autonomous self. During this period, particularly in its earliest stages, there was a strong linking of emotion with embodiment. People were less likely to make the distinction between action and feeling, and did not conceptualize emotions as lying deep within the self: ' "Feeling" still meant both physical and internal sensation; and, at a time when medical authorities made no sharp distinction between psyche and soma, anger and love were seen as having an actual physical presence in the "cold stare" or the "warm embrace" ' (Gillis, 1988: 90–1). Love and affection, for example, were not generally thought about in terms of spiritual transcendence or mystery, but rather in highly tangible, embodied terms.

The conceptual linking of body fluids and emotions as fluids can also be seen in early modern customs around emotions. It was believed that love and hate could be transmitted through bodily orifices, either by their emission by route of body fluids or via ingestion. Exchanging body fluids through sharing a meal or drinking from a common cup, or by exchanging clothing or objects made from body substances such as hair, was thought to bring people together and bind them. This link was not simply symbolic, but literal, in that it was believed that co-mingling fluids was a source of union. One Welsh custom of the time, for instance, involved a young man proving his love to a woman by urinating on her dress, while a French custom involved a courting pair striking each other with 'love slaps'. Love potions used bodily fluids or parts such as blood, saliva, hair and nail clippings to encourage amorous feelings among young men and women seeking a marital partner (Gillis, 1988).

Popular concepts of health into the sixteenth and seventeenth centuries continued to link emotions and health states. The humoral theory remained predominant, and there was also a strong linking of certain bodily parts with the generation and control of the 'passions' (as emotions were often called) (Porter and Porter, 1988: 46). The exact relationship between the emotions and anatomy, however, was the cause of some dispute and confusion. It was held in some English medical texts of the seventeenth century that mental distress or turmoil were transmitted to the heart, where the passions were aroused. Once the emotional climate of the body had been disturbed, the inner temperature was affected, which in turn was believed to cause dangerous mutations in the balance and composition of the humours (MacDonald, 1981: 182). Other physicians and philosophers argued that grave sickness was the outcome of a poisoned imagination, believing that 'the fevers' heat cooked and burned the humors, turning them into a toxic substance called "melancholy adust", whose fumes roiled up from the crucible of the spleen to pollute the mind' (1981: 184).

From the sixteenth century onwards, a growing disdain for and self-consciousness about the body and its products gradually took hold, leading to a heightened focus on emotional and bodily regulation. The individual came to see the self as 'inside', with society and others 'outside'. The subject gradually became 'self-censoring' and an emphasis on voluntary self-control rather than external imperatives or coercive means such as torture or execution developed (Barker, 1984: 10–12). The ideal body became conceptually more 'closed off' from the entry of outside agents or contact with others' bodies. Bodies became privatized and more invisible at the same time as a network of regulations grew concerning how the body should be managed and controlled (Foucault, 1977; Barker, 1984; Elias, 1939/1994). The intimate habits of everyday life, the deportment of the body and the dispersal of bodily wastes became more and more interbound with regulations. Indeed, they became 'intimate' or 'secret' through such regulation, and the emotions of shame, embarrassment and fear became associated with their public display. As an outcome of these processes, by the seventeenth century, 'it was no longer possible to dispose of one's own body as freely as during the preceding centuries' (Muchembled, 1985: 191). Inherent in these approaches towards the body and self was the ideal of the human agent who is able to 'remake himself [*sic*] by methodical and disciplined action' (Taylor, 1989: 159). There emerged a conflation of bodily discipline with the disciplined self: without disciplining the body, the self would be unruly.

The concept of the body as comprising fluidities remained dominant in the early modern period, but from the late fifteenth century a growing number of texts on the moral features of bodily excess were published. In this moralist literature, vices were represented as a kind of inner fluid, threatening to burst forth from the body and requiring discipline:

'Discipline is a kind of "fence" . . . which has but little strength against the untameable brute force of the lusts within' (Roper, 1994: 24). The sixteenth-century Protestant Reformation developed a focus on minimizing the role of nature, sensuality, the body, superstition and the supernatural, all of which were important in medieval Catholicism. Instead, the proponents of the Reformation emphasized rational thought and control of the body and the emotions as the route to knowledge and spirituality. Magic and the supernatural were positioned as evil, and worshipping was seen as more of an individualistic communing via thought and word with God rather than as a sensual embodied experience that took place via communal rituals. Thus, for example, Protestantism insisted upon the 'Word of God' as being more important to spiritual self-identity than the sensual and emotional stimulations offered by such trappings as icons, paintings, statues, chants and incense, and looked askance upon trances, visions and expressions of religious ecstasy. The fleshly passions were viewed as sinful, an impediment rather than a route to the divine, and thus as requiring strict control (Mellor and Shilling, 1997: 42–5).

In the sixteenth and seventeenth centuries, religious notions played an integral role in understandings of emotional states. Godliness was often contrasted with emotions that were considered abnormal. Other supernatural forces, however, were also seen to be at work in emotional states, such as astrological events and witchcraft. Anger was viewed as an evil visited by Satan, and unacceptable thoughts (such as thoughts of suicide) and misery were also often attributed to him. People in despair thought of themselves as having been possessed by a bad spirit and of their good angel as having disappeared (MacDonald, 1981: 144; Stearns and Stearns, 1986: 19–20). In the Catholic literature on exorcism of the sixteenth century, devils were seen as residing within the body. It was believed that these devils must be brought out of the body, expelled into the light, if the sufferer were to be cured. Expulsion of this inner force was thought of as painful, but desirable (Roper, 1994: 24). Fantasies about witchcraft similarly drew on the notion of the disorganized body containing poisonous liquids (1994: 25).

In this literature the elision of distinctions between self and other was represented as terrifying rather than pleasurable. Descriptions of anger at that time often portrayed it in terms of an invasion of bad spirits taking over the individual. In the seventeenth century, one of the Pilgrim leaders in America, John Robinson, described the wrathful man as a 'hideous monster', going on to note that: 'If a wrathful man saw himselfe [*sic*] in glass [a mirror] when his fit was upon him, his eyes burning, his lips fumbling, his face pale, his teeth gnashing, his mouth foaming, and other parts of his body trembling, and shaking . . . he would, and worthly, loathe himself ' (quoted in Stearns and Stearns, 1986: 19).

In his influential work *The Civilizing Process*, first published in German in 1939, the historical sociologist Norbet Elias analysed the emergence of shame and embarrassment around bodily functions that began in the sixteenth century. Elias (1939/1994) suggested that as the feudal order decayed and new social classes were formed during this time, there was an increasing emphasis in the public domain on honour, piety, civility and social order. Life also became more predictable – famines were less common, acts of physical violence reduced in number and sudden or early death was not as prevalent a feature. Elias links changes in the production and expression of the emotions with the emergent notion of *civilité*, or a new obsession with outward bodily propriety – how one behaves oneself in public. The behaviours associated with *civilité* were directed towards self-control, the holding of oneself apart from others, the stifling of displays of bodily function and the regulation of facial expression, table manners, gestures, dress and the disbursement of bodily wastes.

Elias contends that rules about these behaviours became far more complex in the sixteenth century compared with medieval times, and the importance of conforming to good manners because of 'what others might think' more emphatically emphasized. So too, he argues, expressions of aggressiveness, anger, cruelty, joy in battle and fighting, and in the torment and torture of others and of animals became far more controlled than in medieval times, when, as noted above, they were seen as part of the pleasures of life. According to Elias, there developed a far greater sensitivity to cruelty, the suffering of others and the expression of anger, as part of the intensification of emphasis on interpersonal interactions and on 'refinement' of emotional expression. By the nineteenth century, what was once accepted as a source of pleasure, such as the public torturing of humans and animals and public executions, became viewed with horror and revulsion.

Other historical accounts have underlined changes in the ways that people deported themselves and regulations about behaviour during the early modern period. Muchembled (1985), in his history of France between 1400 and 1750, has also identified changes in notions of the self and the body from pre-modern to modern times. He argues that in the fifteenth century there was little evidence of prudishness about the sexual functioning or excretion of the body. By the mid-eighteenth century, however, there had developed new rules of conduct. For example, the bedroom came into being as a separate room in the eighteenth century, and fewer people slept together in one bed, as whole families had done in the fifteenth and sixteenth centuries. People began to wear clothing to bed and nudity became taboo and shameful, compared with the sixteenth century, where they habitually washed, undressed and dressed in public (1985: 189).

Barker-Benfield (1992: Chapter 2) describes the behaviour of privileged men, 'rakes' and 'libertines' associated with the court of the newly installed King Charles II in the late 1600s, who engaged in drinking, fornicating, cockfighting, gambling, bear-baiting and violent assaults upon others, both men and women, for the pleasure of it. Their behaviour was attacked by reformers, who sought to encourage respectable, disciplined behaviour among the privileged and the lower classes. There were about 20 reform societies in London by the end of the seventeenth century, directed at publishing 'dissuasives' and 'cautions' and pressuring authorities such as the Church, local magistrates and central government to encourage reform for the governance of manners and immoral behaviour. These societies also concerned themselves with the regulation of alehouses, taverns, playhouses and brothels.

The 'civilized' person, thus, as the notion developed in early modern European societies, began to be viewed as a privatized individual who could set him- or herself apart as an autonomous, contained entity and who could exert a high degree of control over bodily functions and movements, including the emotions. The 'open' body/self that has been identified as a dominant concept in medieval times became progressively more 'closed' off. Containing one's body boundaries and exerting more control over the disbursement of one's bodily fluids became a central aspect of proper deportment. To lack appropriate control over one's body was to be viewed as 'uncivilized'. By the seventeenth century, people had come to see themselves as divided into two irreconcilable halves: the outward 'civilized' body and the excessive 'grotesque' body, the latter requiring continuing vigilance and work to keep hidden and contained inside oneself (Mellor and Shilling, 1997: 10).

It would be misleading, however, to present a view of subjectivity and social life in the early modern period as completely dominated by rational thought, asceticism and self-control. Roper (1994: 5) argues that in this period there was a renewed interest in magic and the irrational; the late seventeenth century was the time of the witch-hunts in Europe, for example. So too, the supporters of the Catholic Counter-Reformation emerging in early seventeenth-century Europe demonstrated a disaffection with the constraints upon sensual embodied ritual and the rejection of 'carnal knowledge' as a route to spirituality imposed by the Protestant reformers. The counter-reformers sought to introduce a new sensuality into religious practice, with an emphasis on the emotional and the mystical rather than the cognitive (Mellor and Shilling, 1997).

Modern Bodies/Selves

The Enlightenment, a period of change in intellectual thought which began in the late seventeenth century and continued into the eighteenth century in Europe and North America, built on the concerns of the Protestant Reformation in turning away from tradition, 'irrationality' and 'superstition' and towards 'scientific' and 'reasoned' thought in the quest for human progress. From the Enlightenment perspective, the emotions were viewed as 'irrational', the enemy of reason and therefore requiring discipline and regulation. Broad social changes in the wake of the Industrial Revolution, including urbanization on a mass scale, also wrought further changes in notions of the body/self. In the eighteenth century people began to interact with large numbers of other people in unprecedented ways, including strangers and those they did not know very well. In smaller communities, where people knew each other well, external regulation of behaviour was common. For individuals living in larger urban groups, however, this regulation was less effective, and a greater emphasis on inner, or self-regulation developed (Demos, 1988; Stearns, 1988).

The word 'emotion' in the mid-eighteenth century still meant physical movement, but by the nineteenth century it came to denote invisible feeling. Around that time, love and marriage rituals also became far more privatized and more removed from the body, which had become sexualized in relation to romance. Love became a more disembodied feeling, less associated with the act of physical joining, which had been defined for the first time as 'sexual'. It was viewed as 'a powerful inner impulse, as private experience transcendent of all social and moral considerations' (Gillis, 1988: 107). At the same time, concepts of the self, particularly for men, privileged autonomy, individualism and the main-tenance of firm boundaries around the self which could only be dis-solved in a romantic relationship with one's true love and life partner. The body, in concert with the self, had become individualized and viewed as 'owned' by the individual, signifying that person's social position (Duden, 1991: 13).

Even though physicians were beginning to abandon humoralism by the eighteenth century, the legacy of the humoral theory was the notion that the flow of fluids was vital to health and bodily functioning (Porter and Porter, 1988: 52). As the eminent English physician George Cheyne described the body in 1734:

> The human body is a machine of an infinite number and variety of different channels and pipes filled with different liquors and fluids, perpetually run-ning, gliding, or creeping forward, or returning backward in a constant circle and sending out little branches and outlets, to moisten, nourish, and repair the experiences of living. (quoted in Skultans, 1977: 149)

Porter and Porter (1988: 49) note that there was much concern among the British in the seventeenth and eighteenth centuries with the flow of bodily fluids and essences. Great attention was paid to the consistency, colour and thickness of blood, faeces and urine, as a diagnostic means. It was believed that body fluids should be regularly purged from the body to get rid of stale fluids and make sure that proper circulation took place. The British were also concerned with the circulation of the 'animal' or 'vital spirits', 'whose office was to mediate between the corporeal organs and the mind, will, inner senses, and consciousness' (Porter and Porter, 1988: 49). People said that they felt 'up' or 'down', 'high' or 'low', 'in' or 'out' of spirits (1988: 46).

It was commonly believed in these times that illness could be psycho-somatic; that the 'passions', as they were termed, could cause illness. Some people made a link between personality types, the passions they felt, and the resultant bodily effects. Cheyne, for example, argued in his *An Essay on Health and Long Life* (first published in 1724 and reprinted many times), that 'Men of lively Imaginations and great Vivacity, are more liable to the sudden and violent Passions, and their Effects. . . . Thoughtful People, and those of good Understanding, suffer most by the slow and secretly consuming Passions. . . . The Indolent and the Thoughtless suffer least from the Passions: The Stupid and Ideots [*sic*] not at all' (quoted in Porter and Porter, 1988: 64). Humoral theory again underlay these beliefs, in bringing together body, mind, environment and health states.

The concept of 'nerves' also began to gain currency in Britain in the eighteenth century, linking states of agitation, feverishness or depression with internal workings of the body (Porter and Porter, 1988: 68–72). According to this way of viewing ill health:

> If the nerves were 'high', or 'highly strung', the mind was bright, and the body felt sensations acutely; were the nerves 'low', the mind was dull and the body sluggish. Or one could simply be 'nervous' as a blanket term, suggesting a diffused heightened sensibility, febrile delicacy, vulnerability to excessive feeling, and a brittleness of temper. (Porter and Porter, 1988: 70)

Both men and women were said to suffer from 'nerves', including King George III during one of his bouts of insanity (Porter and Porter, 1988: 70). The condition of 'nerves' was, however, believed to afflict only the well-to-do, for having 'nerves' suggested delicate sensibility and refine-ment; although by the beginning of the nineteenth century, lower classes began to talk of 'nerves' (1988: 71).

So, too, in the eighteenth century in Germany there developed a growing fascination with the role played by 'the passions' in health and illness. Prominent physicians who wrote tracts for laypeople about health advocated a 'reasonable lifestyle' in the interests of achieving and maintaining good health, including the avoidance of wild mood swings and excessive emotional states. One school of thought which won many converts argued that there were basically two forms of illness, one caused by over-stimulation and one by under-stimulation (Lindemann, 1996: 264). The Germans also believed it harmful to restrict the flow or 'flux' of fluids around and out of the body. Popular German medical works described the effects of 'hampered evacuations' upon the body, arguing that the stoppage or meagre flow of bodily fluids such as sweat, urine, faeces and menstrual blood caused all sorts of illnesses. The idea was that such fluids, in being unable to escape from the body, banked up unnaturally and then 'corrupted' internal organs such as the stomach, the bowels and the lungs (Lindemann, 1996: 266). Reference was com-monly made in medical treatises of the time to the role played by emotion in causing 'hampered evacuation'. One German physician wrote, for example, that fear, horror and grief could suppress healing secretions and stop up the liver ducts, causing bile to accumulate in the stomach and intestines, resulting in dysentery (Lindemann, 1996: 268; see also Duden, 1991: 142–3).

By the nineteenth century, the 'grotesque' body, the body whose boundaries were not well contained, became viewed as a source of horror and disgust, particularly for members of the bourgeoisie. Disgust for 'grotesque' bodies became a potent means by which the bourgeois sought to distinguish themselves from those they considered socially beneath them, who were marked out as 'Other': as dirty, contaminating and repulsive because of their supposed lack of self-control over their bodies and their general deportment, including over their emotions (Stallybrass and White, 1986: 191). For members of the bourgeoisie in Anglophone and northern European societies, such people included members of the poor and the working class, southern Europeans, people of Middle Eastern cultures and non-whites. In the words of one member of the Victorian bourgeoisie, the 'finer feelings' and sense of morality of the working class and the poor were 'brutalized' by their poverty and the rough living conditions they endured in the city slums (quoted in Finch, 1993: 33–4). Evolutionary theory proposed a theory of emotions 'which married the innate and the acquired, the savage and the child, the man and the woman' (Vincent-Buffault, 1991: 199). According to Darwin, the progressive mastery of tears was a sign of civilization. He placed Englishmen at the peak of progress because of their restraint over the shedding of tears (Vincent-Buffault, 1991: 200).

Early European accounts of foreign peoples were rich in the expression of revulsion for their bodily habits and appearance (Greenblatt, 1982: 2). In colonial discourses, the black man was typically represented as highly embodied, particularly sexually, and as infantile and emotional compared to the white man. Overt racism was evident in the writings of Freud, who described 'savages' as developmentally inferior and as being as incapable of appropriate emotional regulation as are children, demonstrating 'the inclination to exceed every limit in the expression of emotion and to work it off completely in the form of action' (quoted in Kovel, 1995: 218). Bordo (1993: 9–10) points out how colonial and 'scientific' writings on and illustrations of African women often drew attention to their similarity to wild animals, particularly monkeys, in their supposed over-developed sexuality, reliance on instinctive drives and savagery.

Again, however, there is evidence in the late eighteenth century and into the nineteenth century of a counter discourse, particularly expressed in Romantic thought, whose exponents argued that rational control was something which 'may stifle, desiccate, repress us; that rational self-mastery may be self-domination or enslavement' (Taylor, 1989: 116). For the Romantics, the realm of imagination and feeling was viewed as a counter to the formality and discipline of modern society, and the

passions were considered the wellsprings for human action. A sentimental feeling for nature began to emerge in concert with Romanticism.
According to the Romantics, nature awoke and intensified sentiments,
bringing about a more spiritual awareness: 'We return to nature, because
it brings out strong and noble feelings in us. . . . Nature draws us
because it is in some way attuned to our feelings' (Taylor, 1989: 297). In
contrast, rationality was viewed as repressing one's 'true' self by damp-
ening sentiment and inner impulses (1989: 301).

Indeed, while philosophers of modernity, such as Kant, supported the
concept of emotional asceticism in the search for pure reason, writers like
Nietzsche remarked upon the emotional sterility, the numbing of the
passions they saw as being an outcome of western modernity (Hughes,
1996). The Romantic philosopher Rousseau was sceptical of what he saw
as the Enlightenment's obsession with knowledge and the domination of
nature by reason, believing that not all the secrets of nature should be
laid open. Too much knowledge, he contended, may lead to moral
corruption. For Rousseau, society had led to the distortion of human
nature, which humans needed to rediscover through feeling (the inner
voice of the heart) (Lloyd, 1984: 58–64).

There was also a move to reform the 'hard-hearted' scholar and
aristocrat in the eighteenth century by encouraging 'humaneness' rather
than rationality, drawing upon people's 'natural' sympathetic natures
(Barker-Benfield, 1992: 66–7). The term 'sensibility' was used to denote a
particular kind of consciousness, a consciousness that was sensitized to
be more responsive to signals from the outside environment and within
the body, and was invested with spiritual and moral values (1992: xvii).
The eighteenth-century novel and other literature established a 'sentimental fashion', a 'cult of sensibility' which was conterminous with a
cult of refined emotionalism and a cult of benevolence and was associated with a broader culture of sensibility in other spheres of life (1992:
xix). In sentimental fiction of the time, the greatest mark of 'taste' was the
ability to respond to such stimuli as wild landscapes, melancholy poetry,
romance and so on, and even more so to the 'trifles' of human interaction
with tears, blushes and the like (1992: 206).

During this period, melancholy was particularly fashionable among
the upper classes and aristocracy, seen by them as denoting sensitivity of
spirit and gentility. According to Vincent-Buffault (1991), in eighteenth-
century France weeping in public was considered entirely appropriate
for both men and women, as evidence of a fine sensibility: 'The subjective experience of tears presented pleasure as a blend of the body and
the mind, both sensation and internal movement, it was the discovery of
the self, the happiness of feeling one's existence. To cry in private was
also to know how to "take pleasure in oneself " ' (Vincent-Buffault, 1991:
3). That is not to say that it was deemed appropriate to lose oneself
totally in one's emotions. Tears should only be shed selectively, with
nuance, and were therefore highly controlled. There was an 'art' of tears

which avoided dangerous excesses: 'the tears of sensibility referred to a refined culture of the self. A series of aesthetic, ethical and even medical stakes delineated the limits of this developed sensibility' (1991: 53).

Blushes were also considered to be a mark of refined sensibility, as long as they were not too pronounced or frequent. In the British writer Thomas Burgess's *The Physiology or Mechanism of Blushing* (1828), he argued that the blush is the distinguishing mark of humanity, human spirituality and moral value. He believed that blushing was created by God, 'in order that the soul might have sovereign power of displaying in the cheeks the various internal emotions of the moral feelings; so as to serve as a sign to others, that we were violating rules which ought to be held sacred' (quoted in Skultans, 1977: 152). The inability to blush was viewed as a sign of insanity, idiocy or lack of moral development. On the other hand, however, excessive blushing was seen to provide evidence of inner moral derangement and was a sign of the chronic masturbator (1977: 153).

The emergence of the Gothic genre of literature in the late eighteenth century also evinces this turn towards strongly felt emotions and (to some extent) loss of self-control. The Gothic genre, examples of which are Mary Shelley's novel *Frankenstein* and Bram Stoker's *Dracula*, was about excess, the return and haunting of the past, the supernatural, evil, the fantastic, the emotions of both terror and laughter. It called into question the drive towards rationality of the Enlightenment by identifying the underside of humanism. The figures in Gothic literature are constantly expressing and battling with their emotions, succumbing to fits of passion, hate, desire, rage, madness and intense love. It is preoccupied with transgression and anxiety over cultural boundaries, with document-ing the ambivalence of emotions. The Gothic was designed to encourage intense emotional reactions on the part of its readers rather than teaching them a moral lesson or inspiring in them a tastefully 'reasoned' response. As such, this body of literature subverted the accepted mores and manners of 'proper' social behaviour: vice was often shown to win over virtue, disorder over order and desire over reason (Botting, 1996).

The modern subject, therefore, was not defined only by rational control but by this new power of self-expression and engagement with one's own nature and feelings. There was a continuing tension between the privileging of rationality and of free affective expression. This dualism of approaches to the emotions was evident in the Victorian attitude to grief and mourning. Self-consciousness, involving a concern about how one appeared in public, became intense in the Victorian period. It was believed that the inner self could be revealed involuntarily, including one's inner-most thoughts and emotional states, and thus one should always be on one's guard to prevent this occurring (Sennett, 1977; Baumeister, 1987). In this context the home became a refuge, the one place in which some (if not full) relaxation over emotional control could occur (see further discussion of this in Chapters 4 and 5).

Although the Victorians were obsessive about self-control in many contexts, particularly in relation to their appearances in public, they were equally obsessed with grief, funerals and mourning rituals, which were elaborate and lengthy. Outpourings of grief were commonplace in popular culture, and sorrow was represented as intensifying life's experiences and other emotions. Children were schooled to expect grief and loss of loved ones: in the USA, for example, toy manufacturers sold coffins for young girls' dolls (Stearns, 1995: 46). There was the suggestion that wallowing in sorrow was paradoxically pleasurable in its intensity of feeling. As the writer of a family advice manual published in 1882 opined: 'It may truly be said that no home ever reaches its highest blessedness and sweetness of love and its richest fullness of joy till sorrow enters its life in some way' (quoted in Stearns, 1995: 47).

A trajectory of sorts may be traced, therefore, in the development of contemporary notions of the emotions as they relate to dominant concepts of the body and the self from the pre-modern to the modern era. In pre-modernity there is evidence of a concept of the body/self as 'open', a more or less permeable entity. Emotions were conceptualized as fluids within the body/self which may or may not be 'let out' into the world. Rules and taboos may have existed to police the openings of the body/self in pre-modernity, but the pleasures of merging with the external world seemed to have generally held precedence over its terrors. Since the Renaissance and into the Enlightenment period, the body/self became conceptually more 'closed' to the outside world, partly as a result of a greater emphasis on regulation and self-control, and there was evidence of greater anxiety around relaxing or losing control of the boundaries of the body/self.

This is not to argue that the transition from the 'open' to the more 'closed' body has progressed inexorably, without discontinuities and counter-discourses. Indeed, those periods in which there was an intensification of focus on the regulation and control of the emotions have usually been associated with a counter-discourse in which the emotions have been represented as the most powerful source of humanness and self-authenticity. This remains the case in the present day, and the next sections of this chapter explore these competing discourses in greater detail as they are expressed in late-modern societies.

The Unruliness of Fluid Emotion

The notion that the emotions are disruptive and somehow external to the self remains dominant in contemporary western societies. Indeed, we commonly talk about the emotions in terms that suggest that we are passive and even helpless in the face of the power of the emotions, suggesting that we often find ourselves submitting to them or overpowered by them despite our better judgement or our best efforts. As Solomon notes, we tend to 'cast ourselves in the role of helpless martyr,

battling powerful and irrational forces within us' (1976: xv). It was
pointed out in Chapter 2 that when people describe emotion, the notion
that it develops 'inside' the self/body is commonly employed. We are
said to feel the emotion accumulating within us, against which we may
struggle to exert control, or else give in by letting it 'out' of the body. We
'fall in love', are 'paralysed with fear', 'struck with jealousy' and
'plagued with remorse', we are 'heartbroken', 'crushed', 'smitten', 'overwhelmed', 'carried away' and 'undone' by our emotions. All of these
terms suggest that emotion 'happens' to us, that it has the power to
destroy our self-possession and self-control and that this is a painful and
debilitating experience (Solomon, 1976: xv). Alternatively, we may seek
to 'fight' against our emotion; for example, people are said to 'struggle
with', 'battle', 'overcome', 'wrestle with', 'come to grips with', 'subdue'
and 'surrender to' anger (Lakoff, 1987: 392).

The emotions are represented from this perspective as being visceral
and primitive, closer to our animal than our higher side. The emotions
are associated with chaos, with excess, disorder, unpredictability and
irrationality, and even with some degree of social or physical risk for
both oneself and others: 'The chaotic energy of emotions makes them
dangerous to anyone in their vicinity and weakens the person experiencing them' (Lutz, 1986: 291). Lakoff points to the association between
anger and insanity in such expressions as 'he went crazy', 'I'm mad',
'you're driving me nuts', 'he went bananas', 'I went berserk', 'she went
out of her mind', 'he had a fit', 'he got hysterical' and 'insane rage' (1987:
390). Further, expressing anger is often described in terms of taking on
animalistic characteristics: for instance, in the phrases 'bristling with
anger', 'hackles up', 'bare his teeth', 'ruffled her feathers', 'snarling
with anger' (Lakoff, 1987: 393–4). In all these metaphors and discourses,
there is a suggestion that emotions are separate to, as well as part of,
the body and the self. Those who are emotional, who allow their
emotions to 'take over' their selves, are positioned as weak, at the mercy
of their emotions (Lutz, 1986: 294). Underlying this conceptualization is
the notion that 'Reason is that part of the soul that is most our own, the
only part of the soul that is completely under our control' (Solomon,
1976: 11).

There are resonances in these discourses with the ways in which we
perceive our bodies in general, as being part of but also separate from
ourselves, requiring the exertion of discipline to contain unruliness and
disorder (Falk, 1994: 2–3). Heywood (1996) describes what she terms
'anorexic logic' as dominating bourgeois notions of appropriate behaviour in modern Anglo-American cultures. She defines anorexic logic as a
set of assumptions that rest upon a number of integral binary oppositions – mind over body, thin over fat, white over black, masculine over
feminine, individual over community, control over disorder. These oppositions, she argues, are then brought to bear not only upon the ways in
which individuals may deal with eating and other regimes related to the

size and shape of the body, but also how they approach other areas of life, including emotional expression. Anorexic logic is predicated upon the ascetic avoidance of excess, the quest for rationality, the transcendence of desire and the flesh. Emotional states, according to this logic, have the potential to disrupt this sense of self-containment. They are impure, defiling, animalistic, alarming and disgusting.

As noted above, the dominant western notion of the ideal human body is that which is hard, impenetrable, closed-off from the outside world and dry. In contrast to this ideal, the emotional body is often represented as an 'open' or 'grotesque' body, a body that is unable to contain itself in socially acceptable ways, a body that threatens to burst apart its boundaries. The notion of the emotions as fluid entities (see Chapter 2 and above) is related to this discourse. We feel ambivalent about fluids in many contexts, because of their liminal nature, their tendency to seep or ooze and thus challenge control. This is particularly the case of slimy or sticky fluids, which have the status of being not quite solid, not quite liquid. Such fluids are the byproduct of putrescence, decay and dissolution – they seep from rotting matter. Bodies that ooze fluids are a standard of horror, presented as monsters because of their loss of containment, their in-between nature between life and the dissolution of dead flesh. We are both repelled and disgusted as well as fascinated by such bodies and fluids (Wilson, 1995: 247).

As discussed earlier in this chapter, the heightened concern with regulating and policing the openings of the body and what is emitted from them is a specifically modern approach, developed in the wake of the 'civilized' body. Indeed, some commentators would argue that the desire to control one's bodily boundaries, to protect the body's openings from penetration or invasion, has become an over-weening obsession in late modernity. Kroker and Kroker (1988) argue that compared with any previous eras, the late twentieth century is characterized by an increasing panic about contact with what are seen to be contaminating body fluids. They identify a 'Body McCarthyism' that has developed around bodily fluids, intensified by concerns over HIV/AIDS and fears about the destruction of our immune systems, their inability to cope with 'invasion'. Kroker and Kroker see this panic as part of a generalized *fin-de-millénium* mood in contemporary western societies, in which people see themselves as alone in a world which is rapidly breaking down and becoming more dangerous.

In contemporary western societies we are acculturated to find the bodily fluids that are an inevitable part of living embodied experience, such as phlegm, mucous, saliva, sweat, pus, vomit, urine, faeces, semen and blood, for the most part as disgusting and abhorrent, as symbolically polluting matter. As Mary Douglas has noted, the fear and anxiety aroused by such substances, their positioning as 'dirty' and 'contaminating', do not necessarily spring from their idea that they are unhygienic in some way, but more fundamentally from the notion that they are conceptually out of their rightful place according to cultural systems of classification (such as the distinction between self and other) (Douglas, 1966/1980). The inside of the body is considered far more disgusting than the outside, with all its sliminess, its unpleasant sights and smells, and we therefore endeavour to police the orifices of the body as much as possible (Miller, 1997: 52). The emergence of bodily fluids from 'inside' to 'outside' in an uncontrolled manner is a potent sign of the permeability of bodily boundaries, of the inherent animality of the body (Grosz, 1994: 193–4).

Great emphasis is therefore placed on the 'proper' regulation of these substances from early childhood. Their appearance at socially 'incorrect' times or places demonstrates a frightening and disturbing loss of rational control, signalling a return to a state of bodily chaos of infancy. The dribbling, incontinent elderly or disabled body is a nightmarish vision for its lack of control. To allow others to see the bodily fluids that emit from our bodies is, for the most part, to humiliate oneself, while the experience of having contact with others' bodily fluids is replete with danger and potential disgust.

The fluidity of emotions is problematic in that like other fluids (particularly bodily fluids) they tend to dissolve the boundaries between outside and inside. They may therefore be conceptualized as polluting in their challenging of bodily boundaries, inspiring horror and fear. Like body fluids, emotions 'flow, they seep, they infiltrate; their control is a matter of vigilance, never guaranteed' (Grosz, 1994: 194). Tears are perhaps the most symbolically 'clean' of the bodily fluids, related not only to their apparent purity as a clear, water-like fluid, but also because they are emitted from the eyes rather than from more reviled bodily orifices. However, they also tangibly bespeak loss of control, a break-down in the containment of the self. The act of dissolving into tears is evidence of a 'leaky' body, a body that is vulnerable and permeable, characterized by the breaking down of boundaries between 'inside' and 'outside'.

As Leder (1990) notes, the body is often experienced as 'absent'. That is, we are not consciously aware of our bodies unless an experience of hunger, pain or other physical sensation occurs. Emotional states, like pain and illness, bring the body into consciousness by virtue of their sensational dimensions. Indeed, intense emotions feel as if the body has taken over. In moments of extreme emotional experience, bodily sensations are experienced as overwhelming cognitive or 'rational' processes. In anger, the quickened heart rate, the tensed muscles, the rush of adrenalin combine to produce a heightened sense of embodiment. The blush of embarrassment, the churning stomach of nervousness, the elation of joy are all experienced as the body coming to the fore, making itself known, slipping beyond the bonds of the mind or will's control. Leder vividly describes this process of the re-emergence of the body in emotional experience and the accompanied desire to re-establish control:

> I feel these emotions holding sway within me as an alien presence that I cannot shake. Anxiety provides a good example of this phenomenon. Reading a paper at an important conference I discover my hands becoming clammy, my voice beginning to crack. My heart is racing and my breathing takes on a choked quality. Try as I might to focus on my talk, my attention is pulled back to these physical manifestations. I watch and try to control them, breathing deeply to calm myself and modulating my voice so that my nervousness will not show. This anxiety is undoubtedly mine, but is also something from without, fighting my efforts at mastery. (Leder, 1990: 84–5)

Such accounts of emotional experience, in which the 'self' is conceptualized as wrestling with the 'body', are also commonly found in narratives of illness or pain. The body that is in pain, ill or disabled is often conceptualized as both self and not-self, as threatening self-control and rationality. People experiencing such bodily extremes often speak about a symptom of physical distress or part of the body causing pain, sickness or dysfunction as something other than themselves; they externalize the sensation or bodily part while also acknowledging that it is part of oneself. Pain, for example, may be described as a demon, a monster lurking within, a force which streaks around the body and attacks it, but also as a betrayal by one's own body. For those experiencing strong pain, there is often a sense of a split subjectivity, the self against the self (Good, 1994: 124).

So too, the emotions may be experienced as the body taking over the self. To be 'overcome' or 'swept' away by our emotional states, to have them 'explode' or 'gush' out of the body can be a frightening experience if we feel that we have relinquished control. Embarrassment, humiliation, disgust and shame may be created by loss of emotional control, whether in private or even more potently, in public. The fluidity of emotions is such that they threaten order and propriety, they are undignified, they render one open and vulnerable and subject to approbation from others. Hence the discourse on emotions that refers to the fragmentation, the 'break-down' of the self that can occur in heightened emotional states, the references to 'pulling oneself together' and 'picking up the pieces' that are the after-effects of losing self-control.

Emotion, Humanity and Moral Value

I have argued that the discourse privileging emotional control is challenged by a counter-discourse championing the importance of acknowledging and expressing emotions as an essential part of humanity and privileging the free expression of the emotions. As was observed in Chapter 2, emotion is seen to be an essential part of being a human and something that sets humans apart from animals, or from inanimate objects like machines. Emotion is linked to the higher human attributes of spirituality and soulfulness, and is commonly represented as the core of human existence, underpinning systems of meaning and values. Emotions are seen to be 'honest' in their closeness to nature, contrasted with the 'artificiality' of culture. Emotion is positioned against estrangement or disengagement in the same way as life is contrasted with death, community and connection against alienation, the subjective against the objective and the authentic against the contrived (Lutz, 1988: 56–7).

In contemporary western societies, the individual's understanding of the emotional self is an important aspect of ideas of the 'real' or 'true' self. The 'true' self has come to be privileged as a special, individual aspect of subjectivity. It is believed important to seek to identify this authentic self, to allow it to emerge from the depths of consciousness, thence to be worked upon. As Craib has commented:

> We can think about our 'real' or 'true' self as the most important thing about us. It often seems, when we speak of it, to be associated with feelings of fragility and preciousness, as if it were an immensely beautiful and valuable vase that could be easily broken or destroyed. We are careful who we show it to, and we guard it jealously. Sometimes it would not be going too far to suggest that perhaps we feel it as a link with God in an increasingly Godless world. (Craib, 1994: 72)

The positive meanings given to emotion is part of our privileging of the 'true' self. Emotional states are understood as a means of gaining an insight into the 'true' self, for in their very 'naturalness' they are perceived as 'breaking through' the bonds of 'culture'. One's emotions have become the gold standard, revealing to oneself how one is really responding to a phenomenon: 'Whoever has emotions and shows and uses them for his or her own identity strategy is morally in the right, since emotions cannot be disputed in communication processes' (Gerhards, 1989: 749). As noted in Chapter 2, emotions are seen as things that are possessed by oneself, not necessarily available to others unless they are 'let out' in some way and shown to the external world. Lutz points out that the meaning of emotions as subjective and personal gives them a special, even sacred place as the indicator of individuality: 'In this view, the emotions are Me in a way that thoughts are not' (1985: 80).

To lack emotion is to lack the compassion and empathy which are hallmarks and supports of humans' relationships to others. In some social contexts a breakdown in the control of one's emotions may be considered positive, a sign of a warm or sensitive personality or someone who has strong affective ties with others – when tears are shed for the plight of others, for example, or where grief is demonstrated at the loss of a close family member or friend. Emotionality from this perspective is not a sign of weakness, but rather is seen as an indicator of strength of conviction and vitality (Lutz, 1986: 294). In contrast with the emotional ('warm-hearted') personality type is that of the 'cold-blooded' psychopath, the 'animal' who is unable to feel emotion and thus has no remorse in killing others. The concept of the 'emotionless' human or non-human creature is a standard of horror, inspiring fear and loathing:

> In the tradition of horror, lacking a soul, in the manner of a golem or a zombie, means that the creature will be incapable of compassion and will be deaf to your pleas. Machines inspire a similar response. . . . Robots, androids and cyborgs all can create genuine horror effects in part because they can be supposed to behave soullessly, like Cartesian animals, and hence act without pity or compassion. (Wilson, 1995: 246)

The contemporary emphasis on the humanizing nature of feeling appears also to be part of a generalized sense, which began to be dominant in the early twentieth century, that living in a (particularly urban) society is alienating, cutting one off from personal ties and distorting selfhood. In this discourse, society is represented as stifling human feeling and repressing self-autonomy and preventing the achievement of 'true' individuality (Baumeister, 1987: 170). The provenance of the discourse in the Romantic approach to the emotions is obvious – indeed, Solomon (1976) has called it the 'New Romanticism'. He argues, however, that unlike the original Romanticism, the New Romanticism does not separate emotion and reason, or view emotion as irrational, but rather positions it as the proper and most penetrating basis of judgement about one's self and about other people. Solomon himself supports this perspective, claiming that 'The passions are the very soul of our existence; it is not they who require the controls and rationalizations of reason. Rather, it is reason that requires the anchorage and earthy wisdom of the passions' (1976: xvii).

The New Romantic approach to emotion can also be seen in the discourses of several contemporary social movements, such as feminists, right-to-life activists, members of the 'green' or environmental movement, gay and lesbian activists and animal liberationists. These movements have competing and often clashing interests with each other. What unites them, however, is that the emotion propelling people to become activists and to join such movements is typically represented in the discourses of the movements as evidence of appropriate feeling, of allowing the sterility and rationality imposed by society to be overcome by emotion based on empathy and compassion for others or for non-human living creatures and anger for what is seen to be abuses of human power. Maffesoli (1996) has referred to the late modern age as the 'time of the tribes', asserting that the personal and the affective have become viewed as the appropriate basis for ethical and moral judgement. He draws attention to the emergence of affinity- and identity-based political groups as examples of these 'neo-tribes' which are often based on lifestyle preferences. Maffesoli argues that emotional forces are what brings individuals together to form these groups and uses several terms to refer to this energy: *'puissance'*, or the vital force of the people (as opposed to the power of institutions), 'multiple explosions of vitalism', 'emotional glue', 'the social divine' and the Durkheimian 'collective effervescence'.

Another dominant discourse that has resonances in Romantic thought represents the 'emotional personality' as comparatively more refined, more sensitive than those who are 'unemotional'. Those individuals who are seen to be 'emotional' (also referred to as 'nervy' or 'high strung') are believed to be 'closer' to their emotions, to live a life that is wrought with emotional highs and lows. There is the implication in this discourse that people are born with a personality that may predispose them to heightened sensitivity, or else have a more stolid disposition which means that they approach life with equanimity, experiencing neither the transports of anxiety nor those of joy that more 'sensitive' types encounter. These meanings were evident in the words of a psychiatrist quoted in a magazine article about anxiety attacks. He commented that: 'On the one side of the scale are the stoics, those who live on a fairly level plane. On the other side are the emotional, sensitive, more vulnerable types – creative, sensitive, complicated people prone to introspection – and life is more a series of peaks and valleys' (quoted in Hawley, 1997: 18). There is a suggestion in this discourse that people who are 'emotional' somehow gain more from life because of their predisposition to respond to events at the extreme edges of emotion. There are echoes here with the discourse of 'nerves' that was evident in eighteenth-century Britain (discussed above).

Working on the Emotions: The Importance of the 'Psy' Disciplines

As an outcome of the association that is commonly made between emotions and authentic selfhood, we often use our perceptions of the emotional self as rationales for explaining why we behave in certain ways. In this discourse, the unruliness of emotions, the difficulty we have in taming and repressing them, may still be considered problematic, but also serve a useful purpose. In contexts in which our behaviour may be otherwise inexplicable, identifying the emotions we feel provide reasons and sometimes even justification. We do things because we 'can't help it', impelled by emotion over which we have no control. We tend to see ourselves as possessing specific emotional characteristics or an 'emotional identity' – for example, describing ourselves as either 'emotional' or 'unemotional', as 'hot-tempered', 'prone to jealousy' or 'soft-hearted' – and claim that these attributes shape our responses to events and people.

There is a sense that such characteristics persist as part of our personalities throughout our lifespan unless something happens to change them, such as life experiences or via working upon the self. As suggested by some of the interviewees described in Chapter 2, one may become 'more emotional' as one gets older, or through effort of will, by deliberately attempting to express one's emotions more openly. Alternatively, we may seek to suppress or reject aspects of our emotional self that we consider undesirable, such as a tendency to depression, anger or jealous behaviour.

Another dominant feature of late modern understandings of the self and the body is that they have become viewed as 'projects', or endeavours to be worked upon continually, that are never finished or complete. In their writings on relationships in late modern societies, Beck-Gernsheim and Beck (Beck, 1992; Beck and Beck-Gernsheim, 1995) discuss the process of individualization, or the movement in post-industrial societies away from traditional social ties, systems of belief and relationships. This involves not only more flexibility but also new demands and obligations, particularly in relation to choices about such matters as sexual identity, work, family and romantic relationships. Such planning requires a high and continuing exertion of reflexivity upon the ontology and future of one's life course. People are understood to engage in ethical practices that are directed towards the regulation of the self in the interests of 'proper' social deportment and the achievement of life goals. Where once, in pre-industrial society, it was expected that one's destiny was pre-structured through the chance of one's station in life at birth, the life course is now conceptualized as far more flexible and open, albeit through individuals' endeavours rather than the vagaries of fortune.

It is through these notions of the body/self that we understand and experience the emotions. Emotional management and regulation, paying constant attention to how best to deport oneself emotionally, is an integral aspect of reflexive work upon the self. Individuals in contemporary western societies are encouraged continually to examine, and to work upon, their emotional selves. As the interviewees quoted in Chapter 2 observed, it is important to regulate your emotions, to control them as well as express them as the situation permits. It is not socially appropriate simply to display one's emotions as one feels them at all times, but nor is it desirable to maintain too tight a hold over them. As suggested above, however, emotional 'work' is not just about emotional management, but about improving the character of the emotional self, seeking to change it.

American psychologist Daniel Goleman's *Emotional Intelligence: Why It Can Matter More than IQ* (1995) was a best-selling book in countries such as the USA, Britain and Australia in the mid-1990s. Goleman's argument in this book served to underline the notion that an awareness of one's own and others' emotions is an essential part of successful modern living. He claims that there are two forms of 'personal intelligence' that contribute to success: interpersonal intelligence, or the ability to understand other people's feelings and actions, and intrapersonal intelligence, the ability to understand one's self. Both contribute to 'emotional intelligence', which includes the ability to control one's impulses, delay gratification, motivate oneself, handle relationships with others well and empathize with others. Goleman argues that people who score highly on conventional IQ tests may fail to achieve their potential if they lack emotional intelligence. People who lack the skills of emotional intelligence, Goleman asserts, are more likely to fall victim to depression, stress-related illnesses, drug abuse and eating disorders and to behave violently towards others, and are less likely to find success in employment and personal relationships. He locates contemporary social problems among young people such as mass unemployment, illicit drug use and violence as resulting from a general lack of emotional intelligence. Goleman's thesis, therefore, emphasizes the importance of 'emotional literacy' for both men and women, involving working upon the self in relation to the emotions and learning ways of identifying emotions in oneself and in others and of managing one's emotions appropriately to achieve social success.

The notion of the 'true' or the 'authentic' self supports endeavours of self-regulation and improvement. It is through the practices directed at self-knowledge, it is believed, that the 'truth' of the self may emerge. It is expected that individuals seek self-knowledge and engage in reflection throughout their lives so as to achieve the 'best self ' they possibly can: 'What this calls for is the ability to take an instrumental stance to one's given properties, desires, inclinations, tendencies, habits of thought and feeling, so that they can be *worked on*, doing away with some and strengthening others, until one meets the desired specifications' (Taylor, 1989: 159–60, original emphasis). As actor William Hurt commented in an interview in late 1995: 'Everyone is trying to be worth the privilege of life. . . . Life's a gift, given to you to witness, a remarkable thing. Yourself is something that takes a lifetime to achieve' (quoted in the *Sydney Morning Herald*, 25 November 1995).

To define and deal with the project of the self, a new 'expertise of subjectivity' has developed, in which numerous professions (for example, psychologists, psychiatrists, social workers, counsellors, probation officers) have established themselves as expert in 'measuring the psyche, in predicting its vicissitudes, in diagnosing the causes of its troubles and prescribing remedies' (Rose, 1990: 3). The observation and monitoring practices of the human sciences construct the notion of the 'normal' self against which people are urged to measure themselves. If they are found to be deficient, individuals are encouraged to work towards achieving 'normality'. The discourses of humanistic psychology and psychoanalysis, in particular, have had an increasing influence on the ways in which self and the emotions are conceptualized in late modern societies. Humanistic psychology is directed at the maximization of human happiness, using the language of self-actualization and self-acceptance. This approach repeatedly asserts that goodness lies within, as an inherent property of the person, and that any badness comes from outside, as 'imposed' upon the individual and 'distorting' her or his 'true' self (Richards, 1989: 115).

Hollway (1989: 26) has described the changes that took place in academic psychology in the 1960s, in which the 'humanist' approach became an alternative to the rationalist perspective offered by positivist psychology. The humanist approach led to such phenomena as encounter groups, in which participants were encouraged to reveal their feelings to other members as a therapeutic exercise:

> I remember sitting in endless encounter groups where the best intervention to make was supposedly to ask someone, 'Yes, but what do you *feel*?' If some people had difficulty in getting in touch with their feelings, it was because they were hidden under layers of socialization which could be peeled off in the climate of trust that the human relations group was intent on providing. The idea of a core individual, an essence prior to socialization, is central to this model. Feelings then became products of nature and not of culture; bearers of truth about the individual. (Hollway, 1989: 26–7)

This approach is itself based on the Freudian 'talking cure' and the notion of repression, which views nervous or psychological disorders such as hysteria, phobias and obsessions as produced by the repression of threatening or painful impulses, desires or memories of experiences, often related to sexuality, that are stored in the unconscious because they are unacceptable to the conscious mind. The language and concepts of psychoanalysis, particularly in its therapeutic form, had, by the mid-twentieth century, entered everyday life. Such terms as repression and frustration and the key concept of the unconscious had become frequently used by members of the lay public (Berger, 1966).

The dam metaphor, which as noted in Chapter 2 is commonly employed in lay accounts of the emotions, was strong in Freud's writings: 'what Freud felt, listening and struggling with his bourgeois neurotics, was their sense of the forceful flow of their inner desires as they began to burst the dams . . . the consequence of the resulting flood would be the overcoming of intellect by emotion, masculine order by feminine anarchy, rationality by irrationality, reason by desire' (Frosh, 1991: 34). For Freud, it was the individual's struggle to maintain order in the face of this threatening chaos that characterized life in modern society: 'Through the power of these metaphors of nature – dams bursting and volcanos erupting – the unconscious emerges as a primeval entity, full of energy, held back only by the controlling exigencies of nature' (Frosh, 1991: 40). The point of psychoanalytic therapy was to facilitate the release of unconscious emotions through talking to the therapist, thus relieving the pressure.

This therapeutic approach to the confessing of the emotions to others has also successfully moved into current popular discourse on the emotions. The removal of 'repression' has come to be a central theme of modern culture, usually referring to individuals' rights to express their needs, desires and feelings (Craib, 1994: 7). In a widely publicized interview conducted with the late Diana, Princess of Wales, for the British *Panorama* documentary television series in late 1995, the Princess revealed that she had received therapy and counselling for her problems with bulimia, self-mutilation and post-natal depression. In the interview she stressed the importance of being 'open' about one's feelings, of being able to discuss them. She demonstrated approval, for instance, that her estranged husband, Prince Charles, had chosen not to hide his relationship with his mistress: 'I admired the honesty. To be honest about a relationship with someone else, in his position, that's quite something.'

Princess Diana's emphasis on the importance of 'honesty' and 'openness' in revealing one's emotions underlines the commonplace that we should articulate our emotional states, both to ourselves and to others, rendering our feelings into language. Craib argues, indeed, that our culture is obsessed with emotions, particularly around their management and making them 'safe' (1994: 86–7). He claims that seeking counselling or psychotherapy, speculating about emotions and talking about them are now seen as signs of status, particularly in relation to sexuality (1994: 89). He has observed among his patients individuals who come to him to learn to 'be in touch with', talk about and express their emotions. Based on his experiences, Craib contends that there are 'fashions' in emotions. Currently, he argues, vulnerability and fear seem to be 'in' for men and anger for women (1994: 89–90). He has also noticed in his trainees and patients in psychotherapy the belief that voicing feelings and understanding them will mean that they disappear. The assumption is that 'we can talk about the feelings instead of having them, that the talking itself solves emotional conflicts and leaves us at ease and peace with ourselves and others' (1994: 104).

The understanding of the self as 'an assemblage of psychological mechanisms' allows people to deal with themselves in the technical, calculated and rational way that is privileged in industrial production (Berger, 1966: 363; Craib, 1994: 102–3). Seeking expert 'technical' assistance, identifying 'causes' of difficulties so that these might be addressed, becoming more 'organized' and better 'managed', are viewed as solving the 'problem'. According to Craib (1994: 104), in this process there is a denial of the inevitability of disappointment, loss, grief, mourning, death and suffering. Through obsessive discussion, these feelings are often turned into 'positive' things or a 'creative' experience. The positioning of the self through psychological therapeutic discourses also brings together the contradictory desires for soberness, rationality and science with the mystery and magic that was part of religion's appeal. Instead of the 'other world' of religion being 'out there', in psychological thought it is 'inside' the individual, awaiting discovery (Berger, 1966: 363–4).

Intimacy and the Confession

It is not only with 'experts' that people are expected to be 'open' about their innermost feelings. To deal with what is seen to be the increasing complexity of society and social relationships, the semantic field of friendship and love has emerged, involving a proliferation of discourse around intimacy (Luhmann, 1986). Personal relationships are believed to bolster us from 'external' dangers, providing supportive intimacy. They have become represented as a site where one can 'be oneself ', express one's emotions openly without fear of recrimination, and withdraw from the demands of 'false' self-presentation required of people in the 'public sphere' (Sennett, 1977; Stearns and Stearns, 1986). Individuals in close relationships are expected to achieve and maintain intimacy by sharing their emotions with each other, even if these are negative.

It is generally believed that trust can only be achieved by self-disclosure, the ' "opening out" of the self to the other' (Giddens, 1990: 124). Giddens attributes our obsession with the quality of relationships as resulting from this need to work on trust: erotic involvement particularly calls for self-disclosure. To know the other, one must know oneself (1990: 122). Luhmann similarly sees 'intimacy' as involving a high degree of 'interpersonal interpenetration', 'meaning that in relation to each other, people lower their relevance thresholds with the result that what one regards as relevant almost always is also held relevant by the other. . . . Lovers can talk incessantly with each other because everything they experience is worth sharing and meets with resonance' (1986: 158). He notes that other personal relationships are burdened with the expectation that the other will 'know' one intimately, which makes them difficult to sustain and in turn renders the quest for the ideal personal relationship more intense (1986: 162).

The confession of one's innermost feelings, dreams and fantasies to others is, therefore, a major part of the strategies of attaining self-knowledge, directed at the 'showing forth' of the 'authentic' self. The confession was once specifically a religious ritual for the production of 'truth', a mechanism in Catholicism by which one was encouraged to reveal one's sins in private to a priest, who then prescribed means of absolution. Foucault suggests that in contemporary times we have become a 'singularly confessing society':

> The confession has spread its effects far and wide. It plays a part in justice, medicine, education, family relationships, and love relations, in the most ordinary affairs of everyday life, and in the most solemn rites; one confesses one's crimes, one's sins, one's thoughts and desires, one's illnesses and troubles; one goes about telling, with the greatest precision, whatever is most difficult to tell. One confesses in public and in private, to one's parents, one's educators, one's doctor, to those one loves; one admits to oneself, in pleasure and in pain, things it would be impossible to tell anyone else, the things people write books about. One confesses – or is forced to confess. (Foucault, 1978: 59)

The confession is deemed to be a difficult but rewarding process. The 'truth' which emerges from the confession is corroborated by the difficulties and obstacles it has surmounted in order to be formulated. Whether in church or in the counselling session or disclosing oneself to a friend or sexual partner, the confessor is rendered purified through the process. Simply bringing the 'truth' out in the open becomes almost an end in itself, a cathartic experience of the release of what are seen to be 'pent up' thoughts and feelings.

Sexual and intimate behaviour in contemporary western societies, thus, are regulated through less overtly coercive or moralistic restraints than in the past. They are shaped through negotiation between relatively equal parties rather than relations of authority and command, requiring new forms of self-control: '[Intimacy] requires a degree of insistence and sincerity in voicing one's demands (now called "assertiveness"), the surrender of means of physical or economic compulsion, and it requires a readiness to consider the desires of others and identify with them, along with a degree of patience and inventiveness to cope with them' (de Swaan, 1990: 156). Intimacy presupposes a distinction between behaviour in public and in private, requiring the ability and capacity to shift from one to the other, and involves constant self-monitoring (1990: 193). This renders personal relationships more complex, compelling each person to speak up but also to be ready to abandon his or her longings or desires should they impinge upon those of others (de Swaan, 1990; Beck and Beck-Gernsheim, 1995).

The high pitch of emotional intensity invested in love, however, and the degree of expectations surrounding love relationships, has resulted in the ideal of love becoming more and more difficult to attain: 'Love is pleasure, trust, affection and equally their opposites – boredom, anger, habit, treason, loneliness, intimidation, despair and laughter' (Beck and Beck-Gernsheim, 1995: 12–13). The trust that one invests in an intimate other can be severed at any time: through a broken love affair, the intimate other becomes a stranger. Therefore, the 'opening up' of oneself to another is characterized by ambivalence and anxiety: 'Torment and frustration interweave themselves with the need to trust in the other as the provider of care and support' (Giddens, 1990: 144). It is difficult to achieve a balance between autonomy and dependence upon another (Giddens, 1992: 140). The 'shared' nature of an intimate relationship may provide a sense of security, but may also be regarded as 'holding back' individuals, becoming a burden (Craib, 1994: 169). It has been suggested that personal relationships are therefore the site of profound insecurity at the same time as they hold out the promise of ontological security (Giddens, 1990, 1992; Craib, 1994; Beck and Beck-Gernsheim, 1995).

There is evidence of an anxiety around the depth of feeling and emotional ties with others. Such newly discovered psychological conditions as 'co-dependency' and 'sex or love addiction' have pathologized what is seen to be an intense need for intimacy and emotional closeness, representing this need as inappropriate and evidence of individual inadequacy and lack of self-control (see Irvine (1995) for a discussion of the phenomenon of 'sex addiction'). Many popular self-help books on relationships have focused on the problematic of people (usually portrayed as women rather than men) 'who love too much' or who see themselves as 'nothing without a partner', seemingly unable to deport themselves as autonomous individuals.

Two studies of the ways in which intimate relationships have been represented in popular magazines and self-help books have found that there has been an increasing emphasis both on 'emotional communication' between partners and on the need for individuals to avoid over-dependence on another. Treacher (1989) traced the representation of the self from 1950 to 1985 in the British *Woman* magazine. She notes that in the 1950s, the magazine emphasized the rules of good behaviour towards others, advising women to think of others before oneself. The advice given to women in the 'agony aunt' column was generally to control one's emotions, not to let one's heart rule one's head, or to brood upon the self, to forget the past and look to the future, to avoid self-indulgence and self-pity.

By the 1970s, noted Treacher, the advice column was actively encouraging the expression of emotions, understanding the self through expressing emotions. Honesty was represented as the new moral virtue, to oneself and to others, through expressing thoughts and feelings rather than repressing or ignoring them. 'Talking things over' was frequently advised as a solution for problems. Rather than represent women's interests as based solely on their families and husbands, it became recognized that they had a need for self-identity and autonomy separate from marriage and the family as well as in the context of the family. Dependency was represented as a malign force, choking self-autonomy, and other people were represented as invariably prone to letting one down, not being able to meet one's expectations and needs.

Hochschild (1994) has similarly drawn attention to what she describes as a 'cultural cooling' in concepts of emotional management, this time identified in American popular self-help books. This 'cooling' relates to the ways in which readers, particularly women, are invited to manage their emotional needs in intimate relationships and to protect themselves from too great an emotional dependency upon others; that is, from becoming the emotional 'victims' of others. According to Hochschild, while readers of these books are encouraged to communicate their feelings to their intimate others, they are also exhorted to engage in 'cool' emotional strategies, maintaining some degree of emotional distance from others as a self-protective mechanism. Readers are encouraged to be cautious in their dealings with intimate others, to maintain some degree of distrust so as to avoid disappointment and to maintain a balance between engaging in 'healthy communication' of one's feelings and needs and revealing too much to others: 'The postmodern cowgirl has sculpted herself to adjust to a paradigm of distrust. She devotes herself to the ascetic practices of emotional control, and expects to give and receive surprisingly little love from other human beings' (Hochschild, 1994: 11).

It may be argued, therefore, that while there appears to be more freedom and flexibility to 'choose' how one should behave in an intimate relationship, this very flexibility brings with it added burdens and uncertainties. To engage in the continuing project of the emotional self with respect to intimate relationships is to juggle one's need for autonomy with a desire for relatedness, to consider the pros and cons of revealing one's innermost thoughts to an intimate other, to risk vulnerability and loss of emotional control.

'Healthy' and 'Unhealthy' Emotion

It is not only in the interests of self-authenticity that the 'open' expression of emotion is championed in western societies. As argued in Chapter 2, many people also hold the strong belief that repressing emotions is detrimental to one's mental and physiological health. It was noted in that chapter that the mechanical metaphor, incorporating concepts of the body as a hydraulic system and emotions as fluid or steam-like entities flowing around this system, is a dominant way of thinking about the relationship between ill health, the body and emotion. The dam metaphor is also commonly employed to describe the potential ill-effects of emotional containment. Emotions are conceptualized as 'building-up' within the body, as subsequently creating tension and pressure which may lead to internal damage if they are not released.

The influence of earlier, pre-industrial understandings of the body and health states, discussed earlier in this chapter, can also be traced in such contemporary understandings. These include the humoral model of the body and the linking of emotional states with the varying intensities and temperature of humours and other fluids within the body. The notion that evil spirits or demons may enter the body's orifices and cause ill health or bad temper, and thus need to be 'let out' again, also underpins ideas supporting the release of disruptive phenomena from 'inside' into the external world. We may no longer refer directly to humours or demons in our concepts of the body, but we retain the view that keeping bad feelings within the body/self is potentially damaging. To confine one's emotions to oneself, to suppress such negative emotions as anger, frustration and guilt, has commonly been represented as pathological. Far more 'natural' and 'healthy', it is argued, is the free and 'open' expression of emotion. These ideas have received a great deal of attention over the past few decades in both expert forums and in popular culture.

Popular notions about the relationship between health and the emotions are strongly influenced by changes in medico-scientific understandings. The contemporary psychosomatic approach in medicine represents emotion as dysfunctional in terms of promoting ill health. Emotion is seen to exaggerate the effects of physical causes in such conditions as asthma, skin disease, digestive disorders, high blood pressure, and heart and circulatory disease (Wingate, 1988: 392). The argument supporting the psychosomatic approach is that attempts to control or suppress the 'natural', reflex expression of internal emotional states may lead to a disturbance in the equilibrium of the body: 'If, for example, a man is ill because he is constantly afraid, "pulling himself together" may stop him from running away, that is from *behaving* fearfully. But it does not always stop him from being afraid, and it is the internal and uncontrollable effects of fear that make him ill' (Wingate, 1988: 166, original emphasis).

For researchers in the relatively new interdisciplinary field of psychoneuroimmunology, developed to address questions of how mind, body and health states are interrelated, the emotions are also treated as internal agents having various effects on bodily function (or dysfunction). They argue that the immune system may be weakened or bolstered by various emotions: negative emotions, for instance, serve to produce certain hormones which undermine the functioning and effectiveness of the immune system, leading to greater susceptibility to illness and disease (Lyon, 1993). The psychoneuroimmunology perspective, in emphasizing the control that people should exercise over their emotions so as to boost their immune system and thus avoid illness, has supported a view on illness and disease which locates the 'cause' of the condition in the individual's emotional life or personality. The preliminary findings of this research has generated interest in ways of training patients to engage in exercises involving 'positive thinking' as a way of overcoming their illness to supplement or supersede conventional medical therapy. In the discourse of psychoneuroimmunology, therefore, unlike that of psychosomatic medicine, emotions are regarded as potentially subject to the will of the individual, and such control is viewed as having possible beneficial effects for immune functioning and consequent health states. Responsibility for good health is directed at individuals in terms of their ability to manage their emotions.

Ideas of personality and emotional types have featured in understandings of the links between emotion and health since the humoral model first gained currency, and remain dominant today. As a popular book on meditation asserted: 'Consider how a relaxed, happy, easy-going person always seems to have fewer medical complaints than his/her counterpart who is neurotic, bitter and anxious' (Wilson, 1985: 19). Sontag (1989: 20–1) points out that both tuberculosis and cancer have been regarded as diseases related to personality type. The nineteenth-century tubercular personality was popularly portrayed as particularly sensitive and prone to emotional excess. Tuberculosis was thought to be a disease of thwarted passion, particularly romantic love, affecting the reckless and the sensual: 'Fever in TB was a sign of an inward burning: the tubercular is someone "consumed" by ardour, that ardour leading to the dissolution of the body' (Sontag, 1989: 20). By contrast, cancer is conceptualized in contemporary western societies as a disease of insufficient passion or of the steady repression of emotion, afflicting those who are unable to express sexuality or spontaneous violent emotions such as anger. The contemporary 'cancer personality' is portrayed as an isolated and lonely individual who denies her or his negative feelings and does not share them with others because she or he lacks meaningful relationships (1989: 51).

The categorization of 'Type A' and 'Type B' personalities, first developed in 1959 but becoming common in popular discourses in the 1970s and 1980s, is another way of associating personality and physical traits with outcomes of illnesses. People demonstrating a 'Type A behavioural pattern' are described as impatient, anxious, ambitious, competitive over-achievers, always hurrying to complete tasks and never satisfied with their lot. In terms of their physical demeanour, they are characterized as agitated, fidgety, displaying tense muscles and speaking quickly. Those with a 'Type B behavioural pattern', by contrast, are described as relaxed, friendly, non-competitive, easy-going and under-achievers. People who are categorized into the former type of personality are believed to be at greater risk of stress-related illnesses such as coronary heart disease because of their inability to 'slow down' and relax and to engage in emotionally satisfying interactions with others.

There is the suggestion in the literature on 'Type A behaviour pattern' that such 'anti-social' traits and emotions as impatience, hostility, anger, competitiveness, greed, selfishness, egotism and 'unbridled ambition' are undesirable and almost deservedly punished by illnesses such as coronary heart disease. This behaviour pattern is regarded as 'over-conformity with the values of Western capitalist society' and paradoxically as a threat to social ties even as it accords with social norms valuing achievement and hard work. Such individuals are seen to 'bring illness on themselves', to almost invite heart disease by refusing to 'slow down' (Helman, 1987: 97).

The trend towards 'holistic' notions of health emerging over the past three decades in western societies has also supported the idea that the emotions and personality types are implicated in health states. Advocates of holism reject the 'mind–body split' they consider to dominate biomedical understandings of health and illness. Instead, they argue, mind and body should be considered as one entity, with each affecting the other in relation to health. Taking up the approach to health that is evident in the ancient humoral model, supporters of holistic health see illness as an imbalance between individuals and their environment, including their relationships with others and their emotional states. As such, illness and disease should not be treated as if they were localized in only one part of the body (as, it is argued, is the case in biomedical treatment), but the whole body/self should be treated. This philosophy underpins such alternative therapies as naturopathy, homeopathy, Bach flower remedies and aromatherapy. In these therapies it is considered important to document and treat each patient's individual personality profile, including her or his emotional state. In homeopathy, for example, remedies are directed towards certain types of personality. The 'physical makeup' of the patient is directly associated with her or his temperament and the medicines themselves are described in terms of their emotional profiles (Coward, 1989: 72–3).

Contemporary understandings of the relationship between physical and psychological health and the emotions tend to employ the notion of 'stress', a term which has become very common in the expert literature. Thoits (1995: 53) noted that over the previous decade, over 3,000 papers on 'stress and health' had been published in psychological and socio-logical journals. The discourse of social stress assumes that distress is necessarily pathogenic, rather than, for example, a spur to activity, God's will or a test of moral fibre. Distress is viewed as abnormal, something that must be alleviated or removed rather than borne stoically (Pollock, 1988: 381). The psychologization of stress has meant that there is a myriad of potential sources of stress – almost anything can cause stress, if the individual perceives or responds to it in a way that creates stress. It is not the stressor *per se*, therefore, that causes illness, but the individual's perception of it (1988: 387).

Taking up the Romantic viewpoint, the meanings underpinning the discourse of stress point to concern about the alienation and pressures of modern living. Stress is represented as a disease emerging from the maladaption, the disjuncture of the human-made social and built environment (usually urban rather than rural) with humans' biological dispositions. In both popular and 'expert' discourses on stress, it is often contended that the conditions of modern life have served to alienate people from their 'authentic selves', encouraging negative emotions and stifling positive emotions. People are seen as now cut off from their 'natural' biological rhythms and interactions with others, developed thousands of years ago when in a more 'primitive' stage of sociocultural development, the hunter-gatherer stage, and feel alienated and frus-trated with living in modern urban environments. Technologies and built environments are particularly singled out as potentially causing distress because of the clash between 'nature' and 'culture'.

The notion that stress is always 'bad' has become widely accepted in both popular and medical forums. In one interview study conducted in the English city of Nottingham, it was found that the great majority of respondents 'felt that the experience of stress was an inevitable and ubiquitous condition of modern living, and that stress could be the direct cause of illness' (Pollock, 1988: 382). 'Heart attacks' and 'nervous breakdowns' were particularly identified as caused by stress. The respondents tended to invoke the stereotype of the harried executive or businessman (this stereotype is nearly always identified as male) who succumbs to a heart attack because of pressures in the workplace. Nervous breakdowns were thought to be produced through such unfortunate life experiences as disrupted personal relationships. When it came to articulating how it is that stress causes physical illness, the respondents in Pollock's study were rather vague and uncertain. Some evoked the idea that stress in some way forces the speeding up of physiological processes, which eventually becomes too much for the body to cope with. As a result, they suggested, one of the parts of the body (such as the heart) 'breaks down'. Stress was thought by some to cause a nervous breakdown by 'irritating' or 'jangling' the nerves, putting the nervous system out of alignment. It was thought to attack the 'weakest' point in the system.

There was evidence of moral judgement in these accounts concerning the ways in which different individuals respond to stress. It was argued, for example, that some people succumb to illness because they cannot 'bear the stress', because they cannot exert 'mind over matter' or because they have a 'weak' constitution (Pollock, 1988: 382–3). As I noted in Chapter 2, moral judgements concerning people's capacity to 'deal' with their emotions were also apparent in the views of the interviewees in my study when they were discussing the relationship between emotion and health. These moral meanings are very common in contemporary discourses on health and illness generally. The increasing focus placed in medical and health promotional discourses on self-control, taking responsibility for one's health status, monitoring aspects of one's 'lifestyle', such as one's diet, intake of drugs such as cigarettes and alcohol, and exercise, so as to prevent disease, has tended to support and reinforce the notion that ill health is a sign that individuals have failed to engage in the appropriate preventive strategies and thus are responsible for their illness (see Lupton (1995) for further elaboration of these points).

Dominant discourses on emotion and health, therefore, fit into the general notion of the self/body as an unfinished project, requiring careful management, the gathering and use of relevant information and behavioural regulation so as to maximize one's potential and health status. While it is often argued in discourses on health and the emotions that interrelations with others or environmental factors (such as conditions at work or living in a city) may instigate negative emotional states, the responsibility for dealing with these states is frequently turned back upon the individual.

Concluding Comments

I have argued in this chapter that contemporary discourses on emotions, embodiment and subjectivity evince a continual oscillation between acknowledging the importance of carefully regulating and controlling the highly fluid and volatile emotions, and the need to express them, to allow them to 'escape' from the body. Both concepts of the emotions draw upon a culturally specific model of the self which sees it as residing within a 'body-container' filled with intensities and flows and surrounded with borders that require constant vigilance to police, allowing certain phenomena 'in' and others the passage 'out'.

The progressive 'closing' off of the body since medieval times, it has been contended, was associated with a notion of the body/self that privileges autonomy and individualism. Certain bodies/selves, as part of this process, have been identified as less contained, less able to control the flux of fluid emotions into the external world and therefore as less 'civilized'. In the context of western cultures, these include members of disadvantaged social groups such as the poor, the working class, non-whites and women. Their positioning as less 'civilized' and as the repositories of fears and anxieties about the 'grotesque' nature of the body/self, has contributed to their social disadvantage compared with those bodies/selves that have been represented as most closely conforming to the 'civilized' ideal: principally bourgeois men of British or northern European ethnicity. The next chapter takes up the issue of gender and explores in detail the ways in which discourses on the emotions have contributed to the sociocultural meanings of femininities and masculinities.

4

The 'Emotional Woman' and the 'Unemotional Man'

It has become common for social theorists writing on gender to point out the performative nature of femininity and masculinity (for example, Butler, 1990; Connell, 1995). From this perspective, not only is gender seen as an outcome of socialization rather than as inscribed in the genes, but it is also viewed as a dynamic project of the self, something that must be constantly made and re-made as part of everyday life. This emphasis on the dynamic nature of gender allows for a degree of shifting practices of gender within one individual's life course and even within the context of a single day. It is not simply a matter of adopting a male or female 'sex role' and adhering to it throughout one's life span, but rather that of a project of constantly taking up different masculinities and femininities. We perform gender as part of our techniques of the self and the body, including at the most obvious level our dress and hairstyle, our ways of walking and speaking and of otherwise moving and decorating our bodies. The ways in which we experience and express emotions may also be considered part of the performative practices of the gendered self.

In western societies since antiquity concepts of the emotional self have routinely been gendered. One of the pivotal concerns around which gendered notions of emotions are structured is that of the importance of mastery and self-control. As noted in the previous chapter, the ideal of self-control and self-containment has emerged as dominant in late modernity. Mastery of the body/self, as well as mastery over others, has traditionally been constructed as an ideal to which all individuals should aspire but which men rather than women are more likely to achieve. This difference is located in the meanings ascribed to feminine versus masculine bodies. Strong distinctions are routinely made between the ways in which women feel and express emotions compared with men's styles of emotional expression. A major binary opposition in discourses on emotion is that of the 'emotional woman' and the 'unemotional man'.

The distinction that is routinely drawn between the 'private' and the 'public' spheres is also an integral dimension of the ways in which emotion is gendered. The sphere of work is constructed as opposite to the private sphere, or 'the home', where, as I noted in Chapter 3, 'open' emotional expression and the supposed relaxation of emotional management are seen as more appropriate, even as necessary for individuals' well-being. The 'home' has been dominantly portrayed as the sphere of women rather than men, as the domain where they exercise power and hold major responsibility. It has been considered to be women's role, in particular, to maintain emotional equilibrium within the home for their partner and children.

This chapter begins by reviewing the antecedents and meanings of the binary opposition of the 'emotional woman' and the 'unemotional man'. The discussion then focuses on the symbolic and psychodynamic aspects associated with representations of the feminine body as more fluid and less contained than that of the masculine body. Then follows an analysis of the gendered aspects of emotional labour in the context of intimate relationships. As was evident in the accounts of the interviewees described in Chapter 2, there appears to be a change in contemporary concepts of masculinity and emotion. What might be called the 'feminization' of masculine emotionality has become a dominant trend in current concepts of emotion. As this suggests, while there may be a set of hegemonic discourses on gender operating at any one time, these discourses are open to contestation, and indeed may compete and clash with each other. The chapter ends with a discussion of this trend and its implications for assumptions about gender and emotion.

The 'Emotional Woman'

While it may be accepted that all individuals may feel the full range of emotions, in Anglophone and north European cultures in recent times it has been seen as typical and more appropriate for women rather than men to express such emotions as grief, fear, sentimentality, vulnerability, envy and jealousy. Emotions such as anger, rage, aggressiveness or triumph are less expected or condoned in women compared with men: 'Anger in a woman isn't "nice". A woman who seethes with anger is "unattractive". An angry woman is hard, mean and nasty: she is unreliably, unprettily out of control' (Brownmiller, 1984: 209). Friedman (1996: 62) notes that a woman who murders is regarded with far more suspicion and fear than a man, because such an act confounds assumptions about gendered behaviour. Men are often expected to kill in certain situations (such as war): it seems part of an inherent masculinity to have the potential to kill. This is not the case for women, who appear to engage in a perversion of their nature as women when they kill, particularly when they murder their children. A female murderer therefore appears more evil and terrifying, even more out of control, than a male murderer, unless his crime is seen as particularly pathological.

Emotion or emotionality themselves at a general level of meaning tend to be culturally coded as feminine, while rationality or lack of emotionality are dominantly represented as masculine. Brownmiller (1984: 207) refers to a landmark study carried out with a group of professional psychologists (published in 1970), in which such personality traits as 'Cries very easily', 'Very emotional', 'Feelings easily hurt', 'Very easily influenced', 'Very subjective' and 'Unable to separate feelings from ideas' were rated by the psychologists as highly feminine traits. Traits that were rated by the group as highly masculine included 'Very direct', 'Very logical' and 'Never cries'.

This gendering of emotion has conveyed a series of paradoxical meanings. In general, women are expected to display gentleness, to be willing and able to express tender feelings to others and be aware of and empathetic to the feelings of others. These attributes are considered to be an important aspect of dominant forms of ideal femininity. Indeed, women who appear emotionally inexpressive or lacking such traits as tenderness and caring may be viewed as lacking appropriate femininity (Jaggar, 1989: 157). Such expressions of sensitivity or caring have not been demanded of men to the same extent or considered as a vital component of ideal masculinity. Men have typically been considered 'blunter' or 'rougher' in their emotional styles and as less interested in the sensibilities of emotion. As there is such a strong symbolic link between femininity and emotionality, women are regarded as being 'naturally' good at dealing with other people's emotions because they are believed themselves to be inherently emotional and emotionally expressive, while men, on the whole, are not. As some of the inter-viewees in Chapter 2 noted, women 'wear their heart on their sleeves' more than do men. There is a continuing representation of women as closer to their emotional states, and as the guardians of civility, in charge of promoting emotional management: women as 'keepers of the heart, keepers of the sentimental memory' (Brownmiller, 1984: 215).

These 'feminine' emotional attributes are often seen as desirable and appropriate, demonstrating a woman's capacity for emotional sensitivity and caring for others. As discussed in Chapters 2 and 3, these features are in general linked to humanity and refinement of feeling, and repre-sent a major dimension of the positive meanings given to emotion and emotionality. On the other hand, however, women's supposed greater capacity for emotional feeling and emotional expression and their emo-tional lability also bear highly negative meanings, particularly in regard to understandings about women's inferiority compared with men. Emo-tionality, as noted in the previous chapter, is associated with weakness of will, insufficient capacity for reasoned thought and loss of control. Jaggar has pointed to the complex association of a number of binary oppositions linking femininity with emotionality: 'not only has reason been con-trasted with emotion, but it has also been associated with the mental, the cultural, the universal, the public, and the male, whereas emotion has been associated with the irrational, the physical, the natural, the particu-lar, the private, and, of course, the female' (1989: 145).

The continual association of emotion and emotionality with femininity, therefore, associates femininity with the other negative meanings asso-ciated with emotion, such as irrationality, the chaotic nature of the 'grotesque' body, lack of reason and cultivation and membership of lower orders. There is a clear metaphorical association between women's supposed emotional lability and their bodies. Women in general are associated with the body, whereas men have been represented as less 'weighed' down by the flesh, as more of the mind: 'it is commonly agreed that women are tossed and buffeted on the high seas of emotion, while men have the tough mental fiber, the intellectual muscle, to stay in control' (Brownmiller, 1984: 208). The binary opposition that positions women with the body and men with the mind denotes a view of femininity that incorporates the negative meanings associated with the body: 'if, whatever the specific historical content of the duality, *the body* is the negative term, and if woman *is* the body, then women *are* that negativity, whatever it may be: distraction from knowledge, seduction away from God, capitulation to sexual desire, violence or aggression, failure of will, even death' (Bordo, 1993: 4, original emphases).

The association of femininity with 'the private' and 'the home' has also had important implications for women in many spheres of life, including the domain of paid employment. The professional and bureaucratic workplace in particular is culturally associated with masculinity, rationality and self-control, including tight rein over the emotions, which are seen to be destabilizing to efficient production and management. Emotionality is regarded as being out of place in such an environment (Davies, 1996). Bureaucracy, for example, champions 'rationality' and order against what is seen as the disorderly state of emotions, basing authority on tradition, social status or technical competence rather than on emotional ties (Putnam and Mumby, 1993: 41).

The antecedents of the interrelated binary oppositions linking reason with masculinity and emotion with femininity, and positioning the first pair as superior over the second, are rooted in ancient times. Genevieve Lloyd's *Man of Reason* (1984) traced the provenance of these oppositions in western philosophy, in which the construction of dualisms that represented women negatively was a common part of thought: 'From the beginning of philosophical thought, femaleness was symbolically associated with what Reason supposedly left behind – the dark powers of the earth goddesses, immersion in unknown forces associated with mysterious female powers' (Lloyd, 1984: 2). It was argued by the ancients that to achieve reason, femaleness and its associated disorder had to be expunged, driven out. Lloyd gives as an example Pythagorean philosophy, dating from the sixth century BC, where maleness was explicitly linked with the orderly, the bounded, the precise, while femaleness was joined to their opposites – disorder, lack of boundaries, the indeterminate (1984: 3).

Similarly, for Plato maleness was associated with knowable form, accessible to the human mind, femaleness with unknowable matter that must be transcended in the quest for rational knowledge. Related to this distinction was Plato's scorn for the body, which he saw as intruding into and disrupting rational thought (Lloyd, 1984: 4–6). Aristotle, for his part, wrote that 'Woman is more compassionate than man, more easily moved to tears. At the same time, she is more jealous, more querulous, more apt to scold and to strike. She is, furthermore, more prone to despondency and less hopeful than man' (quoted in Brownmiller, 1984: 208). In the thirteenth-century writings of St Thomas Aquinas, a philosopher who attempted to synthesize Greek and Christian thought, women were portrayed as deficient and inferior in the capacity to reason compared with men, as unstable, easily led and too ready to follow their passions (Synnott, 1993: 46). His view is perhaps not surprising, as his teacher, Albert the Great, once wrote that 'Woman is less qualified [than man] for moral behaviour. . . . Her feelings drive woman towards every evil, just as reason impels man toward all good' (quoted in Synnott, 1993: 45).

These portrayals of women as far more manipulated by their emotions than men, and therefore as inferior, continued into the early modern period, when, as noted in Chapter 3, the imperative towards order, self-control and reason again became priorities. Part of the gendering of emotions in the sixteenth and seventeenth centuries was the common representation of women as more duplicitous than men in their emotions. Women were regarded as more easily able to convey a false emotional state, in their efforts to bewitch or betray unsuspecting men. Because women were seen as closer to nature, it was believed that their sensuality and sexuality ruled them and led them to tempt men into losing their reason. As the well-known English writer Robert Burton wrote of women in his *Anatomy of Melancholy* (first published in 1621), women are faithless and display false emotions in the calculated attempt to deceive men. He advised other men that when women protest their love, 'believe them not. Thou thinkest peradventure because of her vows, tears, smiles and protestations, she is solely thine, thou hast her heart, hand and affection, when as indeed there is no such matter, she will have one sweetheart in bed, another in the gate, a third sighing at home, a fourth, etc' (quoted in Rojek, 1993: 61). The Romantic philosophers of the period, such as Rousseau, both championed what they saw as women's closeness to nature, and thus to virtue and truth, and were critical of the disorderliness that was associated with nature, seeing it as requiring some taming and ordering by reason. Women were viewed as being naturally close to nature, while men were seen as requiring reason to see the virtues and truth offered by nature, thus achieving a closeness to nature through reason (Lloyd, 1984: 58–64).

A developing separation of home and work in the wake of industrialization in western societies has been associated in many writers' work with the linking of femininity with the 'private' and 'emotionality' and masculinity with the 'public' and 'rationality'. Part of this distinction between the 'private' and the 'public' spheres was an increasing feminization of the 'domestic', or 'the home', and of the family. The separation of home and work positioned these spaces as sites for the different use

and expression of emotions. Whereas in 'civil' society contractual relations among self-interested individuals dominated as the mode of interaction, the feminized site of the family was seen to have an entirely
different dynamic, involving relationships based on affection, love and
intimacy (Fraser and Gordon, 1994: 100). The economic sphere was
commonly represented as a site in which personal relationships were
impersonal and cold, characterized by competitiveness, calculation,
uncertainty and individualism in comparison to the warm, supportive
private sphere. The home was seen as the dominant private domain,
allowing the expression of 'freer' emotional expression (as long as those
emotions were deemed to be positive).

By the nineteenth century, the family had become idealized as an
intimate refuge with a higher moral value than the public realm (Sennett,
1977: 20). Family relationships were expected to provide enduring and
continuing emotional support. Love and family relationships were
viewed as central human fulfilments and the expression of emotion was
valorized as part of maintaining affective bonds (Taylor, 1989: 293). The
growing schism between the masculine world of commerce and the
feminine sphere of the home in this century, in concert with the growth
of industrial capitalism, encouraged men to take on a harder, cooler
persona, particularly in the late Victorian era. The masculine ideal was to
be independent, self-possessed, dynamic and disciplined. This new ideal,
espoused in such texts as *Tom Brown's Schooldays* (1857), was supported
by the ideals of courage, unemotionality, physical prowess and audacity.
Public schooling for middle-class boys attempted to develop these
attributes in the young men through such strategies as team games, cold-
water washing and spartan accommodation (Segal, 1990: 105–11). The
home was represented as an oasis of calm, a place where men could
retire from the chaotic nature of public life and seek peace and rest.
Cancian quotes, for example, the words of a New England minister,
who asserted in 1827 that 'it is at home, where man . . . seeks a refuge
from the vexations and embarrassment of business, an enchanting repose
from exertion, a relaxation from care by the interchange of affection'
(1987: 19).

The increasing focus into the nineteenth century on the home and
family as havens for the bourgeois man from the pressures of the
commercial world had implications for how women were represented.
According to Lasch, the bourgeois family system 'simultaneously
degraded and exalted women' (1977: 6). Women were encouraged to
succour their men and children with their warm feminine qualities
(Cancian, 1987: 21). This role was generally valorized, supporting
women's claim for moral authority in the private sphere (Barker-
Benfield, 1992: 37). Women were represented as possessing the appropriate innate capacities – gentleness, attention to others, empathy, lack of
aggression, tenderness, love – for playing this role that men did not have.
Even the ways in which women decorated and furnished the home were

viewed as important to maintaining it as a place of comfort, order, softness and warmth, designed to encourage dissociation from the chaos and hardness of the world of commerce (Rojek, 1993: 74). This in turn tended to position women well within the home context, for they were viewed as lacking the appropriate emotional capacities for participating in the 'public' sphere. Such characteristics as aggressiveness, cold-hearted rationality and competitiveness, seen as vital to success in the world of commerce, were split from femininity and positioned as innately and appropriately masculine.

Women's proper role in economic production and the 'public' sphere, therefore, particularly for members of the bourgeoisie, was seen to be in preparing others (husbands and sons) for their work and supporting their endeavours through emotional comfort (working-class women often could not attain this ideal even if they wanted to, forced as they were to engage in paid labour outside the home to support themselves or their families). Mothers were expected to regulate their male children and produce them as rational, dispassionate citizens, even as they themselves were portrayed as irrational and emotional.

The knowledge system of scientific medicine has also played an important part in constructing, disseminating and legitimizing the notion that there are significant differences in the ways that men and women experience emotion. From this perspective, gender differences are principally founded upon anatomical differences between men and women, particularly in relation to their reproductive organs. In medico-scientific discourses, the relationship between women and emotionality has generally been uncritically accepted as a fact, and research within this field has been devoted to proving this 'truth'. For example, doctors, philosophers and novelists in eighteenth-century Britain insisted that women had far more sensitive and delicate 'nerves' and 'passions' than men and that their nervous systems were 'finer textured' (Barker-Benfield, 1992: 26–7). By the last third of that century, tenderness became viewed as a characteristic of well-bred women's sensibility and a high value was placed on this refinement, even though it was associated with a greater susceptibility to nervous disorders (1992: 28). While this linking of a finer sensibility to women suggested their moral superiority, civilized deportment and intensity of imagination, it was also linked to the meanings of physical and mental inferiority (1992: 36).

There is also a strong relationship between gendered notions of sexuality and those associated with the emotions. The patriarchal Victorian approach to feminine sexuality, for example, saw women as chaste, delicate and loving, but considered these attributes to be the socially-refined thin veneer over the wildness and chaotic nature of the female reproductive organs, which were regarded as controlling women both physically and emotionally. As Smith-Rosenberg has observed, the Victorians portrayed women as 'being both higher and lower, both innocent and animal, pure yet quintessentially sexual' (1985: 183).

Women undergoing puberty and during menstruation, pregnancy and menopause were particularly singled out for their lack of self-control over their moods, and during such times were advised by doctors to avoid the display of strong emotions or engaging in stimulating activities (Smith-Rosenberg, 1985: 186–8). Men, in contrast, were seen as possessing far more control over their sexual impulses.

Shuttleworth (1990) notes that in Victorian England, popular medical advertisements and the medical literature itself appeared obsessed with female secretions, in particular menstruation. She argues that in the medical literature of the day, women were described as needing medical help to regulate the flow of their bodily secretions, while men were exhorted to deploy their own internal resources to bring about self-control. Physicians claimed that mental effort could cause a stoppage in the menstrual flow, and therefore women were advised to dull their minds, reducing excitement and stimulation, whether intellectual or emotional, so as to allow their bodies to regulate themselves. Women were also warned against strong emotional states while pregnant, for fear of damaging their infants. It was thought that the child's physical and mental condition would be 'a legible transcript of the mother's condition and feelings during pregnancy' (Shuttleworth, 1993/1994: 38). Some medical authorities considered even breast-feeding to be a route by which mothers could pass on their emotional states to their nursing children. For example, one (male) physician to a woman's hospital cautioned in 1860 against women suckling their infants after recently experiencing strong emotion, employing an anecdote in support of his argument about a woman who had inadvertently poisoned her baby by breast-feeding it soon after she had helped to defend her husband against a violent attack (Wright, 1988: 311).

During the Victorian period, diagnoses of hysteria were common for women aged between 15 and 40 in the urban middle and upper-middle classes. Doctors assumed that hysteria affected only women, because it was seen to originate from a disorder of the uterus. The most characteristic symptom of hysteria was a 'fit', similar to an epileptic seizure, often involving the victim alternately laughing and sobbing violently and perhaps experiencing hallucinations or losing the powers of hearing and speech, followed by a moribund state of passivity (Smith-Rosenberg, 1985: 200–1). By the end of the nineteenth century, the model of the 'hysterical female character' had developed in the medical literature, involving disposition and personality traits rather than physical symptoms: 'Doctors commonly described hysterical women as highly impressionable, suggestible, and narcissistic. They were highly labile, their moods changing suddenly, dramatically, and for seeming inconsequential reasons' (Smith-Rosenberg, 1985: 202).

While hysteria is no longer considered to be a discrete medical condition, or is associated with the uterus, it has its modern-day equivalents. Contemporary discourses on pre-menstrual syndrome and menopause, both medical and popular, commonly portray women as subject to rule by their hormones, including responding in highly emotional ways. The term 'pre-menstrual syndrome' is used to describe a collection of bodily disturbances occurring in the days following ovulation. Like hysteria, pre-menstrual syndrome is seen to include not only bodily symptoms (such as swollen breasts), but also extreme emotional lability, a tendency towards emotional disorders such as depression or panic attacks and generally irrational behaviour. Women suffering from pre-menstrual syndrome are commonly described as regularly becoming animal-like in their loss of control of their emotions, prone to outbursts of temper for no apparent reason (Chrisler and Levy, 1990). Menopausal women are similarly represented as under the sway of their unruly, erratic hormones and are commonly described as experiencing 'brain fogging', forgetfulness, emotional swings, moodiness, irritability, depression or unprovoked rage over which they are seen to have little self-control (Lupton, 1996b).

The 'Unemotional Man'

At the end of the twentieth century, the archetype of the 'unemotional man' (which always gains its meaning by being set in a binary opposition against the archetype of the 'emotional woman') has both positive and negative associations. On the one hand, it represents men as more rational, more of the mind and reason, better controlled and therefore better suited to the public sphere. On the other hand, the increasing attention paid to the importance of emotional expression for both men and women, the privileging of emotional sensitivity and 'being in touch' with one's own emotions (see discussion of this in Chapters 2 and 3) has meant that the 'unemotional man' is also often portrayed as emotionally sterile, lacking self-awareness and putting himself at risk of emotional breakdown or physical illness because of his inability to express emotion. While it is still considered appropriate for men to keep their emotions to themselves in certain situations, such as the boardroom, in many other contexts – and particularly the sphere of intimate relationships – men are encouraged to reveal their emotions, to resist and challenge what is seen to be the damaging and unhelpful archetype of the 'unemotional' man for their own sake as well as that of their partners, other family members and friends. There is, therefore, no single dominant representation of masculinity that defines how men should behave in emotional terms.

Books on masculinity, both popular and academic, routinely describe men's emotional lives as 'stunted'. Men are described as 'strangers' to themselves, cut off from their real emotions, unable to articulate what, why or how they are feeling. The language of emotions is often used in discussions on the social position of men in contemporary western societies. Much of this writing has taken up a 'personal is political' approach that has been often used in feminist writings by incorporating discussion of personal experience with theoretical analysis. Men writing about their responses to social changes, such as the impact of the second-wave feminist movement, describe their feelings of inadequacy, shame, fear, anxiety, stress and vulnerability, and argue that it is important for men not to hide such feelings. Men's oppression and disempowerment is frequently equated with their inability to speak out about their emotions (Yudice, 1995).

Victor Seidler, an academic writer on masculinity, argues, for example, that even if men attempt to be 'more in touch' with their emotions, their acculturation into dominant forms of masculinity makes this difficult: 'We were brought up to kill our feelings at an early age, so that we could survive as men. Often this means that as men we do not know what we feel. We do not have the words to express what is happening to us, nor a sense of how our emotional and personal lives have been disorganized' (1991: 37). While men may feel 'inside' the emotions of fear, frustration, insecurity and anxiety, writers such as Seidler argue that they deny these feelings to present themselves as controlled, disciplined, impenetrable. Roger Horrocks, a psychotherapist, similarly argues that 'men are, in general, emotionally impotent and inarticulate. Men find emotions dangerous things, they fear them and shun them' (1994: 30). Horrocks uses the term 'emotional autism' to refer to men who do not know how to feel, respond to the world intellectually and withdraw from intimacy with others. He contends that this leads to emotional problems for such men, because they feel unable to express their vulnerability, despair, anxiety, fear and dependence on others.

Writers on masculinity have often contended that what they see as the 'feminine' mode of emotional expression is superior to the 'masculine' mode. In his recent writings on love and intimacy, the sociologist Anthony Giddens (1992, 1994) draws a strong distinction between the emotional styles of men and women, championing the latter's approach. He argues that over the previous few decades, women have 'pioneered changes of great, and generalisable, importance' in such relationships (1992: 1–2). Giddens contends that the 'pure relationship' is the ideal to which women have been working. The 'pure relationship', according to Giddens, is a 'relationship of equals' and a 'social relation entered into for its own sake', for each person to derive benefits from the other and the relationship (1992: 58). Giddens argues that when the pure relationship is achieved, 'a relation of equals, organized through emotional communication coupled to self-understanding, becomes possible. . . . Individuals who are at home with their own emotions, and able to sympathize with those of others, are likely to be more effective and engaged citizens than those who lack such qualities' (Giddens, 1994: 193).

According to Giddens (1992, 1994), men lag behind in working towards the achievement of these ideals compared with women. Men have been influenced, as have women, by the notion of the romantic relationship that has emerged over the past two centuries (see the discussion in Chapter 3), but in different ways. Men may fall in romantic love with a woman, but do not see women as their equals. They have generally excluded themselves from the domain of the intimate, interested predominantly in romantic love as it is related to sexual conquest and satisfaction. Rather than develop self-identity through love relationships, men have done so through work achievements. Giddens argues that the role of men in the paid workforce has traditionally meant that they became cut off from their 'emotional lives', while women, confined to the domestic sphere, have became 'specialists in love'.

Men are typically represented in such writings, therefore, as denying the 'true self' in presenting to others the image of the strong, powerful, invulnerable male. In his book *Being a Man* (1990), David Cohen observes that while some emotions, such as triumph and anger, are acceptable for men to express, it is the more negative feelings related to feelings of powerlessness that men find difficult to acknowledge and express openly:

> It isn't that our feelings are less intense than those of women but that certain feelings are shameful. Triumph and success are splendid. If you have cause for any other feelings – misery, fear, worry – it's best to hide them. Put on the mask. Assume the stiff upper lip. How will other people, how will women like and respect you, if you show you're not a man? (Cohen, 1990: 85)

As these words suggest, the latter-day archetype of the 'unemotional man' operating in the 'public' sphere with a cool, hard, self-controlled demeanour fails to acknowledge the emotions of fear, misery and anxiety that men may often feel, even if they do not openly display them.

The historical literature would suggest that men have not always been enjoined to contain their emotions, including those of love and affection as well as anger, and that the archetype of the 'unemotional' man is a more recent construct than is generally acknowledged. For example, the Romantic approach (described in Chapter 3) emerged from the writings of male philosophers, poets and novelists and the privileging of emotional expression as evidence of fine sensibility was supported largely by men. While the emergence of the 'public sphere' of commerce and industry may have encouraged a 'hard' demeanour among men, well into the nineteenth century there remained the capacity for men to demonstrate loving feelings openly towards each other. Richards (1987) notes that in Victorian society, at least until the 1880s when there was greater concern about the evils of homosexuality, manly love was valued rather than mocked. Documents of the time included great outpourings of emotionality between boys at school and men at universities and descriptions of schooldays in particular portrayed them as a romanticized golden idyll of affection and comradeship between boys, conforming to the model of the pure ideals of ancient Greece.

Yacovone (1990) also argues that the history of masculinity has been distorted by focusing only on discourses encouraging boys and men to present an unemotional, cool demeanour. In his study of the social and intellectual history of the anti-slavery community in the USA, Yacovone came across much documentary evidence suggesting that during the Victorian era friendships among the middle-class men involved were as intensely affectionate as those among some women. There was thus a range of masculinities that were considered acceptable, some of which blurred gender distinctions. However, Yacovone argues that by the end of the nineteenth century even these outlets of love and affection became marginalized. The rejection of sentimentality, rapid industrialization, massive immigration, economic transformation and dislocation 'produced a culture that worshipped muscle and might' (1990: 95).

Nor is it the case, as some contemporary commentators have assumed, that men were seen as outsiders to the emotional world of the family since the industrial revolution. While the movement of men into the sphere of paid labour may have reduced the time they spent at home with their families, this was not necessarily viewed as desirable by men themselves or by 'experts' on family health and welfare. There have been regular commentaries in the child-raising literature since the nineteenth century on the importance of men as fathers playing an important role in the care of their children and bemoaning the lack of time men had available to fulfil their duties (Lupton and Barclay, 1997: Chapter 2).

In the late nineteenth and early twentieth centuries, for example, there is evidence of an increasing emphasis on men, as husbands and fathers, having more emotional responsibilities within the home setting. This was partly a result of growing concern about the 'absent father' and the possibility that male children were being feminized through too much exposure to their mothers and not enough to their fathers. There were calls on the part of experts in countries such as Britain and the United States for men to participate more in child-rearing and to provide an appropriate 'masculine role model'. Middle-class fathers, in particular, were encouraged to spend more time with their children and to show them affection for mutual emotional enrichment, rather than acting solely as stern authoritarians. Fatherhood was represented as a possible means of self-expression for men, a way of deriving satisfaction and fulfilment through emotional expression (Marsh, 1990; Griswold, 1993; Tosh, 1996).

The 'unemotional man' archetype also ignores the frequent occurrence of such emotions as anger, aggression, jealousy, frustration and rage, leading in some cases to violence, on the part of men in both the public and the private spheres. As several of the interviewees' accounts in Chapter 2 made clear, men who have disdain for displaying loving emotions may not feel quite so restrained when it comes to anger, rage and violence. Jeff Hearn argues for an alternative construction of men as 'unemotional'. He contends rather that they are 'too emotional, too much out of control (or indeed, too much in control), especially when it comes to anger, sexuality and violence' (Hearn, 1993: 143) and points out that dominance of others can itself be a profoundly emotional experience. Nonetheless, Hearn argues, men often employ the discourse of emotion as something external to the self when attempting to avoid responsibility for behaving violently or angrily. They may represent themselves as 'overcome' or 'swept away' by the emotion, and therefore as not in full control.

Hearn likens this discourse to the 'hydraulic' model of male sexuality, which represents men as being overcome by lust or desire, unable to control their urges despite their best efforts to maintain control (1993: 147–8). While this discourse may represent men as emotionally volatile, it also tends to suggest that such loss of control is either exceptional or is justified in some way. The justification for emotional outbursts is often related to women's behaviour, including the temptations offered by their sexuality or the loss of face resulting from their faithlessness.

Harris (1989) notes that in France during the *fin-de-siècle* era (the final decades of the nineteenth century), in almost half the murder cases committed by men passion was claimed by the defendants as the motive for killing their wives, lovers or rivals. Men on trial for murder often referred to the need to defend their masculine honour against the disloyalty of their female partner or a public affront by another man as the justification for the crime. These accused drew on a discourse of uncontrollable passion causing temporary insanity or a degeneration to a beast-like state, removing moral awareness and allowing them to commit the crime. The duel was a formalized means of satisfying wounded pride and anger, rationalized by the belief that private honour could not be properly avenged through the litigation system. So too, the crime of passion against a lover or rival was presented as an active means of restoring honour and dealing with rage and jealousy.

In the courts of *fin-de-siècle* France, distinctions were still drawn between the passions of men and those of women. Men were far more likely to be exonerated by the courts for resorting to physical brutality in the case of a crime of passion than were the far fewer numbers of women charged with violent crimes. Harris notes that 'The rare exceptions of "husband-beating" produced horrified reactions from investigating magistrate, judge, jury and neighbours, a universal condemnation which suggests that some fundamental norm, almost a taboo, had been transgressed' (1989: 294). Women accused of violent crimes were often described as suffering from hysteria, or being unduly influenced by the bodily states of menstruation, pregnancy or lactation, causing their faculties of reason to be impaired, and therefore as being inherently unstable and emotionally volatile. In contrast, men were portrayed as suffering from only a temporary state of loss of reason, often viewed as being incited by justifiable and legitimate emotional responses to their partner's infidelity.

In the contemporary era, it certainly is the case that most major violent actions and crimes in western countries are committed by men (Connell,

1995: 83; Alder and Polk, 1996: 396). Those crimes that include murder often involve rage initiated by feelings of possessive jealousy in relation to a female partner or despair at being left by that partner. Those crimes involving child abuse or child homicides are associated with anger and loss of control, as well as sometimes with vindictiveness and hate towards the man's female partner. Other such crimes, however, are associated with feelings of powerlessness, loss, sadness and hopelessness on the part of the man (Alder and Polk, 1996).

Some of the dominant forms of masculinity in western societies, particularly in relation to working-class men and younger men, privilege or at least tolerate expressions of violence as part of masculinity. Tolson (1977: 43) has argued that for the British working-class boy, aggression often dominates as 'the universal currency', the basis of 'style' and protecting oneself. More recently, Connell (1995: 98–103) observed among his case studies of young Australian unemployed men from working-class backgrounds that violence was a dominant part of their lives. Canaan (1996: 114) has described her 'horror and fascination' at the stories told her by predominantly white, English working-class young men about their gleeful participation in violence against other young men, often involving the use of a broken bottle to attack them. These young men set out to become drunk so as to lose control and engage in outrageous acts of 'hardness' with their peers. Getting angry while fighting was valued as a means of gathering courage and avoiding feeling pain, and was therefore seen as a way of maintaining control over the situation. Fighting was also regarded by these young men as a way of getting frustrations or anger over other issues 'out of your system'. Both drug use and violence serve as ways to 'let go', to escape the realities of a harsh existence and to construct and perform valued forms of masculinity (Collison, 1996).

Other dominant forms of masculinity, however, tend to position violence as inappropriate. This is particularly the case for men in the privileged classes, who are expected not to express feelings of anger, frustration, fear or loss in violent acts unless they take place in carefully prescribed and controlled places such as the sporting arena. Men in bourgeois organizational contexts, for example, are not encouraged to behave in overtly emotional ways, except perhaps for expressing emotions such as anger and related aggressiveness verbally (through angry or sarcastic words) (Hearn, 1993). This is not to argue, however, that the bourgeois work context is free from strong emotion. The appearance of mastery over one's emotions is itself a form of emotional management, as is dealing with others' emotions in the workplace. As critics such as Roper (1996) have noted, far from emotions being excluded from the masculine persona in the workplace, they are central to it. While the ideal of work organizations may be that of dispassionate rationality, both men and women engage in relationships with others in the workplace in ways that invariably involve emotion, including the desire, friendship and mutual attraction that men may experience in their relationships with other men as well as with women (see Roper (1996) for an account of unacknowledged homoerotic desire and strategies of seduction in male management relations).

Fluidity and the Abject

As discussed in Chapter 3, the contemporary western ideal of the body is that which is contained, dry, set apart from others' bodies, able to police its boundaries effectively. I also contended in that chapter that the fluidity of emotion is one source of the contemporary anxiety around emotionality and emotional expression, because fluidity has anarchic tendencies. It is difficult to contain or control and constantly threatens to breach the boundaries of the body/self. Fluidity or liquidity are also characteristics that are frequently related to femininity. The archetypal female body is culturally represented as more permeable and as less contained from the outside world than are men's bodies. It is conceptualized as inevitably and uncontrollably leaky, prone to seepage (Grosz, 1994: 203). As Grosz has put it: 'the female body has been constructed not only as a lack or absence but with more complexity, as a leaking, uncontrollable, seeping liquid; as formless flow; as viscosity, entrapping, secreting; as lacking not so much of simply the phallus but self-containment' (1994: 203). This lack of containment is seen to reside not only in the fluids emitted by the female body but in its fleshiness. In contemporary times, where thinness and tightness of bodily flesh are privileged, the plump, rounded female body, with its soft, fleshy protuberances that are not tightly 'held down', is culturally represented as ugly and even disgusting in its apparent unruly nature, its lack of self-discipline (Bordo, 1993).

Fluidities of emotion are often associated with embodied feminine emotional response and heat and fire with masculine response. For instance, in a study by Patthey-Chavez et al. (1996) of contemporary erotic fiction written for women, gender differences were noted in the ways women and men were described as responding to passion. Both female and male protagonists were portrayed as struggling against the forces of passion. For men, it was their desire for the woman's body against which they struggled, while for women, it was their own bodies that become an opponent. Characters of both sexes found themselves unable to think clearly, behaving as if drugged. Men were commonly portrayed as experiencing hot, fiery passion, while women responded more passively in terms of fluidities: 'Like fire, wetness courses through the bodies of romance protagonists like a bodily sensation and often becomes a force (for example, a flood) that overwhelms them. . . . Females *melt* and *dissolve* in response to males' heated actions and words' (Patthey-Chavez et al., 1996: 88–9; original emphases).

Men's bodies, real or imaginary, are generally viewed as conforming more to the ideal of the hard, dry body than are women's bodies. The muscular, invulnerable bodies of male fictional screen characters, such as those played by Arnold Schwarzenegger in the *Terminator* films or those of elite sportsmen, represent the apotheosis of this ideal. As Jones has observed: 'such phrases as "bottling it all up inside", "letting it all out" and "holding the tears in" are all metaphors for the masculine ideal of a tight, leakage free, impenetrable body where the body boundary allows no involuntary transference of substances from inside to outside' (1993: 89–90).

Sporting activities are a route by which men from all social backgrounds have traditionally expressed emotions such as anger, aggressiveness, triumph and joy, whether as a participant or as a spectator. They may also serve the opposite purpose: that of demonstrating how certain emotions may be controlled or vented 'productively' by the participant through the exercise of self-discipline. Sports such as boxing, traditionally one of the few means by which men from working-class and black backgrounds have been able to achieve fame and fortune, particularly value the controlled release of aggression, the ability of the fighter both to act violently against his opponent and to demonstrate coolness in doing so, including stoically withstanding pain inflicted by the other. Physical activities such as bodybuilding, in their more autonomous, self-centred mode and their focus on self-discipline rather than emotional expression, are a means by which men may seek to achieve transcendence over the body and the emotions through the exertion of will. The pumped-up muscular development that is the outcome of successful bodybuilding both acts as a testament to a man's masculinity and is a tangible sign of his ability to control and discipline his body. The hard, powerful, muscular body, therefore, is also the idealized contained, restrained body, which nothing, including emotions, can disrupt (Wacquant, 1995).

Miller (1997: 102–3) claims that women's bodies evoke both horror and desire on the part of men, not only because they are conceptualized as 'gaping maws' or because they secrete viscous fluids, but because they are the receptacle of the most highly polluting bodily fluid produced by men's bodies – semen. Semen, he argues, 'makes the vagina the site of rank fecundity and generation that assimilates it to the constellation of images that makes teeming, moist, swampy ooze a source of disgust' (1997: 103). According to Miller, men find semen particularly disgusting and shame-making, not only because it is emitted from the same orifice from which urine comes or because it has a viscous, slimy texture that repulses, but because it is culturally associated with a man's loss of bodily control (1997: 103–4). As argued in Chapter 3, loss of control over bodily fluids is associated with the emotions of disgust, embarrassment, humiliation and horror.

At its most extreme, the woman's body is seen to leak both substances and emotions at the moment of birth, in the form of the foetus which expels itself from the female body in a scene of pain, uncontrolled physical writhing, shouting, moaning, crying and screaming, a scene of high emotion accompanied by floods of fluid: blood, amniotic fluid, mucous, all ejected together with sound from the labouring body. The menstruating or labouring body inhabits the border between civilized and grotesque, between nature and culture, inside and outside, adulthood and infancy, rational being and irrational animal. Menstruation and labour may begin without warning, 'ruled' as they are by the hormones and 'natural' bodily cycles. The embarrassment and disgust generated by menstruation is related again to the lack of control over bodily fluids. Menstruation is not simply loss of control, it represents an absence of control through its sheer unpredictability: 'for the girl, menstruation, associated as it is with blood, with injury and the wound, with a mess that does not dry invisibly, that leaks, uncontrollable, not in sleep, in dreams, but whenever it occurs, indicates the beginning of an out-of-control status that she was led to believe ends with childhood' (Grosz, 1994: 205).

Documentary evidence would suggest that men position women as both inferior and dangerous because of their perception of women's lack of emotional and bodily containment. For example, Theweleit's (1987) examination of the writings of and about men in the Freikorps in Germany, organized by officers returning from the First World War to maintain order and withstand revolution in post-war Germany, reveals the ambivalence that these soldiers held towards women: 'They vacillate between intense interest and cool indifference, aggressiveness and veneration, hatred, anxiety, alienation, and desire' (Theweleit, 1987: 24). Theweleit notes that the metaphor of flood was used to denote the communist threat and the threat posed by women, both of which were conceptualized as having the potential to engulf the body of the soldier. In Freikorps writings, the 'mire' of revolution and 'slime', 'pulp', 'floods' are described in bodily terms, displaying extreme negativity towards bodily secretions, particularly those believed to emanate from women's bodies (floods, red tides, slime). Such substances are hybrid and viscous, absorptive, alive, autonomous, capable of swallowing and engulfing, leaving no traces behind and therefore deceptive (1987: 409). The soldiers saw themselves as needing to prevent the entry or exit of these fluids into or from their bodies by stiffening, hardening and closing themselves off. Theweleit notes that 'For the soldier–male dam, none of the streams we've mentioned can be allowed to flow. He is out to prevent all of them from flowing: "imaginary" and real streams, streams of sperm and desire. . . . All of these flows are shut off; more important, not a single drop can be allowed to seep through the shell of the body' (1987: 266).

In a more contemporary piece of writing, the self-help book for men entitled *Wrestling with Love: How Men Struggle with Intimacy with Women*,

Children, Parents and Each Other (1992), the language used by American psychologist Samuel Osherson makes frequent reference to the shame that intimacy is believed to cause men by using metaphors of fluidity. He argues that yearnings for connection and contact are experienced as unmanly and counter to how a man should feel and behave. Osherson describes the shame provoked by men's needs for intimacy as 'a visceral feeling – we feel "disgusting", "slimy", "pathetic", "smaller than a piece of dust", or "mortified, like I wanted to die" ' (1992: 31). He uses the term 'emotional flooding' throughout his book to describe the experience of being overwhelmed by their feelings that men experience and dislike. He contends that: 'Intimacy not only leaves us feeling exposed or inadequate, it can also disorganize us. We may be flooded with anger, sorrow, hope, or despair, and then feel as if something is wrong with us for being so torn and uncertain, or we may fear fragmenting or falling apart under the pressure of feelings that overwhelm our capacity to contain them' (1992: 32). When this happens, he argues: 'We feel the slimy finger of shame pointing at us' (1992: 40). Osherson goes on to claim that: 'Many men have spent much of their childhood trying to master and get in control of their feelings. Being flooded by them brings a shameful sense of falling apart, of being a "sissy", "wimp", or "faggot" ' (1992: 41).

In the discourses and metaphors used in this writing can be seen the same kind of fear, anxiety and horror concerning the fluidity (and sliminess) of emotion, and the coding of this fluidity/sliminess as feminine, as was evident in the Freikorps texts analysed by Theweleit. In both the Freikorps texts and Osherson's writing it is suggested that the fluid, leaky body, the body that is 'flooded' with emotion, is somehow unmanly, and by corollary, disgusting and shame-inducing, in its liquidity, it lack of containment and its associated femininity.

Some theorists have sought a psychodynamic explanation for why men may approach emotional expression and intimate relationships differently from women. They have contended that at the base of men's positioning of women as overly emotional or uncontrolled is their own fear about becoming too close to others. The project of masculinity, it is argued, is far more tenuous at the psychodynamic level than is that of femininity. As a result, men are more insecure than women about their gender, requiring constant affirmation of their masculine subjectivity, and tend to engage in defensive strategies in the attempt to represent themselves as impenetrable, independent and autonomous. While both men and women may find the emotional dependency that is part of intimacy unsettling and challenging to their sense of self-mastery and autonomy, men in particular are more likely to find this confronting and to deal with their resultant anxiety and feelings of inferiority at the psychodynamic level by splitting them off and projecting them on to the feminine Other.

For Julia Kristeva (1982), the relationship with the mother and the process of individuation is the font of strong emotions, including not only love, hate, frustration, loss and fear, but also disgust. Kristeva's concept of the abject, which she describes as that which 'disturbs identity, system, order' (1982: 2), she locates as originating in the liminality between bodies that first occurs in the mother–infant relationship. Such liminality, she argues, provokes strong and often conflicting emotions. Kristeva draws not only on psychoanalytic theory but also on the work of the anthropologist Mary Douglas, whose writings on the symbolic nature of boundaries and the fear and revulsion incurred by transgression of these boundaries have been extremely influential in sociocultural theory (see Chapter 3). Kristeva seeks to locate the origin of the emotions aroused by the transgression of body boundaries in the process of individuation during infancy (see the discussion of Klein's work on individuation in Chapter 1). She claims that as the infant comes to construct the mother as 'other' as part of individuation, there is an accompanying sense of sorrow at the loss of oneness with the mother's comforting, nourishing and powerful body. But it is only through constructing the mother's body as abject, and thereby rejecting and repelling it, that the infant is able to achieve autonomy. Hence the constant movement between repulsion and attraction of blurring one's boundaries with others' bodies that continues into adult life, as well as both the fascination and disgust occasioned by what is seen to be liminal, to lack self-containment or 'proper' definition between self/other.

The abject threatens self-identity and self-containment because of its in-between nature. The feelings inspired by the abject, the loathing and revulsion, the desire and fascination, are very much at the level of the visceral and their provenance cannot entirely be explained at the conscious level. As Kristeva describes it: 'There looms, within abjection, one of those violent, dark revolts of being, directed against a threat that seems to emanate from an exorbitant outside or inside, ejected beyond the scope of the possible, the tolerable, the thinkable' (1982: 1). Importantly, because of the original link in the unconscious with the mother, the abject is constantly culturally linked to 'the feminine'. Thus, those bodies, substances or things that are considered to be liminal, to breach the boundaries between self and other, that threaten self-containment, are typically coded as 'feminine' (Grosz, 1994).

The influential feminist psychoanalytic theorist Nancy Chodorow (1978, 1989) has also taken up object relations theory to explore the ways in which men differentiate themselves from women in order to realize self-identity and autonomy. Chodorow builds upon the notion that because women take the primary caregiving role of infants, as part of their development children are forced to break away from their mothers (rather than their fathers) and reject the symbiosis with the maternal body that was part of infancy. Boys, in particular, seek to reject their close relationship with their mothers in the quest for masculine autonomy once they come to realize that their mothers are women, and that they themselves must become men. Chodorow claims that as a result, boys reject and deny the maternal figure and the feminine attributes associated with her: intimacy, dependence, emotionality. Masculinity is defined as that which is not feminine; it remains precarious, constantly needing to be proven. Hence the abhorrence of femininity and women often shown by young boys and adult men.

Chodorow argues that men therefore have a highly ambivalent relationship with their mothers, and by extension, with all women: torn between desire and dread, dependence and autonomy, wanting engulfment with the female body but simultaneously fearing it. In their efforts to maintain strong ego boundaries and defend themselves against relatedness as part of their attempts to take up culturally dominant forms of masculinity, many men have difficulties in engaging in empathetic, close and caring relationships with others. Chodorow argues that girls, on the other hand, are loved narcissistically by their mothers, as like themselves rather than other. Girls are therefore more secure in their gender identity but have a weaker sense of autonomy in relation to others. She claims that as women do not have to go through individuation to the same extent as part of their development of femininity, because they are able to identify with the mother as another female, they tend to have a more related sense of self that is less autonomous and less fraught than men with tension between autonomy and dependence. According to Chodorow, when men attempt to deny their need for emotional closeness, they project these feelings on to the women with whom they are involved or else repress them, becoming intolerant to those who express a need for love. Men both look for and fear an exclusive, intense relationship. Women, on the other hand, are more easily able to express these needs.

Chodorow's earlier work on the reproduction of gender via these psychodynamic processes has been criticized by some for demonstrating too structuralist an approach, for implying that there is little diversity or potential for change in the ways in which individuals develop their gendered sense of selves and relate to others. In her more recent work, Chodorow (1995) has emphasized the importance of taking into account the cultural discourses, narratives and fantasies circulating around gender and love, as well as individuals' own personal experiences of living in their family of origin, as also shaping people's responses to intimate relationships. In doing so she brings together a psychodynamic focus on the individual's life experiences and psyche with an awareness that the individual's social position as gendered and as a member of a certain cultural group at a particular historical moment is also a vital component of her or his emotional self:

> Gender is an important ingredient in how men and women love, and all men's and women's love fantasies, desires, or practices are partially shaped by their sense of gendered self. But this sense of gendered self is itself individually created and particular, a unique fusion of cultural meaning with a personal

emotional meaning that is tied to the individual psychobiographical history of any individual. (Chodorow, 1995: 100)

Chodorow emphasizes that people form their emotional responses via a conscious and unconscious appropriation of a cultural repertoire that they learn via their acculturation into society through their parents and other family members, the mass media, the education system and so on. She acknowledges that there are multiple forms of masculinities and femininities that are available even within the one cultural context and upon which individuals may draw. Some of these are hegemonic over others, however, and thus tend to have more cultural resonance and influence. Nonetheless, even these dominant forms of gender are open to contestation and change.

These assertions are supported in Hollway's work, which involved discussions with British heterosexual men and women about relationships (see also the discussion of her research in Chapter 1). Like Chodorow, Hollway (1984, 1989, 1995) emphasizes that individuals' responses to intimacy are structured through the prevailing dominant discourses on emotion and gender as well as through such features of their personal experience as their history of early relationships with their parents and siblings. As a result of the influence of this early individual experience, some people compared with others are able to deal more successfully with their ambivalence between desiring autonomy and control as well as closeness with and dependence on another. Nonetheless, her research suggested that men are more likely than women to find dependency threatening and destabilizing. Hollway found that the men in her study tended to project their need for emotional intimacy on to their female partners and to express their fear of becoming too involved and dependent.

As one of Hollway's male interviewees commented: 'I'm very frightened of getting in deep – and then not being able to cope with the demands that the relationship's making' (1984: 244). He went on to talk about his need to maintain freedom in a relationship and to avoid responsibility even while professing to love his partner. His fear of 'getting in deep', or 'letting go', demonstrate the intense vulnerability men feel about trusting another person, because revealing one's emotions gives power to the other. Another male interviewee similarly commented that 'Once you've shown the other person that you need them, then you've made yourself incredibly vulnerable' (1989: 246). It is this projection of anxiety that men feel upon women, Hollway maintains, which is the source of the continuing discourse that 'women need commitment' while men do not: 'The reproduction of women as subjects of a discourse concerning the desire for intimate and secure relationships protects men from the risk associated with their own need (and the consequent power it would give women)' (Hollway, 1984: 245–6).

The writings of Grosz, Kristeva, Chodorow and Hollway, therefore, serve to identify the psychodynamic provenance of the horror and disgust that are associated with fluidity and the leaky body whose boundaries are seen to be uncontained. It is argued that because the process of individuation from the maternal body that is part of psychic development for both men and women includes the generation of extremely strong emotions – principally love and hate – in relation to this body, women's bodies are positioned as the repositories of these emotions into adulthood. For men in particular, in their attempts to establish and maintain a masculinity that is positioned as the antithesis of femininity, women are represented as more vulnerable, more dependent, more chaotic in their uncontrollable corporeality as part of men's attempts to deny the fluidity and excessiveness of their own bodies/ selves and the emotional dependency that they perceive within themselves (Grosz, 1994: 200).

Women themselves may find threatening or disturbing the meanings of fluidity, emotionality and loss of control that combine to represent femininity as inferior. Some women, such as those who engage in stringent dieting and exercising, or who have eating disorders, may participate in these bodily practices as an attempt to discipline their own unruly (because female) bodies. The melting away of their 'feminine' flesh they see as a symbolic move towards the masculine ideal of the contained, hard, dry body (Bordo, 1993; Heywood, 1996). In interviews with 23 anorexic women, Malson and Ussher (1996) found that they articulated negative attitudes towards both emotionality and the menstruating female body. The women thought of archetypal femininity as involving labile emotionality, which itself was associated by them with vulnerability and loss of control. They said that they wanted to separate themselves from what they saw as their 'alien' menstruating bodies as part of their attempts to overcome the negative meanings of the female body. Controlling their eating was the means they had chosen to work towards this ideal of the contained, disciplined body. Not only does this bodily practice serve to pare the body down, reducing its feminine fleshiness, it also often has the side-effect of amenorrhoea (the absence of menstruation). This was viewed as positive by the anorexic women because it spelt an end to the chaotic emotions and bodily fluidity they associated with menstruation.

Even those women who do not suffer from eating disorders may find disturbing the meanings linking femininity with the inability to regulate the self and the body, and thus work to overcome these meanings. In another study, Lutz (1990) interviewed 15 American men and women and analysed their discourses on emotional control. She noted that the women talked about the control of emotion more than twice as often as did the men. Lutz argues that this discursive pattern may be explained by the negative meanings attached to both emotional loss of control and femininity. Women therefore may perceive themselves as more susceptible to loss of control over their emotions and as requiring greater conscious control compared with men. According to Lutz, because women are aware of the negative associations with loss of control, they therefore position themselves dually as 'controller' and 'controllee' by articulating the importance of maintaining emotional control and dissociating themselves from the stigmatized feminine archetype (1990: 73–4).

As described in Chapter 2, in my own interview study there was evidence of ambivalence among women concerning their positioning as being emotional simply because they were female. Both men and women agreed that being emotionally expressive in some contexts (particularly the sphere of the intimate) was important, and that more women than men tended to have the capacity for such expression. However, they also recognized that in some contexts the association of femininity with emotionality worked against women. Some women, for example, demonstrated concern about being positioned as an 'emotional woman' in the context of the workplace and engaged in deliberate strategies to avoid this. Other women were aware of the negative meanings given to women who express anger, and struggled with this.

Emotional Labour and Intimate Relationships

The term 'emotional labour' has recently been used in relation to gender and intimate relationships. This term is sometimes used interchangeably with the term 'emotion work', but has a more specific meaning. 'Emotion work', as argued in Chapter 1, refers to constituting emotion in response to 'feeling rules' or expectations about what sort of emotion one should feel in particular contexts. 'Emotional labour' is used more specifically in relation to dealing with other people's feelings, particularly as part of the goal of maintaining harmony within a social unit or workplace (see, for example, Hochschild, 1983; James, 1989; Duncombe and Marsden, 1993, 1995, 1998). It has been argued that women engage in emotional labour far more than most men, with the suggestion that this is a feature of women's social and economic disadvantage. Duncombe and Marsden (1993: 234), for example, call the emotional labour that women perform in the home, 'emotional housework' and 'invisible domestic labour'. They contend that many women work a 'triple' shift if their responsibility for maintaining the emotional aspects of family relationships is taken into account, and claim that: 'The search for intimacy and emotional reciprocity is the last frontier of gender inequality' (1995: 165).

The work involved in emotional labour in the family context includes not only continually noting and responding to others' emotional states, but also acting to alleviate distress or regulate others' emotions that are deemed to be 'inappropriate' for that context. It is part of the selfless 'caring' that women are expected to demonstrate for others, particularly members of their families (James, 1989: 26). The purpose of women's emotional labour is thus to preserve and reproduce social order and norms from one generation to another. Ironically, such work is not generally regarded as labour, because it is often unpaid and tied to taken-for-granted notions of the 'natural' roles of women as wives and mothers. As James notes, however, much effort, thought and time must be put into emotional labour: 'When emotions are thought to be "irrational" it is hard to associate them with organization, yet managing them requires anticipation, planning, timetabling and trouble-shooting as does other "work", paid and unpaid' (1989: 27).

Women's role as carers in the marital and family context has been critiqued as perpetuating their place in the 'private' rather than the 'public' sphere at the same time as they support men's participation in the 'public' sphere. It is claimed that men, rather than performing emotional labour in the home, are the recipients of it, allowing them to effectively carry out emotional work at the site of the workplace. As Mulholland asserts, it may be the case that some men 'are emotionally dissociated from domesticity. They refuse to confront and find solutions for familial problems. Their work provides the excuse to evade deeper involvement with problems associated with family life' (Mulholland, 1996: 143). This suggests that the distinction that is commonly drawn between the 'private' and the 'public' sphere is somewhat artificial, for in this case the emotional and other labour performed by women in the 'private' sphere is part of men's continuing engagement and success in the 'public' sphere. Mulholland's (1996) interviews with British men who were 'workaholic' entrepreneurs found that they did indeed see their wives as providing them with much-needed emotional succour when they returned home at the end of the day exhausted from long hours of work. A 'good' wife was seen as relieving men from the burdens of childcare and domestic problems.

I commented in Chapter 3 on the increasing importance that has been placed upon the expression and articulation of feelings as part of the projects of finding and working upon the 'true' self and maintaining close intimate relationships. These activities have been represented as important for both men and women, but it remains the case that women are seen to be far more competent and willing to engage in them compared with men. Research into women's and men's engagement in parenthood supports the notion that women tend to engage far more in caring work and emotional labour, and what is more, are viewed as having a greater capacity for such work. Verheyen's (1987) research with Dutch women and men, undertaken in the early 1980s, found that fathers and mothers judge themselves differently, particularly with respect to the relational and affective aspects of parenthood. She found that for both parents the mother was usually considered to be the 'expert' in the domain of relational and affective aspects of parenthood. Fathers tended to regret their lack of involvement and time to spend with their children. Simultaneously, however, they tended to accept this as inevitable and not subject to change because of their work demands. Verheyen argues that women as mothers are more aware of the relational aspects of all relationships, including those they have with their children, while men as fathers define themselves as separate, even from their children. As a result, she suggests, mothers are more highly aware and self-critical of their affective relationship and their sensitivity to their children's needs than are fathers. (See also the research of Ribbens (1994) and Walzer (1996) for similar conclusions.)

Duncombe and Marsden (1993, 1995, 1998) conducted interviews with British long-term married couples about their relationships. Based on these data, they argue that an asymmetry in emotional expression is evident in many modern heterosexual relationships. Women, they contend, perform most of the emotional labour in such relationships and 'do' intimacy, complaining that men either cannot or will not express intimate emotions to a similar degree. The women in their study, for example, wanted their partners to make them feel emotionally 'special' through the unprompted expression of love and affection, but for the most part they did not feel that their partners offered this. They felt as if men 'deserted' them by giving priority to their work and spending time away from home (see also some of the comments made by women in my own study in Chapter 2 on this issue). For their part, the men in the study appeared not to understand what the problem was, and in some cases found their partners' demands unreasonable, particularly after a hard day at work. While the men acknowledged that they had feelings, they argued that they preferred not to disclose these feelings to their wives.

Critics have argued that women are also typically expected to engage in emotional labour more than men in paid employment and are over-represented in the 'caring' or 'service' industries that involve dealing sensitively with clients or customers (for example, sales clerks, nurses and flight attendants) (Hochschild, 1983; James, 1989). Women in secretarial positions are often expected to 'care' for the person for whom they work almost like a wife or a mother, maintaining the superior's emotional equilibrium and performing the 'back-stage' work that allows their superior to appear in control, efficient and untroubled by disturbing emotional states (Pringle, 1989). Such emotional labour, which tends to be regarded as 'trivial' and is often unacknowledged, serves to support what is seen to be the more important intellectual or revenue-producing activities in the professional or bureaucratic workplace (Davies, 1996). Parkin (1993) also points to the spatial dimension of the expression or containment of emotions in the paid work setting which are often gendered. In universities, for example, secretarial and administrative staff generally work in 'public' areas that are constantly shared by others, allowing them very little, if any, privacy and requiring them to be on 'show' throughout the working day, while permanent academic staff have their own offices to which no one can gain admittance unless invited. The former group of workers are predominantly women, while the latter are predominantly male.

It is important to recognize, however, that emotional labour need not be about inciting emotional expression, calming people down or making them feel happy. It may well be the case that women engage in these types of activity more than men in the paid workplace and the home. But men engage in other types of emotional labour, such as suppressing their feelings for what they see to be the good of the workplace or their intimate relationships. In their most recent writings, for example, Duncombe and Marsden (1998) have pointed out that emotional labour need not be glossed as 'expressing oneself'. Men's participation in emotional labour in the family may involve keeping their anxieties and frustrations (including those related to work) from their partners, so as not to distress or worry them. In the workplace, attempts to keep one's frustrations or feelings of anxiety or anger to oneself or to pretend to like people one heartily dislikes, so as to present a professional self or avoid social disharmony, may also be considered to be a form of emotional labour in which both men and women participate.

While some feminists have criticized what they see to be the negative associations between femininity and emotionality, seeking to disrupt or challenge these meanings, other feminists have taken a different tack by attempting to privilege what they see as women's more highly developed capacity for emotional sensitivity and expression. Emotionality, in this reading, is endowed with the meanings of superiority, and not as being directly opposed to intellectual activity or rationality. It is particularly represented as being related to positive rather than negative emotions; to love, empathy and tenderness, for example, rather than to anger or hate. This feminist discourse also tends to equate emotionality with the capacity for relating to and caring for others in unselfish ways. Emotional labour is represented as a worthwhile activity that has its own rewards.

Exponents of this perspective argue for an understanding of human life as essentially interdependent, lived in emotional relationships to others, and for the privileging of mutuality, relatedness, the ethnic of caretaking and empathy as they are demonstrated by women, particularly mothers. Inherent in their arguments is a disdain for what they see as the masculinized notion of the autonomous, individuated, non-relational self, a model of being they consider to be reductive and limiting compared with that of the 'relational being' (see, for example, Gilligan and Rogers, 1993; Jordan, 1993; Ruddick, 1994). This literature suggests that emotion labour as performed by women in intimate relationships need not be considered in negative terms as contributing to women's disempowerment and socioeconomic disadvantage, but rather as a potential source of women's power and self-fulfilment.

The 'Feminization' of Masculine Emotionality: Towards Equality?

As I have argued above, new writing about masculinity has tended to reproduce the assumption that men should express their emotions to others, particularly intimate others, to a greater extent than they do currently. So too, the increasing attention paid to the 'new' father, in conjunction with the writings of feminist critics calling for a greater participation by men in parenting, has begun to problematize the notion that women are 'naturally' equipped for emotional labour in ways that men are not (Lupton and Barclay, 1997). In both popular and expert forums this move towards the 'feminization' of emotions for men is generally represented as positive, offering the potential to lead to more equitable relationships between men and women and stronger emotional ties between fathers and their children.

In these portrayals, therefore, the 'feminine' or 'open' approach is represented as the most appropriate way to engage in emotional behaviour while the 'masculine' approach is portrayed as stultified, old-fashioned and harmful, both for men and for their intimates. Craib (1994) has noticed a change in his own lifetime in the way that talking about feelings and emotionality is represented. In his childhood, he claims, this practice was often regarded as feminine and inferior, as something that men should avoid. In present times emotionality is still seen as feminine, but it is often claimed as a superior rather than inferior quality (Craib, 1994: 88).

An interest in the emotions of people and their relationships with others as represented in the popular media has been traditionally considered as feminine. The soap opera is the archetypal 'feminine' genre, revolving around domestic scenarios and the ups and downs of intimate relationships, while the archetypal 'masculine' popular entertainment is that which deals with action, physical prowess, political intrigue, crime or sporting activities. Conceptualizing certain media products as 'emotional', however, because they focus on intimate and love relationships, ignores the fact that other media products constantly evoke a range of intense emotions. The stock in trade of television drama about crime and violence, for example, such as 'cop shows', as well as news reports, are such emotions as fear, anxiety and excitement, and as I noted in the Introduction, the coverage of political and sporting events revolve around emotion. In that sense these media products are no less 'emotional' than soap opera, but are less often viewed as such because 'emotionality' tends to have certain meanings that link it to female rather than male interests and behaviours.

Nonetheless, in recent mainstream television and film these binary divisions – between 'feminine', 'emotional' media and 'masculine', 'non-emotional' media – have become more blurred. Despite the very strong cultural linking of femininity and emotionality, there has recently emerged a focus on what Boscagli calls 'masculine emotionality' in the popular media: 'The vision of men barely repressing tears, "confessing," reminiscing about their personal past, and exploring their interiority has taken the stage and convinced the audience that a new generation of sensitive men has come of age' (Boscagli, 1992/1993: 64). This is particularly evident in the ways in which male characters are now often represented in terms of their emotional behaviour and interest in the emotions. While the hardened, muscular action hero of few words and cool demeanour may still feature as a dominant archetype in mainstream film (the Arnold Schwarzenegger *Terminator* archetype), the sensitive, articulate, male character willing to discuss his feelings is also common, in the films of Woody Allen and Hal Hartley, for example. Even action heroes are occasionally represented as able to express tender emotions; for instance, the Bruce Willis character in Tarantino's *Pulp Fiction*, a boxer who is shown engaging in extremely violent activities and escaping from dangerous situations in some scenes and in others as cuddling with his lover and exchanging tender words with her.

Prime-time American television series such as the late 1980s drama *thirtysomething*, the contemporary drama *Party of Five* and the sitcoms *Ellen*, *Seinfeld* and *Friends*, all of which are directed at a male as well as a female audience, portray male characters who are concerned about their personal relationships and interested in talking about them at length with others, both men and women, to seek their advice. So too, in recent years, the archetype of the 'new father' who is devoted to his children and interested in spending time with them, including discussing and advising upon their personal problems, has become popularized in the mass media, with the ultimate exemplar of the Cliff Huxtable character played by Bill Cosby in his highly successful 1980s comedy *The Cosby Show* (see Lupton and Barclay (1997: Chapter 3) for a discussion of media representations of fathers).

A colleague and I found in a previous study on early fatherhood that it was very common for the men who were interviewed to have taken up this discourse of the 'new father'. All the men in the study wanted to 'be there' for their children and to have a loving and intimate relationship with them. They described their own fathers as emotionally distant, and said that they wanted to avoid this in their own fathering practices. While some men were managing to engage at a profound emotional level with their young children, others found themselves frustrated by their lack of opportunity to engage in caring for them and developing an intimate relationship with them. These difficulties were due to a number of factors, including the demands of their paid work and their partner's unwillingness to allow them to play more of a role in their children's care (Lupton and Barclay, 1997).

There is other evidence to suggest that many men are making concerted efforts to express their emotions in response to changing discourses. As I noted in Chapter 2, most of the men interviewed for my study articulated their awareness that they should be emotionally expressive, and that it was important to demonstrate loving feelings to one's family members as well as feeling able to express such emotions as grief and anxiety (rather than 'bottling them up') in the interests of preserving their mental and physical health. Many of the younger men appeared to be comfortable with taking up the discourse of emotional expressivity, finding no difficulty, for example, in weeping in public or describing themselves as 'very emotional'. Several of the older men, however, found this very difficult to achieve, despite their best efforts. This would suggest that although some men may be aware of changes in the 'feeling rules', in which men's expression of their emotions is now incited rather than discouraged, they may experience difficulties in conforming to them. They appear to lack the skills required to present themselves as emotionally expressive.

While in liberal writings on masculinity the notion that men should begin to take up a 'feminine' approach to their emotions and should confront their feelings is generally championed, more conservative writers on masculinity demonstrate an element of hostility to the second-wave feminist movement and the archetype of the 'sensitive new male'. These critics have asserted that men should not be forced to give up what is seen as the 'traditional' attributes of masculinity, such as their aggression and capacity for anger. Robert Bly's mythopoetic writings, such as his well-known *Iron John* book (1990), and the related popular American 'men's movement' are examples of this latter perspective. While Bly and his followers conform to the notion that expression of the emotions is 'healthier' than repressing them, and that therefore men should be allowed to express their emotions to others, they tend to argue for such expression to take place between men as part of men re-establishing their 'deep masculinity' and defending it against the encroachments of feminism. There is much focus placed on the emotional dimensions of men's relationships with their fathers and their need to release cathartically the pain, frustration, aggression and anger they feel towards their fathers and others (via such activities as 'traditional men's rituals' involving shouting and screaming, initiation rites and going into forests to beat on drums and carry spears), in order to become 'real men' again. In the mythopoetic men's movement, the 'feminine' aspect of emotional expression and the notion that men should become closer to women (their mothers or their partners) is marginalized in favour of what is seen to be a more 'authentic' masculine expression of emotion.

Other commentators have been critical of the ways in which some male writers have portrayed themselves as lacking power because of their supposed inability to express emotions. They have drawn attention to the rhetoric of oppression that some men's groups, academics and writers of self-help books for men are using in the attempt to position men as victims, particularly in relation to the women's movement, and the subsequent glossing-over of continuing social inequalities between men and women. They assert that the issue of emotional expression becomes used in this literature as an example of how women are advantaged compared with men. Messner (1993), for example, critiques the simplistic ways in which the mythopoetic men's movement taps into and validates men's emotions of grief, frustration and anger. The movement promises a solution for these feelings, but fails to confront men with their position of power and social privileges and brings men together at the expense of their relationships with women. Messner is also critical of people who urge men to 'open up' in the interests of gender equality and better relationships. As he notes: 'A large part of the naiveté about the emergent New Man is the belief that if boys and men can learn to "express their feelings," they will no longer feel a need to dominate women' (Messner, 1993: 731).

Boscagli (1992/1993) contends that in the postmodern era, men's willingness to display emotions previously stigmatized as 'feminine', such as grief, is a symptom of their anxiety in what they see as a period of crisis of the self. The 'sensitive new male' archetype is often referred to by the mass media as the outcome of two decades of feminism. Men, it is suggested, have responded to changes in gender relations by allowing themselves to become more 'feminine' or else are going through a 'crisis of masculinity' causing them emotional distress. The discourse commonly used by men is that the 'feeling' individual is the universal human: 'I feel, therefore I am' is the creed of the new man (Boscagli, 1992/1993: 73). Boscagli argues that the tears shed by this 'new man' are appropriated as a means of survival, a means by which men are reaffirming their mastery. While it may be more culturally acceptable for men in positions of power to cry, as a display of their humanity and sensitivity (Boscagli uses the example of General Schwarzkopf, the man commanding the American forces in the Gulf War), it remains the case that less privileged individuals, such as women and men from marginalized and disadvantaged social groups, are still stigmatized for their displays of emotionality: 'While a man who cries is a human being, a woman who cries is a woman. By crying she loses her humanity only to become gendered and "particular" again' (1992/1993: 75). The ability for a powerful man to shed a tear in public, therefore, may be considered even greater evidence of his secure and high-status social position rather than destabilizing the traditional sources of men's authority and privilege (see also Messner, 1993: 731–2).

This suggestion would seem to be supported by an empirical study cited by Fischer (1993: 311), in which the participants were asked to evaluate the responses of men and women (crying, laughing or non-emotional) to watching segments from films. The crying man was evaluated more positively than the laughing and non-emotional man, while the crying woman was evaluated more negatively than the non-emotional one. So too, in his interviews with people involved in the animal rights movement, Groves (1995) found that the emotions impelling the men to join the movement were considered differently from those of the women members. Women were generally described by others in the movement as being involved because of their feelings of sympathy and affection for defenceless animals, and therefore as being sentimental. In contrast, men tended to present themselves as being involved because of 'rational', logically derived emotional responses concerning injustice in animal rights, or were admired by others because of their sensitivity and compassion, demonstrating a type of strength in engaging emotionally. Men's emotions were seen as being more legitimate and rational by both the men and women interviewed by Groves.

Concluding Comments

The discussion in this chapter has identified the meanings and discourses contributing to the binary opposition of the 'emotional woman' and the 'unemotional man' and the implications of these archetypes for gendered experience. It has been contended that while certain long-held assumptions around gender and the emotions remain, there is evidence of a blurring of former distinctions between hegemonic notions of masculinity and femininity. In the wake of second-wave feminism, women are now expected to participate in the sphere of paid labour as well as engaging actively in caring activities in the home. While it may be seen to be more difficult for women to achieve the ideal of the contained, autonomous self because of their assumed inherent tendency towards emotionality, it is still expected that they aspire towards this ideal. Conversely, even though men may be thought to be less capable of 'opening up' and revealing their emotions in the intimate sphere compared with women, they are now encouraged (and indeed, expected) to have a strong emotional presence in the family, and to attempt to express their emotions to intimate others.

There is a convergence, therefore, between (particularly bourgeois) notions of ideal masculinities and femininities in relation to emotionality. A 'developed' person now tends to be described as 'someone who combines feminine intimacy and emotional expression with masculine independence and competence' (Cancian, 1987: 8). There is a point, however, at which this convergence halts. Women who take on a highly rationalist, dispassionate or aggressive approach in the workplace are often considered to go too far and to be sacrificing their femininity by 'acting like a man', and women who choose not to have children or to leave most of the child care to their partner are still viewed with some suspicion. So too, the man who appears to have little interest in work, preferring to care for his children, or who goes too far in adopting the 'sensitive new man' persona is often the butt of ridicule and allegations of effeminacy. There is also evidence to suggest that the latest emphasis on emotionality for men is not necessarily overturning the negative meanings associated with the 'emotional woman'. Men in powerful positions may find that their status is bolstered through carefully chosen public displays of feeling, but the social position of women or less powerful men is still undermined through similar displays.

5

Emotions, Things and Places

Surprisingly few empirical studies have sought to identify the nature of
the relationships people have with their material possessions or their
physical environs. Even less research is available which has included a
detailed examination more specifically of the emotional aspects of
people's relationships with objects or with places. As Lunt and Livingstone (1992: 65) have commented, research in the social sciences has
tended to be directed at the relationships people have with each other, or
with social institutions, rather than with objects or things. Miller has
similarly identified this suspicion of objects among critics of mass
culture. He argues that they have tended to be dismissive of attempts
to analyse objects culturally, assuming 'that the relation of persons to
objects is in some way vicarious, fetishistic or wrong; that primary
concern should lie with direct social relations and "real" people' (Miller,
1987: 11). It is clear, however, that human social relationships are
themselves influenced and shaped by objects and spatial environs, just as
the meanings of objects or environments and people's interactions with
them are constituted through social processes and always exist in specific
sociocultural contexts.

In this chapter I take up the issue of the emotional relationship we may
have with things and places. The discussion begins with a review of
consumption and emotion and then focuses specifically on the process
of appropriation, or how we come to incorporate mass-produced commodities into our notion of selfhood. Then follows a discussion of the
ways in which objects may serve as mediators of emotional relationships
with others. I then move on to examine the emotions we may feel about
space and place, particularly in relation to 'home'. The chapter ends with
a review of the emotions incited in leisure activities.

Consumption and Emotion

Most of us have probably experienced difficulty in throwing away
objects to which we have grown emotionally attached but for which we
no longer have a functional use. We can invest our emotions in objects as
diverse and banal as coffee mugs, cars, woolly jumpers, shoes, pairs of
jeans, blankets, stuffed toys, bicycles and kitchen utensils. So too, we can
come to develop a strong emotional relationship with particular places,

whether they be built or 'natural' environments. Human–object relationships may be understood to take place on a number of levels, including
the intrapsychic and the biographical as well as the institutional. The
meanings invested in artefacts are the product of social experiences,
personal biography and memories, cultural myths and fantasies at
both the conscious and the unconscious levels (Lunt and Livingstone,
1992: 67).

Most writers in the area of the sociology and psychology of consumption have made the point that material objects are typically used to
construct and present a certain persona and support membership of sub-
cultural groups (see, for example, Bourdieu, 1984; Featherstone, 1990;
Willis, 1990; Dittmar, 1992). Dittmar, for example, refers to consumer
goods as 'material symbols of identity' (1992: 6). From this perspective,
the active choice and consumption of commodities is integral in the
creation and maintenance of multiple forms of subjectivity:

> Every aspect of life, like every commodity, is imbued with a self-referential
> meaning; every choice we make is an emblem of our identity, a mark of our
> individuality, each is a message to ourselves and others as to the sort of person
> we are, each casts a glow back, illuminating the self of he or she who
> consumes. (Rose, 1990: 227)

Our choice and use of commodities, therefore, may be seen as an integral
aspect of the continuing project of the self, part of our quest for
identifying the 'true' self and working upon it.

This meaning-making process is not all one way, for objects may
change as well as reflect the nature of subjectivity. As Callon contends,
objects can 'order humans around by playing with their bodies, their
feelings or their moral reflexes . . . artefacts are not the enigmatic and
remote objects to which they are often reduced' (1991: 137). The form and
function of things, themselves shaped by their human developers, serve
to direct human action, embodiment and thought in certain ways. The
engagement of emotional states is central to this symbiotic meaning-
making process. For example, Nippert-Eng has discussed the ways in
which the cultural meanings of clothing both draw upon and contribute
to the emotional self. As she points out, the close link of clothing with
our notions of embodiment and the presentation of the self, as well as the
sensual dimensions of clothing next to our skin, combine to render it an
important aspect of subjectivity:

> A number of factors contribute to clothing's essential linkage with self and its
> provocative power. Social images associated with the costume combine with
> the sensual feel and look of the clothing to evoke or 'trigger' a certain
> mentality. In part, this is because clothing is a most immediate mental prop: it
> is unremitting in reminding us of itself. Against our skin and combined with
> the rest of our appearance, clothing provides a more or less constant back-
> ground source of self-awareness. (Nippert-Eng, 1996: 51)

Because objects such as clothing are so intimately tied to our self-
presentation and sense of subjectivity, the choice of clothing can have a

profound effect on our emotional demeanour. We tend to feel differently, for example, if we are wearing old, comfortable casual clothes than if we are wearing a formal business suit. So too, a sense that we are wearing the 'wrong' outfit for the social context can create a profound sense of unease and embarrassment. Physical appearance, including the clothes one is wearing, can have a marked effect on one's mood. If people feel they are wearing the 'right' clothes for the context, and that they are looking 'good', then they are more likely to feel self-confident, while looking 'wrong' and feeling as if one looks unattractive, has the opposite effect. Clothes which make one feel secure and confident, therefore, may be used as 'armour' in situations where the person is feeling insecure, vulnerable or uncertain, such as when in a new or strange environment (Tseëlon, 1995: 60–4).

Many mass-produced commodities are designed to invoke emotional states to attract people to purchase them. For Haug (1986: 7–8), the notion of commodity aesthetics acknowledges the importance of the appearance and appeal of commodities, the desire they stimulate and the subjectivity invested in commodities. Haug defines commodity aesthetics as 'a complex which springs from the commodity form of the products and which is functionally determined by exchange-value – a complex of material phenomena and of the sensual subject–object relations conditioned by these phenomena' (1986: 7). He contends that 'In so far as that which is beautiful about a commodity appeals to people, it engages their sensual understanding and the sensual interest which in turn determines it' (1986: 8). The use-value of the commodity, therefore, is often grounded in its aesthetics, its sensual appeal, provoking desire. As part of their sensual appeal, commodities make promises to consumers, appealing to some kind of 'lack' that the consumers may perceive in themselves, either consciously or unconsciously:

> As we stare at the clothes in a shop window, at the compact discs in a record store, at the motorboats in our leisure magazine, at the mouth-watering dishes pictured in our Sunday newspapers or at our neighbour's smart new car, we experience a feeling which can only be described as desire, a desire which is at once sweet and frustrating, a desire capable at times of convulsing our physical being as though it were purely sexual. Such objects seduce us as though they were sexual objects, sparking off strings of fantasies, which continue to prosper the longer the object remains inaccessible. (Gabriel and Lang, 1995: 113)

The selection of objects, therefore, does not take place simply at the 'rational', conscious level. We may feel a 'pull' towards acquiring an object, some sort of attraction towards it, which we ourselves may find difficult to explain or understand. It is here that the deeper symbolic meanings of objects and of the desire invested in them are important in constituting our responses to and feelings about them. As Dittmar suggests, 'Symbolic meanings may weigh more heavily when people buy "new" things than rational decision-making in terms of costs and resources' (1992: 65). While most of the material objects we purchase and use also have a functional purpose (for example, clothing, cars, watches, furniture, food products), the meanings associated with these objects are integral to our choice (and sometimes are the only reason we choose them). Morley (1992: 214) gives the example of the home computer, often left unused after purchase. He sees the computer as a 'knowledge machine' (similar to a set of encyclopaedias) but also as a totemic object symbolizing 'the future', regardless of whether it was actually used for its overt rational/functional purpose or not.

We draw upon our understanding of the 'image' of an object when selecting one specific thing from the range available to us. Part of this process, whether it takes place at the conscious or unconscious level, is identifying 'who' we are and what is the 'image' we ourselves would like to present to others. Other factors, such as the price we can afford to pay, the appearance of the object and its apparent usefulness compared to other similar objects are clearly important to this selection process. Nonetheless, it may be difficult to distinguish between these factors and the image of the object, for they may be intertwined. For instance, an extremely expensive car such as a Rolls Royce is prestigious partly because of its cost: while many may admire the engineering or design of such a car, only very wealthy people can afford to purchase it.

Advertising strategies around an object or experience rely upon investing the product with symbolic meanings. In doing so, they may seek to evoke both positive and negative emotions. Advertising serves to evoke and work upon anxieties, insecurities and guilt feelings that are culturally shared and are experienced often at the level of the unconscious. Advertisements often seek to address a lack of specific anxieties in members of the target audience, promising to redress these with the attributes given to the product (Williamson, 1978; Richards, 1994). Many of the marketing, advertising and presentation strategies around the consumption of commodities and experiences also emphasize the importance of emotional fulfilment, the narcissistic pleasing of the self rather than others, self-indulgence and pleasure for the sake of it (Featherstone, 1990: 19).

Goods are endowed with these meanings through the process of linking them with abstract values that are not inherently attached to them, and this linking often takes place at a subliminal or unconscious level of association. Advertisements for soft drinks such as Coca-Cola and Pepsi Cola, for example, frequently seek to endow the values of pleasure, happiness and excitement upon the drinks by using such symbols as images of young, carefree, attractive people gambolling in sunny locations. It is suggested that these emotions will be experienced if the drink is consumed. Such images also address people's uncertainties about their sexual attractiveness, their longing to be carefree and joyful, and to be part of a desirable group of people.

Campbell (1995) argues that the consumption experience in general (whether it is of objects or of experiences) is a form of hedonism, of pleasure-seeking. One does not consume most objects or experiences simply because they satisfy basic needs, he argues, but because they provide pleasure in themselves. Thinking, fantasizing or day-dreaming about the objects or the experiences before they are acquired or consumed, placing oneself in 'imagined scenarios' involving consumption, are an important part of the pleasures they evoke. As this would suggest, the emotions that objects or experiences stimulate are integral to the pleasurable dimension of consumption as well as contributing to their cultural meanings. There is often a gap, however, between the fantasies inspired by objects and the reality of their consumption. Indeed, as Campbell (1995) observes, the 'real' objects or experiences may prove disappointing in comparison with the fantasies surrounding them. Consumption, therefore, involves the emotions of disillusionment and even grief or despair as well as strong desire and pleasure. Consumption always requires a new target, a new object of desire, for once an object is possessed it loses its most potent source of desire (Falk, 1997: 79). Falk refers to the consumer's ever-desiring relationship with commodities as similar to 'love addiction', or the pattern of falling in love repeatedly with new partners and then losing interest in them once they return one's affections (1997: 80).

Encountering any type of new consumer commodity may be accompanied by neophilia, 'the bliss of the new'. A major part of the satisfaction of the consumption of new commodities is their novelty and their pristine, apparently 'perfect' state, unsullied by use. Consumption of new commodities, however, may also be accompanied by neophobia, for novelty also suggests strangeness, unfamiliarity, the risks associated with uncertainty (Richards, 1994: 96–101). This may be heightened in individuals' first encounters with such sophisticated mass-produced commodities as personal computers and video recorders, given the mystique that has tended to accompany these technologies, and particularly for those who feel unsure about their capacity to deal with complex, 'intelligent' machines.

In a study a colleague and I conducted into people's relationships with the personal computers they regularly use in the workplace, we interviewed 40 men and women occupied in various positions (both academic and administrative) in an Australian university in late 1995 (see Lupton and Noble, 1997). Among other questions, the participants were asked to describe their early experiences of learning about and using computers and to recount subsequent memorable experiences, both good and bad, of computer use. Most participants recounted strong emotional responses when describing their early experiences of computers, ranging from excitement and pleasure to fear, anxiety and frustration. The feelings of excitement and pleasure that people derived from first learning to use a computer were commonly related to the sense of novelty they experienced in using a new and much publicized technology and the expectation that the use of computers would revolutionize their work practices, making life easier. For other participants, the excitement they felt was related as well to the pleasure of mastery of what was perceived as a 'difficult' or 'complex' machine that required a certain degree of skill and intelligence to use. The task of acquiring mastery over the computer was described as a 'challenge', something that required effort and persistence to overcome. Others spoke about the 'fun' aspects of computer use, presenting their early experiences as ludic.

Those people who felt that the computer technology had been foisted upon them, however, describe far more negative emotional responses, often because they felt inadequate because of their lack of knowledge, and resented having to learn a new way of doing their job. People expressed feeling a lack of agency, fear and anxiety. These feelings were largely provoked by their loss of control over how their job was defined in relation to the introduction of a technology viewed as more mysterious in its technological sophistication than that they were accustomed to using. Many of the participants' worst experiences of computers revolved around dramatic incidents in which important work was lost. Many people said they had learnt 'the hard way' to save their work regularly and to maintain back-up discs religiously.

Feelings of anger, impotence, horror and despair, as well as frustration, were often evoked in these descriptions. For example, one academic talked about his early experiences when he forgot to save, and lost up to six hours of work. His response was: 'Anger, you have learned to understand how people can pick up things and throw them through the window!' In these cases, the ability to 'perform' as an accomplished and 'in-control' worker was undermined. As this suggests, particularly in the workplace, where successful incorporation of new technological artefacts into one's work activities is vital in maintaining one's position, the confrontation with a new commodity like a computer and its associated accoutrements may be experienced with a combination of both neophilia and neophobia.

Appropriation

While advertising and publicity strategies are clearly important in investing emotional meaning in mass-produced objects, they represent merely one dimension of the ways in which those who purchase and use such objects think and feel about them and interact with them. Users bring to commodities pre-established meanings constituted through other forms of mass media, relationships with others, the education system, the workplace, and so on.

While some of the initial attraction of the new commodity may be lost as soon as it is acquired, the modern consumer also wishes to establish long-lasting relationships with her or his commodities, seeking to incorporate them into everyday life and personalize them, make them meaningful. In doing so, 'the objects attain a patina of the mind, they become familiar and find their own places in the private microcosm of the home' (Falk, 1997: 80). When people acquire and make use of material artefacts, they inevitably transform the artefacts in their attempts to personalize and incorporate them into their routines. This has been described by some writers as 'appropriation', or the dynamic processes by which a consumer acquires an 'alien' commodity and proceeds to absorb the commodity into the self to a greater or lesser degree (Miller, 1987; Silverstone et al., 1992).

Commodities are transformed through appropriation from anonymous to personalized objects, and in so doing may become important to subjectivity. This was demonstrated in an interview study of people working in an American science laboratory, focusing on how these people defined boundaries between 'home' and 'work'. As part of the research, Nippert-Eng (1996) talked to people about the type of objects they carried around with them at work and at home. She notes that objects carried in wallets and purses, such as old employee badges, an expired driver's licence from another country where a person may have lived and worked for some time, old membership cards from professional associations, while they are 'useless' in overt functional times, serve to support a particular sense of self: 'We may keep these items purely for ourselves, for their internally integrating, evocative, and sometimes comforting power. Or we may keep them handy as props, to substantiate stories told by others' (Nippert-Eng, 1996: 59). Nippert-Eng gives the example of a scientist working at the laboratory who carries around in his pocket an out-of-date membership card from a left-wing political organization, because he still likes to think of himself as a rebellious political activist, and enjoys showing it to conservative acquaintances.

The notion of appropriation develops a processual, mutually constitutive concept of the relationship between objects and subjectivity. That is, it acknowledges the inherently constructed, dynamic and interrelational nature of the subject–object encounter. Appropriation begins from the time an object is acquired, either by purchase or as a gift, and becomes a possession, a part of the owner's life. When a mass-produced artefact is purchased, it begins as a commodity, an object of trade. Once acquired, however, either by the person who purchased it or by someone else, it may move out of the commodity state through the act of appropriation. When an object becomes 'singularized' or transformed into more of a personal possession through everyday use, it may be regarded as having become 'de-commodified' (Kopytoff, 1986: 65).

Some writers have suggested that as an outcome of appropriation the object may serve as an extension of the self outwards in space, resulting in a 'territory of the self' that surrounds the body (Nippert-Eng, 1996: 34). Examples are clothing, photographs, cars, bags or briefcases, tools, official documents (such as passports and birth certificates) and other personal possessions. In the processes of appropriation, mass-produced artefacts may be reshaped through embodied use. They may take on the imprint of human traces or be deliberately manipulated and changed (within limits) by their owners. In doing so, these objects become autobiographical in bearing the marks of an individual's use, or acting as signifiers and mnemonics of personal events. They become what González (1995) calls 'prosthetics' of the self. She gives as examples of such 'prosthetics': 'Clothing and cloth with all of its scents and residues; furniture with all of its bodily imprints, shapes and sags from years of use; worn silverware and shoes: All of these serviceable objects receive the imprint of a human trace as the autonomy of their purely functional status is worn away by time' (González, 1995: 133).

As a consequence of the changes wrought via appropriation, such objects generally become less attractive as commodities, in terms of their inducements for others to acquire them (major exceptions to this rule are such objects as antiques). Objects which have become individualized are invested with a worth other than monetary, a worth that has very personal significance (Kopytoff, 1986: 83). Because the objects become charged with personal expression, they are also more likely to become charged with emotion. This process of emotional charging does not occur with all, or even most commodities, particularly ephemeral commodities that are used briefly and then discarded. It seems to happen most of all with objects that we wear, that enclose us (our houses or cars), with which we have an embodied interaction on a daily basis (such as furniture) or which have acquired meanings that link us with others (for example, postcards or greetings cards).

Thus, for instance, a pair of shoes that are bought new begin as impersonal commodities, as objects that are identical to all the other mass-produced shoes of the same kind. As such, these objects begin as 'alien' or 'other' to the self – they are not regarded as 'part of the self'. Over a period of use by their owner, however, as their soles take on the marks of the owner's gait, as the leather moulds itself to the shape of the owner's feet (and sometimes as the owner's feet are altered by the shoes themselves), the shoes may become progressively personalized and 'de-commodified'. These particular shoes are now different from others of the same kind with which they were produced, marketed and sold. They have become singularized, bearing the stamp of individuality and everyday experience of their owner, and move more towards the ontological state of 'self' (subject) than of 'other' (object). In doing so, however, these objects lose their exchange value as commodities: they become less attractive to other consumers.

Objects may be used as ways of bringing the emotional dimensions and relationships from one particular site to another site, acting as reminders of one's 'other life'. This use of objects seems particularly to take place in the paid workplace. In Nippert-Eng's (1996) study on how people define the boundaries between 'home' and 'work', she found that for several of her interviewees introducing artefacts and memorabilia from home, such as family photographs or paintings by one's children, gave them a means of evoking emotions and presenting the self that helped to render the workplace more comfortable and pleasant. Nippert-Eng gives the example of the machinists working at the laboratory which was the focus of her study. These men did not have access to personal office space as did the clerical, research and administrative staff, but they nonetheless managed to display photographs of their wives, children, pets and even of their homes, boats or cars by attaching notice-boards to the backs of their tool boxes. Such artefacts also serve to mark out a particular space at work as an individual's specific domain; that is, to designate a 'territory of the self '.

While people may sometimes seek to deny that they have an emotional relationship with the things that they possess, the ways in which they talk about or think about the objects may often betray a tendency to anthropomorphize them or animate them in some way. This is particularly clear in the case of such technologies as cars. Cars are readily anthropomorphized because they envelop drivers and passengers, and respond to the driver's bodily movements in what comes to be experienced as an almost synergistic relationship between self and machine. The object of the car combines thrusting masculine power with maternal protectiveness and sleek feminine body, providing a womb-like internal environment, a private zone within a public space (Richards, 1994). As Richards points out, a car

> is a large moving object which we can enter and control, and it has a sort of metabolism and creates waste products. . . . It suffers from a variety of ailments and breakdowns, and it ages quite visibly. There are not many objects which can invite us so directly to experience them in somatomorphic ways, that is to exercise to the full our tendency to experience things as if they were bodies. (Richards, 1994: 71)

So too, the design of personal computers encourages anthropomorphism, albeit in somewhat different ways: 'Its experts do not think that it is "alive". But it is a medium onto which lifelike properties are easily projected. It supports the fantasy that "there is somebody home" ' (Turkle, 1988: 43). Personal computers, unlike many other machines in constant use as part of the routines of everyday life, often 'speak' to their users, either through the use of words on the screen or, on some personal computers, literally with sound effects that may include human voices that the user has programmed into her or his computer. Many personal computers have personalized welcoming messages that automatically appear on screen each time the computer is booted up, greeting the user by name. Macintosh computers use icons with smiling faces to facilitate the representation of their computers as friendly, human-like creatures.

Computers are also positioned in an embodied relationship with their users that encourages a more personal relationship than with many other technologies. For instance, when operators are using personal computers, the monitor is only centimetres away from their face, and they may stare at the monitor for hours at a time. The keyboard provides an opportunity to translate users' thoughts into words on the screen, and their manipulation of the mouse has a direct relationship with movement of icons on the monitor. This has the effect of suggesting that the computer is responding in an interactive way to the user's thoughts. It is not surprising, therefore, that people who use personal computers may come to see them as an extension of the self, as human-like with moods and personalities (particularly when they fail to work as expected), and may even give them names.

As we found in our study of computer users, even though most people denied that they saw their computers as being more than 'tools' or 'inanimate objects', they often talked about them in ways which suggested a degree of anthropomorphism. The computers were commonly described as being like humans in being 'stupid', 'intelligent' or 'friendly', having a certain 'life', as likely to 'die' and as 'deliberately choosing the moment' to malfunction so as to cause maximum disruption for the user. One woman described her computer as 'too smart for its own good' and talked about the early Macintoshes as 'the babies' and her current computer as 'the old fella'. A 33-year-old male academic, although insisting that he did not see his computer as having a personality, did admit that 'I suppose I might jokingly pat my computer when it is very slow with the World Wide Web, sometimes I pat it and say, "Come on, come on, you can do that" . . . I talk to it in that sense, yes' (see Lupton and Noble (1997) for further details).

To some extent, as Latour (1992) has asserted, this tendency towards the anthropomorphism of technologies is inevitable, given their very nature as artefacts developed by humans for human use. Latour points to the etymology of the word anthropomorphic, a combination of *anthropos* and *morphos* meaning either 'that which has human shape' or 'that which gives shape to humans'. Technologies are invested with human qualities because they have been developed to substitute for the actions of humans, as delegates occupying the position of humans, and because they shape human action in the terms of their use (Latour, 1992: 235–6). Further, as noted in Chapter 1, theorists such as Lakoff (1987, 1995) have suggested that because humans experience the world as embodied subjects, most ways of conceptualizing abstract phenomena (such as the internal workings of a computer) rely upon metaphorical relations dealing with the human body. I would extend this point to suggest that humans, as emotional beings and as individuals accustomed to interactions with others that arouse emotions and require constant assessment of others' interior states, will inevitably invest emotions, moods and agency in objects such as computers as a metaphorical strategy in the process of making sense of the world.

The activity of collecting artefacts is an example of how the acquisition and use of objects may be a highly emotional, personal experience as part of a hobby. Artefacts within a collection may often have no practical use outside their role as part of the collection, but their linking with the notion of 'my collection' is the source of their value and the pleasure they give. In their research on collectors, Danet and Katriel focused on the metaphors used to describe collecting, in interviews with collectors themselves as well as in manuals for collectors and other popular literature on collecting. They found that collectors are often considered as eccentric by others because they talk about the items in their collections as if they were family members or children, and openly attribute emotions to the objects.

As Danet and Katriel note, 'irrational' impulses and emotional responses to the objects appear to dominate collectors' experience, but others may find this difficult to understand: ' "Falling in love" with objects, treating them as if they were children or pets, spending large amounts of time, money, and energy in their pursuit can all be difficult to justify' (1994: 31). Collectors themselves may fear that they are becoming too obsessive, that they are losing control over their desire to acquire more items for their collection, that they are 'going overboard'. Nonetheless, they simultaneously relish the feelings of engagement and passion that propel them, and find the activity of purchasing, handling and ordering the items in their collection absorbing and calming but also energizing and invigorating:

> Via objects, collectors can pursue the imaginary, allow themselves to experience chaos, take on the challenge of an open-ended agenda with many unknowns, surrender to irrational impulses, enjoy the thrilling risk of being out of control, and luxuriate in a deeply engrossing solo activity whose sensuous components are prominent, and which singularizes them as unique, 'interesting' individuals. (Danet and Katriel, 1994: 34)

It is not just people who see themselves as 'collectors', of course, who accumulate possessions and attribute personal and emotional meaning to them. As part of our everyday activities and relationships we all collect artefacts for a multitude of reasons, whether functional, aesthetic, affective or a mixture of all three. There has been some research, mainly within the field of social psychology, which has sought to identify the meanings people give to their possessions. One of the most interesting and influential studies is that carried out by Csikszentmihalyi and Rochberg-Halton (1981), who interviewed people living in Chicago about their home belongings. In so doing, they constructed a typology of the kinds of belongings that people say they cherish or consider special in some way.

Csikszentmihalyi and Rochberg-Halton found, for example, that for some people a certain piece of furniture was considered special because it reminded them of the early days of their marriage, or because it was given to them by a valued friend or because they themselves had made it. As one interviewee commented, she valued two upholstered chairs in her living room because 'They are the first two chairs me and my husband ever bought, and we sit in them and I just associate them with my home and having babies and sitting in the chairs with babies' (quoted in Csikszentmihalyi and Rochberg-Halton, 1981: 60). Indeed, emotional reasons were most often mentioned by people who said that they considered some of their furniture to be special possessions, while only a small proportion stressed utilitarian reasons. Commodities, thus, may come to embody meanings that go far beyond those that they may have had when first purchased.

As part of a study with similar objectives, seeking to determine why people value certain personal possessions over others, Dittmar (1992) distributed a questionnaire to a sample of British respondents in three groups: business commuters, unemployed people and students. She asked the respondents to list five personal possessions they considered important and to describe in their own words why each possession was important to them. Her findings revealed that those objects Dittmar categorized as 'sentimental items' (mainly photographs, gifts and jewellery) were the second most often listed possessions. Slightly more often listed possessions were those she grouped under 'leisure objects' in which category music equipment was foremost, and slightly less often listed were 'utility possessions', such as household equipment and appliances. In terms of the reasons given by the respondents for their choices, as a group they predominantly supplied instrumental, use-related and sentimental reasons. Dittmar found that women tended to give many more sentimental reasons than men, while men gave more instrumental and use-related reasons. Sentimental reasons included the emotions associated with the objects as well as their symbolic link to personal relationships. The instrumental reasons, however, also included aspects to do with emotional expression, such as the possessions facilitating relaxation or mood changes.

As these studies suggest, the emotions that we feel about these objects are generated in different ways. Personal possessions can act as the repositories of memory, standing as a tangible record of personal achievements, successes, relationships with others and shared biographies with others. Virtually any object can play this role: photographs, greeting cards, letters, furniture, clothing, jewellery, kitchen utensils and crockery, records and compact discs, scents, theatre programmes and books may all be associated with past people or events or places in which an individual has lived or has visited. We may associate particular objects with other people with whom we have had intimate relationships, evoking feelings of love, hate or jealousy. Certain pieces of music or songs, for example, may remind us of a time in our lives when such a relationship was important to us. Other things may evoke strong emotions because they are associated with our early family life, or because of their links with time spent at school or university. Some objects help us to enter into emotional states that we find pleasurable and to cast off distressing emotions. Objects such as kitchen utensils, domestic technologies such as televisions and other technologies such as cars or computers may evoke emotions because they are part of our everyday lives, and we have become familiar with them as inherent in our everyday routines. Their loss or failure to operate may evoke feelings of anxiety and anger because of the disruption this causes to our routines.

Objects as Mediators of Emotion

Objects not only serve as means by which notions of style and membership of sub-cultural groups may be communicated to oneself and others. They may also function as part of social relations, supporting emotional bonds between people. Some objects are vital to the development and maintenance of emotional relationships between people. Instruments of communication, such as writing implements and greeting cards, fulfil the function of directly conveying how someone feels via words, as do electronic technologies such as computers that are interlinked and the telephone. Objects such as photographs serve the function of reminding us of how a loved one looks, reinforcing feelings of affection or love. Other things, such as gifts, serve to express and reproduce emotional ties in a less direct manner: as the slogan has it, 'Say it with flowers'.

In a study of Australian women telephone users of diverse ages and social backgrounds, Moyal (1989) found that they considered the telephone to be a vital means by which they participated in and sustained intimate relationships with friends or family members. This was particularly the case, Moyal found, for older women and their adult daughters, many of whom commented that they found their regular telephone calls a way of preventing or alleviating loneliness, depression, boredom, anxiety and worry. Women used the telephone to seek or provide advice from their close relatives or female friends in times of crisis, such as following the break-up of a marriage, a death or during illness, or when they found themselves spending long periods at home with little contact with other adults, as was often the case for the elderly or young mothers caring for small children. Women who were grandmothers commented on the integral role that telephone contact played in their relationships with their young grandchildren, whom they were not able to see regularly. The participants in Moyal's study noted that as a technology the telephone offers a different quality of communication from other forms that do not involve face-to-face contact. As one woman commented: 'The telephone is very important to me because suburban home life is lonely and the phone is a link with colour and variety and with people one loves. There's a need to communicate feeling and caring: the telephone is more personal than letters. What I want to know is how my friends "feel" and I can hear this on the telephone' (quoted in Moyal, 1989: 14–15).

The Internet, a system of computer networks interlinked with each other across the world via telephone or fibre-optic lines, is increasingly becoming a means of communication between those who have access to the appropriate technologies. The Internet not only allows very fast communication of messages between people using email (electronic mail), but also has the capacity for interactive, real-time discussion groups and fantasy game-playing. Much has been made in the mass media and cultural studies writings on this new technology of the ways that intimate, even romantic and erotic relationships may develop via the Internet. The last few years have witnessed a proliferation of networks with tantalizing names such as 'Throbnet' and 'Sleazenet' that allow users to engage each other in explicit erotic chat (otherwise known as 'cybersex') in complete anonymity (Wiley, 1995; Springer, 1996: 54–5). On such networks, users may present themselves in sexual or romantic terms in any way they wish. Some people who meet via the networks go on to exchange photographs and cards and to arrange face-to-face meetings, and even decide to live together or get married.

While some writers have presented the opportunities for interrelationships with others via the Internet in a utopian fashion, heralding a new way of establishing and maintaining intimacy and participating in 'virtual communities', others have been more doubtful, seeing computer-mediated relationships as more sterile and somehow less 'authentic' than those involving face-to-face encounters. Some have claimed that such interaction, reliant as it is on verbal communication using standardized computer fonts, is far less capable of denoting emotion than many other forms of communication because there is no capacity for cues that are conveyed by such aspects as verbal tone or pitch or by facial expression: 'The "asides" that are conveyed in face-to-face or telephone communications, like laughter or tone of sarcasm, must be included in a written text' (Wiley, 1995: 151).

There is evidence in these more pessimistic discourses of a fear that those who use computers for such purposes will prove unable to form 'proper' relationships with others. As one critic has suggested: 'The more that the use of computers is demanded of us, the more we shall be taken away from truly deep human experiences' (Lakoff, 1995: 124). There is the suggestion in such accounts that computer use is dehumanizing, perhaps involving the progressive transformation of those who use computers into 'machine-like' subjects who are unable to experience or understand the full range of emotions that are considered to be part and parcel of intimate relationships with others. Turkle's (1996) research suggests that for some people who spend a great deal of time engaging in interactive fantasy games, the virtual world is perceived as more easily manipulable and less complex than face-to-face relationships – computer-mediated relationships are seen as 'reliable' and 'predictable' in ways that others are not. However, even these enthusiasts tend to express concern that playing such games could lead to a form of 'addiction' which threatened to cut them off from 'real relationships' and everyday responsibilities.

Photographs are obvious mementoes of people, places and things, recording but also acting to shape recollections of these phenomena. In their study, Csikszentmihalyi and Rochberg-Halton (1981) found that personal photographs were highly valued by their interviewees because of their links with close relationships, emotions and memories and because they were considered irreplaceable. They note that for older people in particular, 'More than any other object in the home, photos serve the purpose of preserving the memory of personal ties. In their ability to arouse emotion there is no other type of object that can surpass them' (1981: 69). When describing what it would mean to them to lose a cherished photograph of a deceased family member, for example, several participants found themselves weeping at the thought. When those we love are still living, photographs help to trigger thoughts and emotions about them when we can gaze upon their visages. Photographs of intimate others – particularly partners and children – are often displayed by people in the workplace in the attempt to bring the close relationships of their home lives into their workaday lives (Nippert-Eng, 1996: 71–2).

The symbolic status of gifts is interesting to reflect upon, because of the role played by gifts in the emotional economy of friendships and family relationships. Gift-giving is an important ritual in the main-tenance of such close relationships and is understood to be inspired by the conventional emotions that go with them, such as friendship, love and gratitude: 'All three emotions involve the actor in identifying with others, so that for certain purposes the boundaries between self and other are denied, and a collective identity is defined *vis-à-vis* outsiders' (Cheal, 1988: 18). Gifts are understood to communicate these positive emotions as well as defining the nature of the relationship between the giver and the receiver. As Gabriel and Lang (1995: 58) note, 'Gifts are a highly delicate area of consumption' because of their role in relation-ships. Making misjudgements about the price or quality of a gift can inspire a range of emotions for both giver and receiver, including embarrassment, humiliation and resentment.

Under the ideology of love, it is believed that 'gifts are given spontan-eously, as a result of the natural affections of one person for another' (Cheal, 1988: 106). However, as an outcome of the importance placed upon gifts as symbols of love and affection, in modern western societies there are tensions around the notion of the 'perfect gift'. One tension is that the perfect gift is not judged on its monetary value or its material form, but by the sentiment it expresses: 'The good gift is the spontan-eous, unfettered expression of the real inner self and inner feeling' (Carrier, 1990: 32). The more individualized and 'non-commercial' the gift, the more it is valued as a 'real' gift that is presented out of disinterested love and affection. As commodities are anonymously mass-produced, the expectation that such a gift expresses the giver and the receiver's personal identity is difficult to fulfil.

Carrier (1990: 30) notes, for example, that while Christmas gifts are typically wrapped in festive paper, so as to conceal their identity as mass-produced objects and to individualize them, gifts which are home-made food items, such as jams and breads, tend not to be fully wrapped, often sporting simply a bow and card. He asserts that such gifts need not be fully wrapped because they were not acquired as commodities and therefore do not require the festive wrapping to transform them from commodity into gift. It is in the context of the family that the ideology of the pure gift tends to be most conformed to. For example, parents tend to give gifts at Christmas to their children that far exceed the gifts they receive in return, and gifts are far more personalized than they are in other settings, such as the office (Carrier, 1990).

While the ideology of the gift tends to disavow the importance of the actual nature of the gift itself ('it's the thought that counts'), there are several mass-produced commodities in western societies that signify specific emotions. Giving someone chocolates, for example, tends to suggest romantic love, and is therefore a mainstay of Valentine's Day gift-giving. Sending flowers also has the same meaning, particularly if they are red roses, although they are also given in other contexts, such as when people are hospitalized or to mothers on Mothers' Day. According to the claims of advertising, a man presenting a diamond to his (female) partner is signifying his eternal romantic love, for 'diamonds are for-ever'. Champagne tends to be bought and consumed as a symbol of celebration and the related emotions of excitement and pleasure.

Topophilia: Emotion and Place

Humans may have emotional relationships not only with things, but also with places or landscapes, including built environments such as cities and towns as well as non-urban environments. The human geographer Yi-Fu Tuan calls this phenomenon 'topophilia', or 'the affective bond between people and place or setting' (1974: 4; see also Tuan, 1977, 1979). Space and place are central features of the experience of 'being-in-the-world' as an embodied subject, for embodiment is always experienced through spatial dimension. Just as people are able to shape aspects of their physical environment, so does the environment shape subjectivity. As I argued in Chapter 1, the perceptions of place and space that individuals gather from their senses – the sights, sounds, smells, tastes and feel of the environment – have a potentially powerful role in the production of emotion. Accreted personal experience is also an import-ant part of the emotions inspired by the place.

Tuan (1974: 27–9) has observed how spatial categories incorporate powerful emotional associations. Open space, for example, signifies freedom, the promise of adventure, light, the public realm, formal and unchanging beauty, while enclosed space signifies the security of the womb, privacy and darkness. Because of these dominant cultural meanings, we tend to experience specific emotions when in these types of space. So too, we tend to describe environmental features using emotional terms. Mountains, for example, are said to 'soar', ocean waves 'swell' and Greek temples are 'calm'. Places may inspire feelings such as affection, hope and nostalgia, but also dread, disgust or fear. In western cultures, for example, those places that are considered 'natural' landscapes (such as forests, lakes, seas and open countryside) have been portrayed both as the source of authenticity and pure feeling, inspiring the emotions of awe, delight and joy for their beauty, and promoting relaxation, but also as the site of terror and danger, of violence and desolation, where 'nature' overwhelms the civility of 'culture' and where strange things can happen once one has ventured from the beaten track.

The Bible features many examples of landscapes which signify particular emotional states in relation to communion with God. The 'wilderness' has two dominant contradictory meanings. The Bible describes encounters with God as typically occurring in desolate scenes away from the distractions of human or other living things, with the stark, desert landscape mirroring the asceticism and purity of faith. The 'wilderness' also holds a particular meaning in the Bible as a place condemned by God. People are routinely driven into the wilderness as a punishment when they have transgressed God's law. Desolate areas are not just places for spiritual contemplation but also places of temptation and attack by the devil (Tuan, 1974: 109–10).

Cities and large towns also have attracted opposite meanings. On the one hand, they are portrayed as places of freedom, refinement and civilization, where 'culture' may best flourish, and as the site of pleasurable activities as part of large groups of people. On the other hand, however, cities and towns have also often been portrayed as dirty, polluted, frightening, the site of disease and crime, the cause of stress, and as impersonal, alienating and overwhelming because of the large number of fleeting interactions one has with strangers. Small towns or villages are associated with the positive meanings of community and safety, as places where people know each other and 'look out' for one another, but also as suffocating and boring, the hotbeds of petty gossip and jealousies.

Few sociologists have turned their attention to the emotional dimension of the built environment. One of the most influential of those who have done so is the early sociologist Georg Simmel (1903/1969), who, writing in the early years of the twentieth century on the topic of 'The metropolis and mental life', discussed the impersonal, disorienting and overwhelming nature of urban living. Simmel argued that the intensity of city-dwelling combined with anonymity, a large number of human

contacts, the lack of soul, and the lack of coherence in human relationships led to the fragmenting of identity. Urbanites, he thought, experience an excess of 'psychic stimulation', causing them to respond
defensively by repressing their emotions and fragmenting their lives into
small compartments so as to deal more easily with the complex nature of
everyday life. Simmel was not wholly negative about metropolitan life,
however. He also remarked upon the city as offering the potential for
new and more sophisticated forms of refined sensibility and discrim-
ination.

It is easy to think of particular towns, cities or regions as having a
certain 'character' that tends to promote certain emotions over others
and contributes to a sense of local identity that may be associated with a
particular world view. In England, for example, cultural distinctions are
often made between the North and the South of that country. The North
is associated with the working class, the periphery, bleak countryside,
industry and factories, rugged, outdoors leisure pursuits, a wetter, colder
climate and with neighbourliness and emotional community. The South,
in contrast, is associated with the centre, economic and social elites,
tamed, benign countryside, the occupations of stockbroking and management, high culture, a warmer, gentler climate and institutions, money
and power (Shields, 1991: 231). In the USA, there is also a 'North' and
'South' divide, with residents of the colder northern states presented as
more cultured, intelligent and emotionally contained compared with the
more emotionally volatile, down-to-earth and unsophisticated south-
erners dwelling in balmier climes. In Australia, the cultural meanings
given to the 'North' and the 'South' are exactly opposite, but make the
same associations between climate and emotional disposition. The northern regions of Australia are the most tropical and its denizens are
portrayed as 'rougher', less concerned with the niceties of etiquette and
even as slightly mad ('gone troppo'). The further south one travels, the
colder the weather becomes and the more serious and emotionally
contained the people are seen to be.

A related distinction is routinely made between the two largest (and
very competitive) cities of Sydney and Melbourne in terms of the 'types'
of people who live there. In the popular imagination, Sydney residents
are viewed as far more hedonistic and brash, more interested in indulging the fleeting pleasures of the body than nourishing the intellect.
Sydney is dominantly portrayed as a sunny city, its sub-tropical climate,
lush vegetation, be⁻utiful harbour and plentiful beaches contributing to
feelings of well-being and relaxation, and supporting a predominantly
outdoor lifestyle. It is renowned for its vibrant gay culture, including the
annual Gay and Lesbian Mardi Gras parade held in the summer,
featuring much exposure of flesh by the participants. In contrast, the
residents of Melbourne are often portrayed as more intellectual and
serious about life, with a more 'European' approach. This is linked to the
layout of Melbourne, with its well-planned street grids, its relative lack

of beaches and its colder (in Australian terms) weather. These aspects of Melbourne are seen to contribute to a more insular but also cultured ambience, in which people gather together in pubs, cafés, bookshops, cinemas or theatres rather than seeking pleasure in outdoor activities (with the major exception of attending matches of Australian Rules football, a sport which has many ardent followers in Melbourne).

In their book examining 'local feeling' in the northern English cities of Manchester and Sheffield, Taylor et al. (1996) draw upon focus-group discussions with local residents to explore the emotions people harbour towards their neighbourhoods and the city in which they live generally. This 'local feeling' (the concept of which is drawn from Raymond Williams's notion of 'structures of feeling') is viewed by Taylor et al. as emerging from a combination of factors: residents' lived experiences of the place in which they live, including their relationships with others as well as with space, place and objects; memories and myths associated with living in a particular place; issues to do with gender, nationality, ethnicity, occupation and social class; cultural representations of the city in such forums as the mass media; local climate and topographical features, the architectural and physical layout of the city; and the broader historical, demographical and economic dimensions which influence the conditions and style of living within the cities. All of these dimensions interact in a dynamic fashion to produce and shape the feelings that people have about their local environs.

In the post-industrial cities of Manchester and Sheffield, Taylor et al. (1996) claim, the residents' feelings about their cities have been strongly shaped by such factors as the grimy nature of the physical space which was the outcome of their provenance in heavy industry (cotton and textiles in Manchester, steel in Sheffield), the recent decline of this industry leading to the growth of unemployment and an associated increase in poverty. These broader changes have led to a sense, particularly among older people, of nostalgia for 'better times', a pessimistic feeling that their city was decaying and declining, and a feeling that life has become much more uncertain and perilous. The locals were acutely aware of particular public spaces in their neighbourhood or the city as a whole that they considered 'dangerous' and where they feared being the victim of crime: as Taylor et al. put it (1996: 174), they had a 'mental map' by which they categorized certain places as 'safe' or 'unsafe'. These judgements tended to be made based on features of the space itself and others who tended to occupy it (such as 'the poor', 'drug addicts', groups of younger people and 'beggars' or homeless people) as well as such aspects as the time of day.

At a more specific level of focus, Sibley (1995) has used his own memories and experiences of growing up in London in the 1940s to explore the spatial and temporal dimension of childhood. As he argues, the boundaries, related to the built environment constructed by those in charge of a child (parents, other family members, teachers), play an integral part in the emotions children feel, particularly in relation to transgression. Sibley notes that 'These boundaries are elements of a geography which is partly experienced and defined by sensations – fear, anxiety, excitement, desire – which shape the developing child's relation-ship to people and places' (1995: 124). He recalls his own experiences and feelings in relation to places such as the school playground, which was a place to fear and avoid because of the presence of bullies, and a cat meat shop on the way to his school, the smell of which provoked disgust. Sibley points out that children often have very little control over the ways in which they can use space and time in such settings as the home or the school, subject as they are to injunctions and the privileged wishes of adults. Tensions may arise between child and adult concerning the use of space and time (for example, the untidy bedroom, the time to go to bed), the frustrations of which may be acutely felt by the child in ways that are often forgotten from the perspective of adulthood: 'As adults, we forget what it felt like to be in a new place which looked and smelled different to anything experienced before, or to be late for school or to be sent to bed' (1995: 136).

The Emotional Meanings of 'Home'

In a recent article published in a weekend newspaper colour supplement, the Australian journalist Deborah Hope expressed her fond memories of her own family home in Sydney. She nostalgically recounted childhood games in the large garden and joyful family celebrations at Christmas, comparing her feelings about her childhood home with those she holds about her current disorderly home life: 'The unchanging order, the sameness of routine and comfort, the safety of traditional family values and sense of timelessness mean my parents' home is now not just an idyll, but an ideal that contrasts sharply with the chaos of my own adult domestic life' (Hope, 1996: 24). Hope went on to describe how her cousin had watched her own family home knocked down to make way for a new house, and the emotions associated with this experience:

> 'It was very distressing to see it as rubble, to see the places which had been ours, the walls my parents had painted, intimately exposed to the street,' she says. 'I walked through the rubble trying to find any object I could take with me, but I couldn't find anything. I stood there trying to imagine how it had been. It was a devastating sense of loss. It's very distressing to think about it. It was like it was being violated.' (quoted in Hope, 1996: 24)

Other people interviewed by Hope for the article reiterated their strong emotional attachment to the homes in which they had grown up, the meanings of security, comfort and permanence that were attached to these sites, and the grief and distress that resulted from their loss or destruction. As Hope argued, one's home 'is the blend of association, experience and history woven into the fabric of ourselves' (1996: 28).

In contemporary western societies, the concept of 'the home' has particular resonances for the 'authentic' emotional self. As noted in

Chapter 4, with the progressive divide following industrialization between what has been represented as the aggressive, impersonal world of paid labour or the 'public' sphere, and the 'private' domain of the family and intimate relationships, the home has become portrayed as a place of security, control over one's environment, warmth, comfort, creativity and freedom. Sennett (1977: 3) comments that modern public life is a matter of formal obligation that seems non-authentic to us, while private life is the realm in which we attempt to behave in an authentic manner, to be 'true' to ourselves. Family relationships and the site of the home are commonly represented as providing comfort and security for family members, allowing them a safe place to retreat from the dangers of the outside world.

In contrast to this cosy portrayal of the home and the family, the outside world, particularly the urban environment, is constructed in ambivalent terms as exciting and stimulating but also full of danger and hazard. These include such dangers as accidents, pollution and crime but also those posed by people with whom one interacts in terms of their lack of trustworthiness, their tendency to dissemble (Frosh, 1991). Individuals whose houses are burgled and ransacked by thieves typically respond to this experience with great distress, including feelings of personal violation akin to those aroused by sexual assault (Dittmar, 1992: 46). This response may also be linked to the meanings associated with 'home'.

Nippert-Eng (1996: 18–22) describes how 'home' and 'work' are understood as conceptually different spaces that have different rules about behaviour, appearance and so on. 'Home' is idealized as a safe, welcoming haven, a feminine realm in which the love of the mother/wife provides security and bodily and emotional nourishment and restoration from the day's rigours. 'Work', in contrast, is a place of wage labour, self-control and self-discipline, a more masculine space, a public activity requiring a public presentation of the self. As Nippert-Eng notes, 'As a private realm, however, "home" ideally is the place where we can "be ourselves", "put up our feet", "let down our hair", "relax among those who see us", "warts and all" but aren't supposed to hold it against us' (1996: 20). She goes on to argue that: 'Home is where we seek the predictable continuity of families' presence and their long (and rather unforgiving) memories of who we are. It is the place we expect to most thoroughly embed ourselves, past, present, and future' (Nippert-Eng, 1996: 22).

The home is also commonly portrayed as a site in which people may exercise power, one of the few places which one can alter according to one's needs and tastes. The meanings of creativity and self-expression relate to activities such as home improvement, restoration and decoration. Through such activities, as well as through routine interactions with the spaces and things within the home, the home may become part of the 'territory of the self '. 'A home', assert Csikszentmihalyi and Rochberg-

Halton, 'is much more than a shelter; it is a world in which a person can create a material environment that embodies what he or she considers significant. In this sense the home becomes the most powerful sign of the self of the inhabitant who dwells within' (1981: 123). Many of their interviewees tended to describe their homes as 'comfortable', 'cozy' or 'relaxing' when asked about its characteristics (1981: 127). They also demonstrated a strong emotional attachment to their homes, even representing them in anthropomorphic terms. One 15-year-old girl described her home in the following way: 'This house seems gentle to me, like loving . . . to put it plainly, there's really no home like your own. I am used to it and I know every little stitch around here . . . sometimes sadness is all around, then happiness is all around. Wonderful, this house is wonderful' (quoted in Csikszentmihalyi and Rochberg-Halton, 1981: 130). As this girl's words suggest, if we have positive emotions about our home, we can feel as we enter it that we are 'embraced' by it almost as one is enfolded within the arms of the mother figure. The concept of 'warmth' is often employed to describe homes that make us feel comfortable, loved and protected from the ravages of the 'cold' outside world.

Privacy is also an essential element of western understandings of the home, allowing people to remove themselves from the scrutiny of others (apart from intimate family members): 'Being "at home" means (among other things) that an individual can feel safe and in command, free from the intrusion and direction of others' (Allan and Crow, 1989: 3). This privacy can hold negative as well as positive implications, however, particularly in the case of people who feel as if they are confined to the house and isolated, such as some women with young children, the elderly or the unemployed, where the house can become like a 'prison' (1989: 6).

The positive meanings of home have also been problematized and destabilized by a series of threats and dangers that have been identified as emerging within intimate and family relationships, including violence and sexual abuse on the part of men towards their partners and children, women's subjugation within the home and the economic and emotional side-effects of marital and family breakdown. At the end of the twentieth century it would seem that while the discourse of the home and intimate relationships as providing a 'haven' and 'refuge' from the outside world has continued to dominate, the obverse of this holds an equally strong resonance, perhaps in part because it counters so dramatically the first discourse.

Despite the potentially negative emotional associations of home, many people find leaving their house, their neighbourhood or their country to be a disorienting and distressing experience. Tuan notes that 'To be forcibly evicted from one's home and neighbourhood is to be stripped of a sheathing, which in its familiarity protects the human being from the bewilderments of the outside world' (1974: 99). In his book *Returning to*

Nothing: The Meaning of Lost Places (1996), historian Peter Read presents interviews with Australians who had lost their homes through various disasters, including fires and cyclones, or who had been forced to leave their homes because they were to be flooded as part of the building of a dam or demolished to make way for a new freeway. He also talked to people who had left their earlier homes voluntarily as migrants from other countries or who had owned properties as farmers but had to leave them for various reasons, including retirement or bankruptcy. The accounts given by the people with whom Read spoke were redolent of the near spiritual relationship that people had with houses, and the urban, suburban or rural landscapes in which they had lived and to which they had become emotionally attached. They emphasized the interrelationship between individuals' personal biographies, their memories, their relationships with others and their experiences of living in houses and landscapes.

The emotional attachment we have to our homes and surrounding landscapes develops from everyday, embodied interactions with objects in these environments, with their smells, their textures, their sounds and their colours. Through use of or focused attention upon the many individual items within a home (what Csikszentmihalyi and Rochberg-Halton (1981: 184) describe as the investment of psychic energy in possessions), a *gestalt* is created that communicates a sense of 'home'. The attachment is grounded, therefore, in sensory experiences repeated over time, to which we become familiar and accustomed, and in our emotional feelings about the people with whom we share these spaces, both good and bad. In terms of individuals' life histories, pivotal events surrounded with strongly felt emotion and personal significance frequently take place in the home context, perhaps more than in any other site. As one woman interviewed by Read said of her family home in the city of Perth (Australia):

> The more I think about this, the more I realise that important events happening in a place make that place more memorable. I can't get away from that. In my Perth house, both my grandmother and my uncle, they both died in that house. It's all those things that add up to it being a home, something special. (quoted in Read, 1996: 115)

When we leave our homes, whether by choice or involuntarily, it can be an emotionally wrenching experience. This was clear in the words of one of the people interviewed by Read, who left a rural property where she had lived with her husband all her married life, almost 40 years, to retire to a nearby town: 'the actual physical feeling of leaving it was quite hard. You felt all those feelings of despair, physically, in your stomach almost' (quoted in Read, 1996: 15). She went on to describe how the pain of leaving never quite left her: 'Just when your feelings were under control this can take you by surprise, there's a real physical tie to the land and a feeling that is part of your spirit that's divorced from all arguments of logic and reason and behaviour, just something that assails you' (quoted in Read, 1996: 20).

For people who have left their home in one area or country and moved to live permanently in another, the use of objects they have brought with them to the new place is a means of nostalgia, of maintaining a tie with their previous place of residence. So too, people living as part of marginalized groups in their country of origin may use objects of memory such as photographs and souvenirs in their homes in the attempt to construct a new sense of 'home'. The objects that people take with them when they move house provide a feeling of grounding, stability and a sense of home in what is initially an unfamiliar and 'unfriendly' territory and maintain a continuity with their previous lives, dwelling places and identities (González, 1995: 145–6). As González puts it, 'Objects that symbolically or indexically represent a "homeland", whether actual or ideological, in this case serve to support a communal sense of "self". Memories are made manifest in a material form' (1995: 138).

Emotional Escapes: Leisure Activities

While the 'civilized' body began to be valued over the 'grotesque' body in western societies after the Middle Ages (see Chapter 3), Mellor and Shilling (1997) identify a third type of body in late modernity. They call this the 'baroque' body, which marries the controlled tendencies of the 'civilized' body with a growing tendency towards valuing sensual and emotional experience. The intensification of self-control and bodily discipline that was the outcome of modernity has, as its corollary, the incitement of the pleasures of transgression. The imposition of rules in themselves produce the possibilities for lack of conformity, for transgressive possibilities, generating a constant interaction between desire and prohibition (Roper, 1994: 8). As Mellor and Shilling observe, 'A desire for unmediated experiences and feelings, for a body which provides a sense of home, is understandable in a culture whose internal referentiality has made it banal' (1997: 26).

Carnivals, fairs and festivals have historically provided the settings for cultures of excess, emotional expression and 'the direct and vulgar grotesque bodily pleasures of fattening food, intoxicating drink and sexual promiscuity', as Featherstone (1990: 14–15) has described it. In such settings, boundaries are crossed, taboos are deliberately subverted, the everyday world is turned upside down for the sheer pleasure of it. Featherstone gives the examples of the city, the seaside resort, the music hall of the nineteenth century, exhibitions, department stores and shopping malls as other sites where the emotions associated with the carnivalesque may be incited and experienced through lavish or exotic sensual stimuli.

Campbell (1995) argues, however, that while traditional, pre-modern hedonism was concerned primarily with opulence, luxury, abundance and revelry, contemporary hedonism is also achieved via 'new', exciting experience, which may involve danger, grief, hardship and fear. Many commentaries on the nature of human existence at the end of the twentieth century remark on the ceaseless search for new and exciting experiences, the lack of satisfaction, that appears to be part of this existence: 'Images of consumers as explorers, restless and impatient, driven by insatiable curiosity, constantly looking for difference, underscore the ideas of numerous prominent cultural theorists' (Gabriel and Lang, 1995: 72). Examples of such experiences include viewing horror, suspenseful or tear-jerking films, visiting theme parks that include thrilling rides, engaging in adventurous holidays involving 'roughing it', or playing computer games. Such hedonism goes beyond sensory arousal to the use of the imagination to evoke emotions such as excitement and nostalgia: 'since the stimulation which creates pleasurable arousal can as easily derive from an imagined internal source as a real external one, day-dreaming about possible novel pleasant experiences can become a more than acceptable alternative to repeating already experienced real ones' (Campbell, 1995: 118).

In the contemporary era, travel and tourism are typically represented as experiences which involve removing the consumer from one emotional site to another. The emotional experiences offered by holidays are one of their most prominent selling points. Advertisements for holidays typically employ the language of emotion in their attempt to appeal to potential customers: a holiday destination may provide 'relaxation', an 'opportunity to unwind', or else may provide 'excitement' and even a sense of danger. The appeal is made to the audience of escaping the humdrum realities of everyday life, so as to immerse oneself in an environment in which sensation is heightened.

Rojek (1993: Chapter 4) describes the enormous capital investment in the 1970s and 1980s in escape areas organized around spectacle and sensation in Europe and the USA. These include tourist attractions based on sites where well-known or a large number of people had met with a sudden or violent death (such as the American highway where James Dean was killed in a car accident and Auschwitz), heritage sites which attempt to recreate events and ways of life of former times, literary landscapes, involving the exploitation of areas where famous novelists lived or about which they wrote (for example, 'Brontë Country' in Yorkshire) and theme parks organized around serialized spectacles and exciting rides (such as the Universal Film Lot in California and the Disney theme parks). These sites work upon not only the emotions of excitement and happiness, but also those of nostalgia, terror, sorrow or grief and the desire for authenticity, extreme sensation, adventure, the exotic and novelty as well as curiosity. Much of the pleasure evoked by these sites, Rojek argues, is associated with time–space compression, 'giving the consumer the "experience" of stepping across continents in seconds or shedding centuries in minutes' (Rojek, 1993: 164).

More banal, everyday sites such as cinemas, theatres, restaurants, bars and pubs provide places where certain types of emotion – pleasure, excitement, relaxation, enjoyment – might be invoked and savoured. This may occur partly because of the environment established to engender such emotions (such as the provision of music and comfortable seating, allowing for interaction with others), but also by the pre-established cultural meanings around 'going out'.

Going outside the home to eat is a major form of leisure. Eating out, whether it is in fast-food chains such as McDonald's or in more upmarket and expensive restaurants, is associated with the meanings of pleasure, excitement, relaxation and enjoyment:

> When dining out, we are pursuing a variety of needs and desires; in addition to the prosaic need for bodily sustenance, we look for a sense of excitement as we change routines, a feeling of participation in the on-going stream of social life as we carry on our affairs within the physical proximity of others, and a sense of self-enhancement which is supposed to derive from conspicuous consumption and the display of fiscal strength. (Finkelstein, 1989: 64)

Those dining establishments which advertise their products often seek to draw attention to these positive emotions as part of the experience they offer, showing families and young people laughing together as they consume their meals, enjoying each other's company. The architecture and decoration of such establishments, and the packaging of their products, are also designed to evoke a sense of fun and play, particularly for children. These emotions are in turn linked to the sense of novelty of eating out and the luxury that accompanies not having to cook or clean up for oneself at home, particularly for women. We often choose to eat out to celebrate special occasions such as birthdays or anniversaries as part of the ritual of marking these occasions as 'out of the ordinary' and as a way of indulging oneself through unusual sensory pleasures. Eating out is also more strongly associated with the weekend, the time of leisure, rather than with the working week day.

Like the tourist experience, eating out experiences are often presented to the consumer as a means of engaging in an exciting activity, both through the experience of consuming interesting, delicious and different cuisine that one cannot usually prepare for oneself at home, and also through the experience of being present in the restaurant itself. I found in a study including interviews with people about food that they frequently referred to the excitement and pleasure of discovering 'exotic' cuisines and of trying new dishes (Lupton, 1996a). Eating out, however, is not necessarily an enjoyable experience. Some people may find the eating-out experience, particularly when it takes place in an expensive restaurant, a little confronting or anxiety-provoking because it demands of them certain formalized ways of behaviour with which they may feel unfamiliar. Compared with engaging in the more familiar and less public family meal, eating out 'is often experienced by individuals as a more demanding experience, requiring of them a display of *savour faire* about what to order and how to eat it' (Lupton, 1996a: 99). Being 'shown up' as not possessing this knowledge can evoke strong feelings of embarrassment. So too, disappointment caused if the food is not to one's liking or is poorly cooked, the social relations are not as happy or relaxed as one's hopes, or because the staff at the restaurant are rude or too slow in dealing with orders, may be part of the eating-out experience. These experiences counter the expectation that the restaurant meal will be special, creating happiness and pleasure. Further, some people feel threatened or even repulsed by meals offered to them in restaurants that use unfamiliar ingredients or flavours (see Lupton, 1996a: 101–2).

The very concept of leisure depends on the temporal and spatial separation of the workaday world with that of the world of relaxation and enjoyment. Certain times and spaces are designated as belonging to one or the other: the weekday versus the weekend, the office versus the pub, day versus night. Commodities are often used to help define and reproduce these distinctions. For example, for many people in Anglophone societies such as the USA, Britain and Australia, coffee is culturally associated more with work than with leisure, while alcohol holds the opposite meanings. Coffee is consumed periodically throughout the working day, often beginning first thing in the morning, to mark settling down to work: 'we associate the image of someone drinking coffee with people who are fighting natural states of mind to engage in the utmost artificial activity: important, hard work' (Nippert-Eng, 1996: 129). In contrast, alcohol tends to be consumed out of work hours, in the evenings and particularly at the end of the working week, as a means of defining leisure time (Gusfield, 1987). People may have the habit of sitting down with an alcoholic drink soon after arriving home from work, using it as a transitional drink to help them 'unwind' from their work-related pressures and preoccupations (Nippert-Eng, 1996: 129). Coffee is associated with the meanings of self-control, clear-headedness and rational thinking, while alcohol bears the meanings of loss of self-control, self-indulgence and disinhibition. Both commodities, therefore, are believed to create and sustain particular emotional moods.

For some, entering the world of the bar or pub provides a means of escaping the realities of the working world (or for the unemployed, the non-working world). As Willis notes of young English men who regularly go to the pub:

> The direct effect of alcohol relaxes the self and distances the real world, as does the warmth, size, comfort and protection of the pub. . . . For many young men the entry into the pub, especially on a Saturday night, is also the start or the promise of a kind of adventure, reflected symbolically in some of the more outlandish 'theme styling' of refurbished 'leisure pubs'. The adventure or promise is about the suspension of the given, the mundane and the everyday. It starts in the head and in the immediate social group with the physical effects of alcohol, but it produces changes there whose ripple can and does spread to make waves outside. (Willis, 1990: 101)

Elias and Dunning (Elias and Dunning, 1986; Dunning, 1996) have pursued a similar theme by focusing on the emotions aroused by sporting and leisure activities. These activities, they claim, take people out of the dull, predictable routines of their everyday lives, providing a degree of insecurity to conditions in which people normally seek security. Risk, tension, anxiety and uncertainty are valued for their disruptive and 'uncivilized' nature. Elias and Dunning also emphasize the 'mimetic' aspect of the emotions involved in leisure activities, or the ways in which the emotions may be experienced as pleasurable in that context because they are not related to 'real' events directly affecting the participant. They contend that the public arousal of excitement is usually severely controlled in western societies, and that the opportunity to experience emotions in mimetic contexts is therefore sought:

> One can vicariously experience hatred and the desire to kill, defeating opponents and humiliating enemies, making love to desirable men and women, the anxieties of threatened defeat and the open triumph of victory. In a word, one can – up to a point – tolerate the arousal of strong feelings of a great variety of types in societies which otherwise impose on people a life of relatively even and unemotional routines, and which require a high degree and great constancy of emotional control in all spheres of life. (Dunning, 1996: 195)

These emotions, Elias and Dunning argue, are a paler version of the emotions felt in 'real life' because there is some distance from the event inspiring the emotion, there is a mediating factor. Thus, for example, even feelings of fear, horror and hatred may be experienced as enjoyable through leisure. Participants are provided with the opportunity to experience emotions which in other situations they would find distressing. Viewers of the horror film, for instance, seek out the sensory thrills of fear and disgust in their viewing of death, mutilation and gore, finding enjoyment in these sights because of their transgressive nature (Tudor, 1995). The suspense, excitement and physical tension built up and released as audiences witness monsters or psychopaths stalk and attack their human prey are pleasurable in their intensity because one's own safety is never threatened.

Participating as a member of a group can also contribute to the emotional experiences engendered in leisure activities. While Durkheim's concept of 'collective effervescence', or the intense emotion generated through embodied interactions with others, referred to religious rituals (see Chapter 1), it may also be applied to more secular activities. Percy and Taylor (1997) have commented on the strong similarities that football fandom has with charismatic religion. Both football fans and religious devotees, they argue, typically have feelings of communion with others, enjoy participating in a large group in the suspension of reality, engage in hero-worship and devotion to charismatic leaders (players) and experience heightened 'effervescent' emotion, even ecstasy. Football supporters, they point out, often sing solemn, hymn-like songs such as the Liverpool supporters' 'You'll never walk alone'. According to Percy and Taylor, for religious devotees and football fans, 'The belief is in a God, or in a team: both are there to perform, bless, lead and bring victory to the believer' (1997: 40). Both groups are able to find a common identity, a sense of hope and meaning, and participate in narratives of possibility as part of their experience.

Those individuals who engage in more physically risky activities may derive pleasure from their status as dangerous or prohibited, from flouting the rules of self-deportment to which most people adhere. Young men, for instance, particularly those from the 'underclass', tend to engage in risk-taking activities which go beyond mimesis of emotional states to actual engagement in violence and criminal acts and threats to health, such as drink-driving and fast driving and taking drugs in large quantities (Collison, 1996). The pleasure of such activities stem from the heightened sense of 'being in the moment', the excitement of the senses: 'Being on the edge, or over it – beyond reason and in passion – is momentarily to grasp a spiritual and romantic utopia' (Collison, 1996: 435). There are few public places, however, where people may completely relinquish emotional control. Featherstone (1990: 17) notes that the enjoyment of such experiences involves not a total removal of control over the emotions, for some degree of self-control is still expected. Rather, it is more accurately a 'controlled de-control' of emotions, for all such sites or occasions still have a set of written or unwritten rules and procedures for policing these, concerning how people should deport themselves.

Concluding Comments

I have argued in this chapter that the relationship between people, things and places is often saturated with emotion. Advertisers and marketers set out deliberately to evoke various emotions in their target audience to incite them to purchase their commodities or experiences. Emotional states accompany the desire or longing we may feel for an object we have not yet acquired or for an experience we would like to try. Objects are used to alter emotional states or moods, promoting relaxation or conversely, excitement. Some objects act as the mediators of emotional relationships between people. Engagement in leisure 'experiences' is often a source of emotional intensity, an opportunity for people to transcend momentarily usual norms and constraints of behaviour and self-management, and to engage in collective sociality, albeit in controlled settings.

At a more fundamental level, through the processes of appropriation, objects are incorporated into our subjectivity via consumption, everyday use and memory. The emotional relationship that we experience with things may involve anthropomorphizing objects, investing them with similar emotions to those we have with human intimates. Even if we do not anthropomorphize our objects, we may come to have similar feelings and attachments for them as we may hold for people, and to mourn for them if we lose them. Space and place, too, are profoundly intertwined with our emotional selves, and we can develop strong emotional attachments to space and place. We invest our selves in our things and in the spaces and places we inhabit and through which we move, and in turn, things, spaces and places shape us – our selves, our bodies and our emotions.

Conclusion

At the beginning of this book I commented on the slipperiness of the concept of emotions. Having examined the everyday, popular discourses on the emotions emerging in people's own explanations and experiences and in the mass media, and the expert discourses articulated in professional forums such as the 'psy' disciplines, as well as identifying some of the historical underpinnings of these discourses, emotions still remain somewhat elusive. This is inevitable, given the complex interrelationships of discourse, embodiment, memory, personal biography, sociocultural processes and thought that constitute and give meaning to emotional states. Due to the shifting state of these interrelationships, definitions of emotion are always liable to change – emotion is, therefore, a moving target. More interesting, for me at least, is coming to a better understanding of the ways in which we seek to define emotions and to explain our emotional experiences to ourselves as part of the continuing project of subjectivity, and how acculturation into particular sociocultural contexts shapes and reshapes concepts of emotion.

I have argued that the experience of emotion involves the interpretation of physical sensations mediated through a body image that is culturally contingent. These physical sensations themselves should not be viewed as 'natural' or 'inherent', but rather as produced as part of one's being-in-the-world, one's location as an embodied subject in a particular sociocultural milieu. A bodily feeling or sensation may be experienced as 'internal' but the way in which we interpret it as evidence of an 'emotion' is always already a product of acculturation into a particular society. So too, the production of this feeling or sensation is always in response to a specific situation, a response that is itself phrased through a particular manner of acculturation. Acculturation, therefore, both influences certain bodily responses experienced by an individual and also shapes the way in which those bodily responses are then interpreted as an emotion (or not).

I have further contended that the ways in which we feel, think about, talk about and experience emotions position them in both highly negative and highly positive ways that echo the binary oppositions constructed between culture and nature and mind and body. The emotions tend to be associated with nature and the body rather than with culture and the mind. The cultural meanings of emotions, therefore, intersect with those of nature and the body. Like nature and the body, emotions are considered to be authentic and given, uncontaminated by society, but also, more negatively, as unruly, irrational and disruptive. As with discourses on the body, our discourses on the emotions constantly slip between positioning them as self and as other, as things with which we are born, which are inevitably part of us, but also as things that require conscious control lest they overwhelm or betray us, making us appear less 'civilized' than we would wish.

More specifically, like the bodily fluids that are seen to slosh around inside our bodies and emerge from our bodies at intervals in more or less controlled ways, emotions are commonly conceptualized as liquid entities. It is thought that emotions begin as generated and contained within the body but may emerge outside. Sometimes this is because we deliberately allow them out, but other times they leak or even burst out in spite of our best efforts to contain them. Releasing these fluid entities outside the body, it is believed, may provide pleasure and relief from pent-up pressures or tightness. But emotions may also embarrass or humiliate us by their entry into the social world, and threaten to break down our sense of autonomy, to challenge notions of self-control, independence and separateness from others.

In a world which is experienced as uncertain and changing, being able to cling to the notion of an 'emotional self' that is at least partly stable provides some degree of certainty about the self. As Craib has commented, 'we need to try to hold on to some idea of ourselves as maintaining some consistency beneath the multitude of things that we do, that happen to us, that we experience, or our world will feel as if it is collapsing' (1994: 94). The constantly shifting meanings around the emotions, however, mean that it may be difficult to maintain a sense of coherence and certainty in relation to selfhood. New demands of emotional work may emerge over the course of an individual's life. The emotional self is dynamic, responsive to changes in sociocultural meaning and representation and in individuals' own biographies of interactions with others as well as with inanimate things (such as places and objects).

The management and experience of the emotional self operates at different levels, including unconscious responses and semi-conscious habituated action as well as highly conscious and calculated strategies. Many of the modes of emotional management into which we are acculturated become routine, so that we may barely be aware of them. We engage in them as a dimension of our everyday life without needing to think much about them or problematize them in any way. Emotional management is part of our 'habitus', or the set of dispositions and bodily techniques, modes of behaving and deporting oneself, that is passed on from generation to generation (Bourdieu, 1984). Sometimes, however, we are highly conscious of the decisions we need to make about the emotions we feel, particularly when we identify an emotion that seems in some way to be unusual, strange, particularly strong or potentially disruptive. Even when they are alone, individuals may assess their emotional state, seeking to work upon it in certain ways. An emotion that one finds unsettling or unusual in some way is often interrogated with a set of questions. Is this emotion appropriate, based on the social context? Is it authentic? What does it tell me about myself, my relationships and my life? Should I tell others about my emotional state or reveal it in other ways? Is the emotion damaging or destructive? Will it hurt others or myself should I reveal it? Should I attempt to repress it, or change it into another emotion?

These conscious 'emotion work' strategies, however, are not always successful. Emotion constantly evades our attempts to govern it. Conscious thought and attempts at self-control are underpinned and often destabilized by unconscious desires and fantasies. Because emotion also operates at the unconscious level, we may experience emotions as 'coming out of the blue', as making no 'rational' sense that we can understand. We may harbour mixed or contradictory feelings and find that our emotions do not correspond with what is expected in some situations. Discourses on expected emotional behaviour in a particular sociocultural context may be contradictory, making competing demands on people. People may deliberately flout dominant 'feeling rules', finding them inappropriate, unjust or irrational.

Several important sociocultural trends concerning the management and expression of one's emotions are related to the contemporary contrasting and competing notions of emotion. One of these is the trend towards revealing one's emotions and celebrating such revelation that is evident in late modern societies. Another trend is a move towards the 'emancipation of emotions' as part of a long-term process of informalization 'in which behavioural, emotional and moral codes have relaxed and differentiated' (Wouters, 1992: 229). In many social contexts, less formality is required of people, people are required to consider the feelings of others to a greater degree, and 'feeling rules' have diversified, acquiring more nuances, over the past century or so (Gerhards, 1989; de Swaan, 1990; Wouters, 1992). Part of both these trends is the endless discussion of emotional states in institutions, therapeutic environments, the mass media and the informal culture of conversation. As I have argued, people are now generally expected to be more 'in touch' with their emotions and those of others, to devote time and energy to identifying their emotions and listening to intimate others discuss their feelings.

Another dimension in these trends is the notion that emotional control should at times be relinquished. As I have shown, social conditions in which there is a focus on the importance of self-discipline in relation to the emotions invariably produce a counter-discourse championing freer emotional expression. In a context in which many people feel as if they are subject to a high degree of social regulation, the emotions are seen as allowing people to experience life vividly, to transcend the constraints of social expectations. The more we perceive ourselves as being regulated via social norms and expectations, the more we assume that this is somehow distorting our 'true' selves. Wouters (1992) claims that individuals are aware of the high degree of emotional management required of them and respond by seeing such regulation as involving an increasing distance from emotions themselves: 'people have found themselves more often in situations where they feel obliged to create and to endure differences, even contradictions between their emotions and their emotion management' (1992: 40). As a consequence, he argues, people seek behaviour that is experienced as 'natural', 'spontaneous' and 'authentic', and experience a nostalgic yearning for intense, non-violent emotions that feel as if they overwhelm the self, such as love. Beck and Beck-Gernsheim have also pointed to the way that love, above all emotions, is regarded as the supreme source of self-fulfilment, the opposite of instrumental, rational behaviour, giving life significance and meaning:

> Loving is a kind of rebellion, a way of getting in touch with forces to counteract the intangible and unintelligible existence we find ourselves in. Its value lies in the special, intense experiences it offers – specific, emotional, engrossing, unavoidable . . . [love] is the only place where you can really get in touch with yourself and someone else. (Beck and Beck-Gernsheim, 1995: 178)

The intensity of lived emotions, such as love, fear and anger, provide a depth of experience – they make us aware that we are alive, and underline our humanity. Emotions may be viewed as destabilizing and unsettling, but these very properties are also those that we may seek in our project of 'true' selfhood. Normative rules and self-consciousness may simply be swept away by the strength of emotions – in episodes of extreme pain, during the heights of sexual pleasure, while experiencing abject terror, grief or joy. Indeed, it is this very aspect of the emotions which constitute them in discourse as 'authentic', as part of nature rather than culture.

While there may be relatively few occasions when self-consciousness and emotional management are completely relinquished, we constantly seek experiences in which we may feel as if there is some relaxation of usual norms. In contemporary western societies, the sensual pleasures and excitements that were integral to the medieval carnivalesque body are evoked through a host of activities. Buying new consumer goods, drinking alcohol, smoking and taking other drugs, having sex, dancing, swimming, participating in or attending sporting events, going to parties, playing with one's children, listening to music, watching television or films, going to the theatre, gambling, singing, playing computer or video games, travelling to foreign places, religious activities, eating favourite foods, falling in love, to name but some activities, are all routes to emotional intensity and bodily abandon, transcending the rhythms, routines, boredoms and restrictions of 'ordinary' life for a while. While some of these activities can be carried out on one's own, many others incite the 'collective effervescence' of embodied sociality.

This view of emotion presents a 'Romantic' perspective on the importance and pleasures of emotional expression, of occasionally flouting
social norms about emotional restraint. However, there is also evidence
in western societies of greater concern about the expression of what are
considered to be inappropriate or negative emotions, including frustration, anger, jealousy, envy, hate and rage. These emotions are generally
viewed as personally or socially destructive or both. It is no longer
thought acceptable to display violence, to inflict humiliation or express
arrogance or feelings of superiority; to do so is to risk a loss of face and
status. Nor it is generally considered appropriate to express scorn for the
defects of others or display racism and sexism (Gerhards, 1989; de
Swaan, 1990; Wouters, 1992). As this suggests, even though emotion
rules may have been 'informalized' and some emotions may be considered appropriate to articulate and express openly, there are many
others which are seen to require tighter control.

The emphasis on controlling the expression of 'negative' emotions
comes at a time when there appears to be a growing sense that modern
(particularly urban) life, seen as replete with pressures and unpleasant
experiences, is increasingly alienating and distressing people and producing emotions such as frustration, resentment, envy, aggression and
anger. Public attention has been focused on the apparent dangers created
by the crumbling of the welfare state in western countries and the
resultant growing divisions between the advantaged and the disadvantaged, including the foment of anger and violence among members of
socially and economically disadvantaged groups. As Allison and Curry
(1996) note, rage has become a central cultural construct by which the
daily existence of some marginalized groups in the USA is defined,
particularly in the mass media. While more liberal-leaning commentators
may view the rage and violence of the marginalized as the justified (if
unfortunate and destructive) outcome of social inequity, those from a
politically conservative position are more likely to call for greater social
controls to contain violence and crime.

Although members of disadvantaged groups have been singled out as
particularly affected by social change, the pressures of modern living
are generally seen to affect negatively all members of western societies
in some way or another. The attention that has recently been given in
countries such as Britain, the USA and Australia to 'road rage', or the
expression of anger on the part of drivers via hostile or violent actions
against other drivers or pedestrians, is an example of this concern about
the production, intensification and expression of negative emotions as
part of modern life. As one Australian newspaper article put it, 'middle-
class, mild-mannered drivers' are transformed by 'road rage' into 'monsters in metal cocoons', going on to describe such people as 'the Jekyll
and Hydes of the highway who terrorize thousands of their fellow
motorists every day as they explode into road rage' (*Sun-Herald*
(Sydney), 20 October 1996). Media coverage of 'road rage' frequently

points to the pressures of driving in urban streetscapes as the precursor to these feelings of aggressiveness, frustration and anger. The expression of such emotions in this context is generally represented as inappropriate because it is seen as socially destructive. While it is recognized that road conditions may often incite these feelings, drivers are expected to control them.

'Emancipation' and 'informalization' of emotional expression, therefore, does not imply a complete relaxation in emotional control or a lessening in emotion work. Rather, it denotes a growing complexity around the norms of emotional expression and the need to devote even greater energy to emotion work. There is a heightened degree of emotional sensitivity required on the part of individuals, an ability to distinguish between the appropriate contexts in which to express or contain one's emotions. Some emotional states are incited, their open expression encouraged in at least some situations, while it is expected that others should be restrained, kept 'inside' the self, whatever the situation. In this context, being a 'civilized' person in terms of the presentation of the emotional self means being cognizant of when it is appropriate to repress the expression of one's feelings and when it is appropriate to reveal them, and to act accordingly.

Appendix: Sociodemographic Details of the Interview Study Participants

- Female community worker aged 30, Australian-born, Anglo-Celtic ethnicity
- Female officer manager aged 62, Australian-born, Anglo-Celtic ethnicity
- Female academic aged 31, Australian-born, Anglo-Celtic ethnicity
- Female market stall holder aged 40, Australian-born, Anglo-Celtic ethnicity
- Female beauty adviser aged 44, British-born, Anglo-Celtic ethnicity
- Female shop owner aged 47, Australian-born, Anglo-Celtic ethnicity
- Male customer services worker aged 49, British-born, Anglo-Celtic ethnicity
- Male clerk aged 25, Australian-born, Anglo-Celtic ethnicity
- Female clerk aged 41, Australian-born, Anglo-Celtic ethnicity
- Female property manager aged 46, Australian-born, Anglo-Celtic ethnicity
- Male community worker aged 44, Australian-born, Anglo-Celtic ethnicity
- Female hairdresser aged 30, Australian-born, Anglo-Celtic ethnicity
- Male building investor aged 43, Australian-born, Anglo-Dutch ethnicity
- Male clerk aged 34, Australian-born, Anglo-Maltese ethnicity
- Female unemployed worker aged 50, Australian-born, Anglo-Celtic ethnicity
- Female receptionist aged 38, Australian-born, Anglo-Dutch ethnicity
- Female teacher aged 49, Australian-born, Anglo-Celtic ethnicity
- Male solicitor aged 30, Australian-born, Anglo-Indian ethnicity
- Female customer services manager aged 36, Australian-born, Anglo-Celtic ethnicity
- Male tree lopper aged 55, Australian-born, Anglo-Celtic ethnicity
- Female retired worker aged 66, Australian-born, Anglo-Celtic ethnicity
- Male entertainment manager aged 45, Australian-born, Anglo-Celtic ethnicity
- Male sales clerk aged 54, Australian-born, Anglo-Celtic ethnicity
- Female book-keeper aged 50, Australian-born, Anglo-Celtic ethnicity
- Male customer services worker aged 21, Australian-born, Anglo-Italian ethnicity
- Female photo-journalist aged 25, Australian-born, Anglo-Celtic ethnicity
- Male university student aged 19, Australian-born, Indonesian-Dutch ethnicity
- Female retired worker aged 58, Australian-born, Anglo-Celtic ethnicity
- Male university student aged 20, Australian-born, Anglo-Celtic ethnicity
- Male retired worker aged 68, Australian-born, Anglo-Celtic ethnicity
- Female community worker aged 45, Australian-born, Anglo-Celtic ethnicity
- Male fitter aged 21, Australian-born, Anglo-Celtic ethnicity
- Male promotions manager aged 29, Australian-born, Anglo-German ethnicity
- Female sales clerk aged 45, Australian-born, Anglo-Celtic ethnicity
- Female housewife/retired worker aged 55, Australian-born, Anglo-Celtic ethnicity
- Female health consultant aged 25, Australian-born, Anglo-Celtic ethnicity
- Male retired worker aged 66, British-born, Anglo-Celtic ethnicity
- Female health education officer aged 41, Australian-born, Anglo-Celtic ethnicity
- Male developer aged 47, Australian-born, Anglo-Celtic ethnicity
- Female craft adviser aged 20, Australian-born, Anglo-Celtic ethnicity
- Female retired worker aged 72, Australian-born, Anglo-Celtic ethnicity

References

Abu-Lughod, L. and Lutz, C. (1990) 'Introduction: emotion, discourse, and the politics of everyday life', in C. Lutz and L. Abu-Lughod (eds), *Language and the Politics of Emotion*. Cambridge: Cambridge University Press. pp. 1–23.

Alder, C. and Polk, K. (1996) 'Masculinity and child homicide', *British Journal of Criminology*, 36 (3): 396–411.

Allan, G. and Crow, G. (1989) 'Introduction', in G. Allan and G. Crow (eds), *Home and Family: Creating the Domestic Sphere*. Basingstoke: Macmillan. pp. 1–13.

Allison, T. and Curry, R. (1996) 'Introduction: invitation to rage', in T. Allison and R. Curry (eds), *States of Rage: Emotional Eruption, Violence, and Social Change*. New York: New York University Press. pp. 1–11.

Armon-Jones, C. (1986) 'The thesis of constructionism', in R. Harré (ed.), *The Social Construction of Emotions*. Oxford: Basil Blackwell. pp. 32–56.

Bailey, P. (1996) 'Breaking the sound barrier: a historian listens to noise', *Body and Society*, 2 (2): 49–66.

Bakhtin, M. (1984) *Rabelais and His World*. Cambridge, MA: The MIT Press.

Barker, F. (1984) *The Tremulous Private Body: Essays on Subjection*. London: Methuen.

Barker-Benfield, G. (1992) *The Culture of Sensibility: Sex and Society in Eighteenth-Century Britain*. Chicago: University of Chicago Press.

Baumeister, R. (1987) 'How the self became a problem: a psychological review of historical research', *Journal of Personality and Social Psychology*, 52: 163–76.

Beck, U. (1992) *Risk Society: Towards a New Modernity*. London: Sage.

Beck, U. and Beck-Gernsheim, E. (1995) *The Normal Chaos of Love*. Cambridge: Polity Press.

Bedford, E. (1986) 'Emotions and statements about them', in R. Harré (ed.), *The Social Construction of Emotions*. Oxford: Basil Blackwell. pp. 15–31.

Berger, P. (1966) 'Towards a sociological understanding of psychoanalysis', *Social Research*, 32: 26–41.

Bly, R. (1990) *Iron John: A Book about Men*. New York: Addison-Wesley.

Bordo, S. (1993) *Unbearable Weight: Feminism, Western Culture, and the Body*. Berkeley, CA: University of California Press.

Boscagli, M. (1992/1993) 'A moving story: masculine tears and the humanity of televised emotions', *Discourse*, 15 (2): 64–79.

Botting, F. (1996) *Gothic*. London: Routledge.

Bourdieu, P. (1984) *Distinction: A Social Critique of the Judgement of Taste*. London: Routledge and Kegan Paul.

Brownmiller, S. (1984) *Femininity*. New York: Fawcett Columbine.

Butler, J. (1990) *Gender Trouble: Feminism and the Subversion of Identity*. New York: Routledge.

Callon, M. (1991) 'Techno-economic networks and irreversibility', in J. Law (ed.), *A Sociology of Monsters: Essays on Power, Technology and Domination*. London: Routledge. pp. 132–61.

Campbell, C. (1995) 'The sociology of consumption', in D. Miller (ed.), *Acknowledging Consumption: A Review of New Studies*. London: Routledge. pp. 96–126.

Canaan, J. (1996) ' "One thing leads to another": drinking, fighting and working-class masculinities', in M. Mac an Ghaill (ed.), *Understanding Masculinities*. Buckingham: Open University Press. pp. 114–26.

Cancian, F. (1987) *Love in America: Gender and Self-Development*. Cambridge: Cambridge University Press.

Carrier, J. (1990) 'Gifts in a world of commodities: the ideology of the perfect gift in American society', *Social Analysis*, 29: 19–37.

Cheal, D. (1988) *The Gift Economy*. London: Routledge.

Chodorow, N. (1978) *The Reproduction of Mothering*. Berkeley, CA: University of California Press.

Chodorow, N. (1989) *Feminism and Psychoanalytic Theory*. New Haven, CT: Yale University Press.

Chodorow, N. (1995) 'Individuality and difference in how women and men love', in A. Elliott and S. Frosh (eds), *Psychoanalysis in Contexts: Paths between Theory and Modern Culture*. London: Routledge. pp. 89–105.

Chrisler, J. and Levy, K. (1990) 'The media construct a menstrual monster: a content analysis of PMS articles in the popular press', *Women and Health*, 16 (2): 89–104.

Cohen, D. (1990) *Being a Man*. London: Routledge.

Collison, M. (1996) 'In search of the high life: drugs, crime, masculinities and consumption', *British Journal of Criminology*, 36 (3): 428–44.

Connell, R. (1995) *Masculinities*. Sydney: Allen and Unwin.

Corbin, A. (1994) *The Foul and the Fragrant: Odour and the Social Imagination*. London: Picador.

Coward, R. (1989) *The Whole Truth: The Myth of Alternative Health*. London: Faber and Faber.

Craib, I. (1994) *The Importance of Disappointment*. London: Routledge.

Craib, I. (1995) 'Some comments on the sociology of the emotions', *Sociology*, 29 (1): 151–8.

Crossley, N. (1996) *Intersubjectivity: The Fabric of Social Becoming*. London: Sage.

Csikszentmihalyi, M. and Rochberg-Halton, E. (1981) *The Meaning of Things: Domestic Symbols and the Self*. Cambridge: Cambridge University Press.

Danet, B. and Katriel, T. (1994) 'Glorious obsessions, passionate lovers, and hidden treasures: collecting, metaphor, and the Romantic ethic', in S. Riggins (ed.), *The Socialness of Things: Essays on the Socio-Semiotics of Objects*. Berlin: Mouton de Gruyter. pp. 23–62.

Darwin, C. (1872) *The Expression of the Emotions in Man and Animals*. London: John Murray.

Davies, C. (1996) 'The sociology of the professions and the profession of gender', *Sociology*, 30 (4): 661–78.

Demos, J. (1988) 'Shame and guilt in early New England', in C. Stearns and P. Stearns (eds), *Emotion and Social Change: Toward a New Psychohistory*. New York: Holmes and Meier. pp. 69–86.

Denzin, N. (1984) *On Understanding Emotion*. San Francisco: Jossey-Bass.

de Swaan, A. (1990) *The Management of Normality: Critical Essays in Health and Welfare*. London: Routledge.

Dittmar, H. (1992) *The Social Psychology of Material Possessions: To Have Is To Be*. London and New York: Harvester Wheatsheaf/St Martin's Press.

Douglas, K. (1996) 'Cherchez la différence', *New Scientist* (supplement), 27 April: 14–16.

Douglas, M. (1966/1980) *Purity and Danger: An Analysis of Concepts of Pollution and Taboo*. London: Routledge and Kegan Paul.

Duden, B. (1991) *The Woman Beneath the Skin: A Doctor's Patients in Eighteenth-Century Germany*. Cambridge, MA: Harvard University Press.

Duncombe, J. and Marsden, D. (1993) 'Love and intimacy: the gender division of emotion and "emotion work" ', *Sociology*, 27 (2): 221–41.

Duncombe, J. and Marsden, D. (1995) ' "Workaholics" and "whingeing women": theorizing intimacy and emotion work – the last frontier of gender inequality?', *Sociological Review*, 43 (1): 150–69.

Duncombe, J. and Marsden, D. (1998) ' "Stepford Wives" and "Hollow Men"? Doing emotion work, doing gender, and "authenticity" in intimate heterosexual relationships', in G. Bendelow and S. Williams (eds), *Emotions in Social Life: Critical Themes and Contemporary Issues*. London: Routledge. pp. 211–27.

Dunning, E. (1996) 'On problems of the emotions in sport and leisure: critical and counter-critical comments on the conventional and figurational sociologies of sport and leisure', *Leisure Studies*, 15: 185–207.

Durkheim, E. (1912/1961) *The Elementary Forms of the Religious Life*. London: Allen and Unwin.

Elias, N. (1939/1994) *The Civilizing Process*. Oxford: Blackwell.

Elias, N. (1991) 'On human beings and their emotions: a process-sociological essay', in M. Featherstone, M. Hepworth and B. Turner (eds), *The Body: Social Process and Cultural Theory*. London: Sage. pp. 103–26.

Elias, N. and Dunning, E. (1986) *Quest for Excitement: Sport and Leisure in the Civilizing Process*. Oxford: Blackwell.

Fairclough, N. (1992) *Discourse and Social Change*. Cambridge: Polity Press.

Falk, P. (1994) *The Consuming Body*. London: Sage.

Falk, P. (1997) 'Humans, objects and other beings', in V. Grano (ed.), *Tangible Commodities (Esineiden Valtakunta): Recollecting Collectors*. Oulu, Finland: Pohjoinen. pp. 79–82.

Featherstone, M. (1990) 'Perspectives on consumer culture', *Sociology*, 24 (1): 5–22.

Finch, L. (1993) *The Classing Gaze: Sexuality, Class and Surveillance*. Sydney: Allen and Unwin.

Finkelstein, J. (1980) 'Considerations for a sociology of the emotions', *Studies in Symbolic Interactionism*, 3: 111–21.

Finkelstein, J. (1989) *Dining Out: A Sociology of Modern Manners*. Cambridge: Polity Press.

Fischer, A. (1993) 'Sex differences in emotionality: fact or stereotype?', *Feminism and Psychology*, 3 (3): 303–18.

Folkman, S. and Lazarus, R. (1988) 'The relationship between coping and emotion: implications for theory and research', *Social Science and Medicine*, 26 (3): 309–17.

Foucault, M. (1977) *Discipline and Punish: The Birth of the Prison*. London: Allen Lane.

Foucault, M. (1978) *The History of Sexuality: An Introduction – Volume 1*. New York: Random House.

Fraser, N. and Gordon, L. (1994) 'Civil citizenship and civil society in Central Europe', in B. van Steenbergen (ed.), *The Condition of Citizenship*. London: Sage. pp. 90–107.

Freund, P. (1990) 'The expressive body: a common ground for the sociology of emotions and health and illness', *Sociology of Health and Illness*, 12 (4): 452–77.

Friedman, V. (1996) 'Over his dead body: female murderers, female rage, and western culture', in T. Allison and R. Curry (eds), *States of Rage: Emotional Eruption, Violence, and Social Change*. New York: New York University Press. pp. 62–73.

Frosh, S. (1991) *Identity Crisis: Modernity, Psychoanalysis and the Self*. Basingstoke: Macmillan.

Gabriel, Y. and Lang, T. (1995) *The Unmanageable Consumer: Contemporary Consumption and its Fragmentations*. London: Sage.

Game, A. and Metcalfe, A. (1996) *Passionate Sociology*. London: Sage.

Gergen, K. (1995) 'Metaphor and monophony in the 20th-century psychology of emotions', *History of the Human Sciences*, 8 (2): 1–23.

Gerhards, J. (1989) 'The changing culture of emotions in modern society', *Social Science Information*, 28 (4): 737–54.

Giddens, A. (1990) *The Consequences of Modernity*. Cambridge: Polity Press.

Giddens, A. (1992) *The Transformation of Intimacy: Sexuality, Love and Eroticism in Modern Societies*. Cambridge: Polity Press.

Giddens, A. (1994) 'Living in a post-traditional society', in U. Beck, A. Giddens and S. Lash *Reflexive Modernization: Politics, Tradition and Aesthetics in the Modern Social Order*. Cambridge: Polity Press. pp. 56–109.

Gilligan, C. and Rogers, A. (1993) 'Reframing daughtering and mothering: a paradigm shift in psychology', in J. van Mens-Verhulst, K. Schreurs and L. Woertman (eds), *Daughtering and Mothering: Female Subjectivity Reanalysed*. London: Routledge. pp. 125–34.

Gillis, J. (1988) 'From ritual to romance: toward an alternative history of love', in C. Stearns and P. Stearns (eds), *Emotion and Social Change: Toward a New Psychohistory*. New York: Holmes and Meier. pp. 87–122.

Goleman, D. (1995) *Emotional Intelligence: Why It Can Matter More than IQ*. London: Bloomsbury.

González, J. (1995) 'Autotopographies', in G. Braham and M. Driscoll (eds), *Prosthetic Territories: Politics and Hypertechnologies*. Boulder, CO: Westview Press. pp. 133–50.

Good, B. (1994) *Medicine, Rationality, and Experience: An Anthropological Perspective*. Cambridge: Cambridge University Press.

Greenblatt, S. (1982) 'Filthy rites', *Daedalus*, 3: 1–16.

Griffiths, M. (1995) *Feminisms and the Self: The Web of Identity*. London: Routledge.

Griswold, R. (1993) *Fatherhood in America: A History*. New York: Basic Books.

Grosz, E. (1994) *Volatile Bodies: Toward a Corporeal Feminism*. Sydney: Allen and Unwin.

Groves, J. (1995) 'Learning to feel: the neglected sociology of social movements', *The Sociological Review*, 43 (3): 435–61.

Gusfield, J. (1987) 'Passage to play: rituals of drinking time in American society', in M. Douglas (ed.), *Constructive Drinking: Perspectives on Drink from Anthropology*. Cambridge: Cambridge University Press. pp. 73–90.

Harré, R. (1986) 'An outline of the social constructionist viewpoint', in R. Harré (ed.), *The Social Construction of Emotions*. Oxford: Basil Blackwell. pp. 2–14.

Harré, R. (1991) *Physical Being: A Theory for a Corporeal Psychology*. Oxford: Basil Blackwell.

Harré, R. and Gillett, G. (1994) *The Discursive Mind*. Thousand Oaks, CA: Sage.

Harris, R. (1989) *Murders and Madness: Medicine, Law and Society in the Fin de Siècle*. Oxford: Oxford University Press.

Haug, W. (1986) *Critique of Commodity Aesthetics: Appearance, Sexuality and Advertising in Capitalist Society*. Minneapolis, MN: University of Minnesota Press.

Hawley, J. (1997) 'Deadlocked', *Good Weekend*, 31 May.

Hearn, J. (1993) 'Emotive subjects: organizational men, organizational masculinities and the (de)construction of "emotions"', in S. Fineman (ed.), *Emotion in Organizations*. London: Sage. pp. 142–66.

Heelas, P. (1986) 'Emotion talk across cultures', in R. Harré (ed.), *The Social Construction of Emotions*. Oxford: Basil Blackwell. pp. 234–66.

Helman, C. (1987) 'Heart disease and the cultural construction of time: the type A behaviour pattern as a western culture-bound syndrome', *Social Science and Medicine*, 25 (9): 969–79.

Henriques, J., Hollway, W., Urwin, C., Venn, C. and Walkerdine, V. (1984) *Changing the Subject: Psychology, Social Regulation and Subjectivity*. London: Methuen.

Herzlich, C. and Pierret, J. (1987) *Illness and Self in Society*. Baltimore, MD: Johns Hopkins University Press.

Heywood, L. (1996) *Dedication to Hunger: The Anorexic Aesthetic in Modern Cultures*. Berkeley, CA: University of California Press.

Hochschild, A. (1979) 'Emotion work, feeling rules, and social structure', *American Journal of Sociology*, 85 (3): 551–75.

Hochschild, A. (1983) *The Managed Heart: Commercialization of Human Feeling*. Berkeley, CA: University of California Press.

Hochschild, A. (1994) 'The commercial spirit of intimate life and the abduction of feminism: signs from women's advice books', *Theory, Culture and Society*, 11: 1–24.

Hollway, W. (1984) 'Gender difference and the production of subjectivity', in J. Henriques, W. Hollway, C. Urwin, C. Venn and V. Walkerdine, *Changing the Subject: Psychology, Social Regulation and Subjectivity.* London: Methuen. pp. 227–63.

Hollway, W. (1989) *Subjectivity and Method in Psychology: Gender, Meaning and Science.* London: Sage.

Hollway, W. (1995) 'Feminist discourses and women's heterosexual desire', in S. Wilkinson and C. Kitzinger (eds), *Feminism and Discourse: Psychological Perspectives.* London: Sage. pp. 86–105.

Hollway, W. (1996) 'Masters and men in the transition from factory hands to sentimental workers', in D. Collinson and J. Hearn (eds), *Men as Managers, Managers as Men: Critical Perspectives on Men, Masculinities and Managements.* London: Sage. pp. 25–42.

Hope, D. (1996) 'Home: there's still no place like it', *The Australian Magazine*, 14–15 December: 22–31.

Horrocks, R. (1994) *Masculinity in Crisis.* New York: St Martin's Press.

Hughes, B. (1996) 'Nietzsche: philosophizing the body', *Body and Society*, 2 (1): 31–44.

Irvine, J. (1995) 'Reinventing perversion: sex addiction and cultural anxieties', *Journal of the History of Sexuality*, 5 (3): 429–50.

Jackson, S. (1993) 'Even sociologists fall in love: an exploration in the sociology of emotions', *Sociology*, 27 (2): 201–20.

Jaggar, A. (1989) 'Love and knowledge: emotion in feminist epistemology', in A. Jaggar and S. Bordo (eds), *Gender/Body/Knowledge: Feminist Reconstructions of Being and Knowing.* New Brunswick, NJ: Rutgers University Press. pp. 145–71.

James, N. (1989) 'Emotional labour: skill and work in the social regulation of feelings', *Sociological Review*, 37 (1): 15–42.

Jones, A. (1993) 'Defending the border: men's bodies and vulnerability', *Cultural Studies from Birmingham*, 2: 77–123.

Jordan, J. (1993) 'The relational self: a model of women's development', in J. van Mens-Verhulst, K. Schreurs and L. Woertman (eds), *Daughtering and Mothering: Female Subjectivity Reanalysed.* London: Routledge. pp. 135–44.

Kemper, T. (1987) 'How many emotions are there? Wedding the social and the autonomic components', *American Journal of Sociology*, 93 (2): 263–89.

Kemper, T. (1991) 'An introduction to the sociology of emotions', in D. Strongman (ed.), *International Review of Studies on Emotion: Volume 1.* Chichester: John Wiley. pp. 301–49.

Klein, M. (1979) *Envy and Gratitude and Other Works 1946–1963.* London: Hogarth Press.

Kopytoff, I. (1986) 'The cultural biography of things: commoditization as process', in A. Appadurai (ed.), *The Social Life of Things: Commodities in Cultural Perspective.* Cambridge: Cambridge University Press. pp. 64–91.

Kovel, J. (1995) 'On racism and psychoanalysis', in A. Elliott and S. Frosh (eds), *Psychoanalysis in Contexts: Paths between Theory and Modern Culture.* London: Routledge. pp. 205–22.

Kristeva, J. (1982) *Powers of Horror: An Essay on Abjection.* New York: Columbia University Press.

Kroker, A. and Kroker, M. (1988) 'Panic sex in America', in A. Kroker and M. Kroker (eds), *Body Invaders: Sexuality and the Postmodern Condition.* Montreal: Macmillan. pp. 10–19.

Lakoff, G. (1987) *Women, Fire and Dangerous Things: What Categories Reveal about the Mind.* Chicago: University of Chicago Press.

Lakoff, G. (1995) 'Body, brain, and communication (interviewed by I. Boal)', in J. Brook and I. Boal (eds), *Resisting the Virtual Life: The Culture and Politics of Information.* San Francisco: City Lights Books. pp. 115–30.

Lasch, C. (1977) *Haven in a Heartless World: The Family Besieged.* New York: Basic Books.

Latour, B. (1992) 'Where are the missing masses? The sociology of a few mundane artifacts', in W. Bijker and J. Law (eds), *Shaping Technology/Building Society: Studies in Sociotechnical Change.* Cambridge, MA: MIT Press. pp. 225–58.

Leder, D. (1990) *The Absent Body.* Chicago: University of Chicago Press.

Lindemann, M. (1996) *Health and Healing in Eighteenth-Century Germany.* Baltimore, MD: Johns Hopkins University Press.

Lloyd, G. (1984) *The Man of Reason: 'Male' and 'Female' in Western Philosophy.* London: Methuen.

Luhmann, N. (1986) *Love as Passion: The Codification of Intimacy.* Cambridge: Polity Press.

Lunt, P. and Livingstone, S. (1992) *Mass Consumption and Personal Identity.* Buckingham: Open University Press.

Lupton, D. (1995) *The Imperative of Health: Public Health and the Regulated Body.* London: Sage.

Lupton, D. (1996a) *Food, the Body and the Self.* London: Sage.

Lupton, D. (1996b) 'Constructing the menopausal body: the discourses on hormone replacement therapy', *Body and Society,* 2 (1): 91–7.

Lupton, D. and Barclay, L. (1997) *Constructing Fatherhood: Discourses and Experiences.* London: Sage.

Lupton, D. and Noble, G. (1997) 'Just a machine? (De)humanizing strategies in personal computer use', *Body and Society,* 3 (2): 83–101.

Lutz, C. (1985) 'Depression and the translation of emotional worlds', in A. Kleinman and B. Good (eds), *Culture and Depression: Studies in the Anthropology and Cross-Cultural Psychiatry of Affect and Disorder.* Berkeley, CA: University of California Press. pp. 63–100.

Lutz, C. (1986) 'Emotion, thought, and estrangement: emotion as a cultural category', *Cultural Anthropology,* 1 (3): 287–309.

Lutz, C. (1988) *Unnatural Emotions: Everyday Sentiments on a Micronesian Atoll and Their Challenge to Western Theory.* Chicago: University of Chicago Press.

Lutz, C. (1990) 'Engendered emotion: gender, power, and the rhetoric of emotional control in American discourse', in C. Lutz and L. Abu-Lughod (eds), *Language and the Politics of Emotion.* Cambridge: Cambridge University Press. pp. 69–91.

Lyon, M. (1993) 'Psychoneuroimmunology: the problem of the situatedness of illness and the conceptualization of healing', *Culture, Medicine and Psychiatry,* 17: 77–97.

Lyon, M. (1995) 'Missing emotion: the limitations of cultural constructionism in the study of emotion', *Cultural Anthropology,* 10 (2): 244–63.

Lyon, M. and Barbalet, J. (1994) 'Society's body: emotion and the "somatization" of social theory', in T. Csordas (ed.), *Embodiment and Experience: The Existential Ground of Culture and Self.* Cambridge: Cambridge University Press. pp. 48–66.

MacDonald, M. (1981) *Mystical Bedlam: Madness, Anxiety, and Healing in Seventeenth-Century England.* Cambridge: Cambridge University Press.

Maffesoli, M. (1996) *The Time of the Tribes: The Decline of Individualism in Mass Society.* London: Sage.

Malson, H. and Ussher, J. (1996) 'Bloody women: a discourse analysis of amenorrhea as a symptom of anorexia nervosa', *Feminism and Psychology,* 6 (4): 505–21.

Marsh, M. (1990) 'Suburban men and masculine domesticity', in M. Carnes and C. Griffen (eds), *Meanings for Manhood: Constructions of Masculinity in Victorian America.* Chicago: University of Chicago Press. pp. 111–27.

Marx, K. and Engels, F. (1848/1982) *Manifesto of the Communist Party.* Reprinted in *Marx/ Engels: Selected Works.* Moscow: Progress Publishers.

Mellor, P. and Shilling, C. (1997) *Re-forming the Body: Religion, Community and Modernity.* London: Sage.

Merleau-Ponty, M. (1962) *Phenomenology of Perception.* London: Routledge and Kegan Paul.

Mesquita, B. and Frijda, N. (1992) 'Cultural variations in emotions: a review', *Psychological Bulletin,* 112 (2): 179–204.

Messner, M. (1993) ' "Changing men" and feminist politics in the United States', *Theory and Society,* 22: 723–37.

Miller, D. (1987) *Material Culture and Mass Consumption.* Oxford: Basil Blackwell.

Miller, W. (1997) *The Anatomy of Disgust.* Cambridge, MA: Harvard University Press.

Minsky, R. (1996) *Psychoanalysis and Gender: An Introductory Reader*. London: Routledge.

Morley, D. (1992) *Television, Audiences and Cultural Studies*. London: Routledge.

Moyal, A. (1989) 'The feminine culture of the telephone: people, patterns and policy', *Prometheus*, 7 (1): 5–31.

Muchembled, R. (1985) *Popular Culture and Elite Culture in France, 1400–1750*. Baton Rouge, LA: Louisiana State University Press.

Mulholland, K. (1996) 'Entrepreneurialism, masculinities and the self-made man', in D. Collinson and J. Hearn (eds), *Men as Managers, Managers as Men: Critical Perspectives on Men, Masculinities and Managements*. London: Sage. pp. 123–49.

Nippert-Eng, C. (1996) *Home and Work*. Chicago: University of Chicago Press.

Nutton, V. (1992) 'Healers in the medical market place: towards a social history of Graeco-Roman medicine', in A. Wear (ed.), *Medicine in Society: Historical Essays*. Cambridge: Cambridge University Press. pp. 15–58.

Osherson, S. (1992) *Wrestling with Love: How Men Struggle with Intimacy with Women, Children, Parents and Each Other*. New York: Fawcett Columbine.

Parkin, W. (1993) 'The public and the private: gender, sexuality and emotion', in S. Fineman (ed.), *Emotion in Organizations*. London: Sage. pp. 167–89.

Patthey-Chavez, G., Clare, L. and Youmans, M. (1996) 'Watery passion: the struggle between hegemony and sexual liberation in erotic fiction for women', *Discourse and Society*, 7 (1): 77–106.

Percy, M. and Taylor, R. (1997) 'Something for the weekend, sir? Leisure, ecstasy and identity in football and contemporary religion', *Leisure Studies*, 16: 37–49.

Plutchik, R. (1982) 'A pyschoevolutionary theory of emotions', *Social Science Information*, 21 (4/5): 529–53.

Pollock, K. (1988) 'On the nature of social stress: production of a modern mythology', *Social Science and Medicine*, 26 (3): 381–92.

Porter, R. and Porter, D. (1988) *In Sickness and in Health: The British Experience, 1650–1850*. New York: Basil Blackwell.

Pringle, R. (1989) *Secretaries Talk: Sexuality, Power and Work*. London: Verso.

Putnam, L. and Mumby, D. (1993) 'Organizations, emotion and the myth of rationality', in S. Fineman (ed.), *Emotion in Organizations*. London: Sage. pp. 36–57.

Read, P. (1996) *Returning to Nothing: The Meaning of Lost Places*. Melbourne: Cambridge University Press.

Ribbens, J. (1994) *Mothers and Their Children: A Feminist Sociology of Childrearing*. London: Sage.

Richards, B. (1989) *Images of Freud: Cultural Responses to Psychoanalysis*. London: J.M. Dent.

Richards, B. (1994) *Disciplines of Delight: The Psychoanalysis of Popular Culture*. London: Free Association Books.

Richards, J. (1987) ' "Passing the love of women": manly love and Victorian society', in J. Mangan and J. Walvin (eds), *Manliness and Morality: Middle-Class Masculinity in Britain and America 1800–1940*. Manchester: Manchester University Press. pp. 92–122.

Rodaway, P. (1994) *Sensuous Geographies: Body, Sense and Place*. London: Routledge.

Rojek, C. (1993) *Ways of Escape: Modern Transformations in Leisure and Travel*. Basingstoke: Macmillan.

Roper, L. (1994) *Oedipus and the Devil: Witchcraft, Sexuality and Religion in Early Modern Europe*. London: Routledge.

Roper, M. (1996) ' "Seduction" and "succession": circuits of homosocial desire in management', in D. Collinson and J. Hearn (eds), *Men as Managers, Managers as Men: Critical Perspectives on Men, Masculinities and Managements*. London: Sage. pp. 210–26.

Rose, N. (1990) *Governing the Soul: The Shaping of the Private Self*. London: Routledge.

Rose, N. (1996) *Inventing Our Selves: Psychology, Power, and Personhood*. Cambridge: Cambridge University Press.

Ruddick, S. (1994) 'Thinking mothers/conceiving birth', in D. Bassin, M. Honey and M. Kaplan (eds), *Representations of Motherhood*. New Haven, CT: Yale University Press. pp. 29–45.

Rutherford, J. (1992) *Men's Silences: Predicaments in Masculinity.* London: Routledge.

Scheff, T. (1990) *Microsociology: Discourse, Emotion, and Social Structure.* Chicago: University of Chicago Press.

Scheper-Hughes, N. and Lock, M. (1987) 'The mindful body: a prolegomenon to future work in medical anthropology', *Medical Anthropology Quarterly,* 1: 6–41.

Segal, H. (1995) 'From Hiroshima to the Gulf War and after: a psychoanalytic perspective', in A. Elliott and S. Frosh (eds), *Psychoanalysis in Contexts: Paths between Theory and Modern Culture.* London: Routledge. pp. 191–204.

Segal, L. (1990) *Slow Motion: Changing Masculinities, Changing Men.* London: Virago.

Seidler, V. (1991) *Recreating Sexual Politics: Men, Feminism and Politics.* London: Routledge.

Sennett, R. (1977) *The Fall of Public Man.* London: Faber and Faber.

Shields, R. (1991) *Places on the Margin: Alternative Geographies of Modernity.* London: Routledge.

Shuttleworth, S. (1990) 'Female circulation: medical discourse and popular advertising in the mid-Victorian era', in M. Jacobus, E. Keller and S. Shuttleworth (eds), *Body/Politics: Women and the Discourses of Science.* New York: Routledge. pp. 47–68.

Shuttleworth, S. (1993/1994) 'A mother's place is in the wrong', *New Scientist,* 25 December/1 January: 38–40.

Shweder, R. (1985) 'Menstrual pollution, soul loss, and the comparative study of emotions', in A. Kleinman and B. Good (eds), *Culture and Depression: Studies in the Anthropology and Cross-Cultural Psychiatry of Affect and Disorder.* Berkeley, CA: University of California Press. pp. 182–216.

Sibley, D. (1995) 'Families and domestic routines: constructing the boundaries of childhood', in S. Pile and N. Thrift (eds), *Mapping the Subject: Geographies of Cultural Transformation.* London: Routledge. pp. 123–37.

Silverstone, R., Hirsch, E. and Morley, D. (1992) 'Information and communication technologies and the moral economy of the household', in R. Silverstone and E. Hirsch (eds), *Consuming Technologies: Media and Information in Domestic Spaces.* London: Routledge. pp. 15–31.

Simmel, G. (1903/1969) 'The metropolis and mental life', in R. Sennett (ed.), *Classic Essays on the Culture of Cities.* New York: Meredith. pp. 47–60.

Skultans, V. (1977) 'Bodily madness and the spread of the blush', in J. Blacking (ed.), *The Anthropology of the Body.* London: Academic Press. pp. 145–60.

Smith-Rosenberg, C. (1985) *Disorderly Conduct: Visions of Gender in Victorian America.* New York: Alfred A. Knopf.

Solomon, R. (1976) *The Passions.* Garden City, NY: Anchor Press/Doubleday.

Sontag, S. (1989) *Illness as Metaphor and AIDS and its Metaphors.* New York: Anchor.

Springer, C. (1996) *Electronic Eros: Bodies and Desire in the Postindustrial Age.* Austin, TX: University of Texas Press.

Stallybrass, P. and White, A. (1986) *The Politics and Poetics of Transgression.* London: Methuen.

Stearns, C. and Stearns, P. (1986) *Anger: The Struggle for Emotional Control in America's History.* Chicago: University of Chicago Press.

Stearns, P. (1988) 'Anger and American work: a twentieth-century turning point', in C. Stearns and P. Stearns (eds), *Emotion and Social Change: Toward a New Psychohistory.* New York: Holmes and Meier. pp. 123–50.

Stearns, P. (1995) 'Emotion', in R. Harré and P. Stearns (eds), *Discursive Psychology in Practice.* London: Sage. pp. 37–54.

Stein, H. (1985) *The Psychodynamics of Medical Practice: Unconscious Factors in Patient Care.* Berkeley, CA: University of California Press.

Strongman, K. (ed.) (1992) *International Review of Studies on Emotion: Volume 2.* Chichester: John Wiley.

Synnott, A. (1993) *The Body Social: Symbolism, Self and Society.* London: Routledge.

Taylor, C. (1989) *Sources of the Self: The Making of the Modern Identity.* Cambridge: Cambridge University Press.

Taylor, I., Evans, K. and Fraser, P. (1996) *A Tale of Two Cities: Global Change, Local Feeling and Everyday Life in the North of England – A Study in Manchester and Sheffield*. London: Routledge.

Theweleit, K. (1987) *Male Fantasies. Volume 1: Women, Floods, Bodies, History*. Cambridge: Polity Press.

Thoits, P. (1995) 'Stress, coping, and social support processes: where are we? What next?', *Journal of Health and Social Behavior*, extra issue: 53–79.

Tolson, A. (1977) *The Limits of Masculinity*. London: Tavistock.

Tosh, J. (1996) 'Authority and nurture in middle-class fatherhood: the case of early and mid-Victorian England', *Gender and History*, 8 (1): 48–64.

Treacher, A. (1989) 'Be your own person: dependence/independence, 1950–1985', in B. Richards (ed.), *Crises of the Self: Further Essays on Psychoanalysis and Politics*. London: Free Association Books. pp. 131–46.

Tseëlon, E. (1995) *The Masque of Femininity*. London: Sage.

Tuan, Y.-F. (1974) *Topophilia: A Study of Environmental Perception, Attitudes, and Values*. Englewood Cliffs, NJ: Prentice-Hall.

Tuan, Y.-F. (1977) *Space and Place: The Perspective of Experience*. London: Edward Arnold.

Tuan, Y.-F. (1979) *Landscapes of Fear*. Oxford: Blackwell.

Tudor, A. (1995) 'Unruly bodies, unquiet minds', *Body and Society*, 1 (1): 25–41.

Turkle, S. (1988) 'Computational reticence: why women fear the intimate machine', in C. Kramarae (ed.), *Technology and Women's Voice*. London: Routledge. pp. 41–61.

Turkle, S. (1996) *Life on the Screen: Identity in the Age of the Internet*. London: Weidenfeld and Nicolson.

Turner, B. (1996) *The Body and Society: Explorations in Social Theory* (second edition). London: Sage.

Verheyen, C. (1987) 'Mother knows best: for him the play, for her the rest', in T. Knijn and A.-C. Mulder (eds), *Unravelling Fatherhood*. Dordrecht: Foris. pp. 37–47.

Vincent-Buffault, A. (1991) *The History of Tears: Sensibility and Sentimentality in France*. Basingstoke: Macmillan.

Wacquant, L. (1995) 'Why men desire muscles', *Body and Society*, 1 (1): 163–79.

Walter, T., Littlewood, J. and Pickering, M. (1995) 'Death in the news: the public invigilation of private emotion', *Sociology*, 29 (4): 579–96.

Walzer, S. (1996) 'Thinking about the baby: gender and divisions of infant care', *Social Problems*, 43 (2): 219–34.

Wetherell, M. (1996) 'Romantic discourse and feminist analysis: interrogating investment, power and desire', in S. Wilkinson and C. Kitzinger (eds), *Feminism and Discourse: Psychological Perspectives*. London: Sage, pp. 128–44.

Wiley, J. (1995) 'No BODY is "doing it": cybersexuality as a postmodern narrative', *Body and Society*, 1 (1): 145–62.

Williamson, J. (1978) *Decoding Advertisements: Ideology and Meaning in Advertising*. London: Marion Boyers.

Willis, P. (1990) *Common Culture: Symbolic Work at Play in the Everyday Cultures of the Young*. Milton Keynes: Open University Press.

Wilson, P. (1985) *The Calm Technique: Meditation without Magic or Mysticism*. Elwood, Victoria: Greenhouse Publications.

Wilson, R. (1995) 'Cyber(body)parts: prosthetic consciousness', *Body and Society*, 1 (3/4): 239–60.

Wingate, P. with Wingate, R. (1988) *The Penguin Medical Encyclopedia* (third edition). London: Penguin.

Wouters, C. (1992) 'On status competition and emotion management: the study of emotions as a new field', *Theory, Culture and Society*, 9: 229–52.

Wright, P. (1988) 'Babyhood: the social construction of infant care as a medical problem in England in the years around 1900', in M. Lock and D. Gordon (eds), *Biomedicine Examined*. Dordrecht: Kluwer. pp. 299–330.

Yacovone, D. (1990) 'Abolitionists and the "language of fraternal love" ', in M. Carnes and C. Griffen (eds), *Meanings for Manhood: Constructions of Masculinity in Victorian America*. Chicago: University of Chicago Press. pp. 85–95.

Yudice, G. (1995) 'What's a straight white man to do?', in M. Berger, B. Wallis and S. Watson (eds), *Constructing Masculinity*. New York: Routledge. pp. 267–83.

Index